Early Victorian House Designs

William H. Ranlett

Dover Publications, Inc.

Mineola, New York

Bibliographical Note

This Dover edition, first published in 2006, is an unabridged republication of the work originally published in 1847 by William H. Graham, Tribune Buildings, New York, under the title *The Architect, A Series of Original Designs, for Domestic and Ornamental Cottages and Villas, Connected with Landscape Gardening, Adapted to the United States: Illustrated by Drawings of Ground Plots, Plans, Perspective Views, Elevations, Sections and Details,* Volume I.

The only significant alterations consist in omitting the blanks from the original edition in order to accommodate the pagination for the Dover reprint; and moving the Frontispiece from the interior of the book to the inside front cover. Original folios have been retained because of internal page references and the Index on the last page of the book. Keeping in mind the age of the source, the reproduction merely reflects the condition and imperfections of the original work.

Library of Congress Cataloging-in-Publication Data

Ranlett, William H.
   [Architect]
   Early Victorian house designs / William H. Ranlett.
      p. cm.
   Originally published: The architect : a series of original designs for domestic and ornamental cottages and villas, connected with landscape gardening, adapted to the United States : illustrated by drawings of ground plots, plans, perspective views, elevations, sections and details, Vol. I. New York : William H. Graham, Tribune Buildings, 1847.
   Includes index.
   ISBN 0-486-44863-0 (pbk.)
   1. Architecture, Domestic—United States—Designs and plans. 2. Architecture, Victorian—United States—Designs and plans. I. Title.

NA7207.R36 2006
728'.37022273—dc22

2006040176

Manufactured in the United States of America
Dover Publications, Inc., 31 East 2nd Street, Mineola, N.Y. 11501

INTRODUCTION.

In a new country, the first objects of attention are the *simple necessaries* of life. As improvements progress and property accumulates, the opportunity and means are afforded to add conveniences, comforts and ornaments. In the first settlement of a country, the buildings are necessarily rude and inconvenient; but as soon as the means are at hand, domestic demands will be met by improved dwellings and other buildings. The republican equality of our institutions, offers to all, the opportunity of being the proprietors of their own houses; and it cultivates a laudable ambition to enjoy the *independence* of such a position; and the unfettered freedom and general intelligence of our citizens, afford great opportunities for the cultivation of the finer feelings of our nature. As naturally as plants assume the ornaments of flowers, do human beings adorn their persons and appendages, to gratify their innate faculty of perceiving and appreciating beauty; which faculty is called taste.

Our mental and physical tastes are equally the product of Divine Power and Wisdom, and equally designed by the Creator to be exercised in lawful gratifications: hence, æsthetics, or the science of beauty, is as legitimate a study as the culinary art. Indeed, it may be said, now to possess the highest rank in human science, in the grade universally assigned to poetry, painting and sculpture. It is, moreover, important to cultivate a proper balance in taste, especially in the ordinary ranks of society; for while an artist is excusable in being absorbed in one of its departments, there is something repulsive and bordering upon the monstrous, in a development of it, which, like Shenstone's, cultivates and ornaments, in a high degree, the garden and other grounds, and neglects the dwelling to the manifest discomfort of the family and guests.

But the most important feature of this subject, is its moral aspect. There is so intimate a connection between taste and morals, æsthetics and Christianity, that they, in each instance, mutually modify each other: hence whatever serves to cultivate the taste of a community, will be likely to improve their morals; and whatever promotes their knowledge of beauty, will give to Christianity increased opportunity and means of charming the heart and governing the life. From this view, it follows that he who corrects a vicious or improper development of public taste; or opens the way or provides the means of proper æsthetic gratification, is to be looked upon as a public benefactor.

While the products of Painting and Sculpture are necessarily limited and selfish in their effects—being shut in from public gaze, and designed to gratify only the proprietor and his chosen friends and guests—Landscape Gardening is claimed as producing a far greater amount of public good, by spreading its beauties before the public eye—allowing the rich and the poor alike to look upon them and be delighted.

Still more diffusive is the influence of the department of the fine arts principally treated of in the following pages; for while the beauties of the garden are of a high order, their lowly position requires a near approach that they may be appreciated; but many of the beauties of architecture are reared aloft, as if—in the sunlight of heaven—to challenge the gaze and delight the minds of passers-by far and near.

Architecture, having no patterns in nature, is the most difficult and least regulated of all the fine arts. Painting and Sculpture are imitations of nature, and the perfection of the Arts, is only the ability to make the imitations perfect. Poetry is a sublime and measured expression of the author's conceptions of grandeur and beauty. Landscape Gardening was, formerly, the imitation of geometric figures; hence the ancient mode of it is called the geometric style of gardening. In late improvements, it consists in the imitation of nature, in curved walks and winding waters, and trees and clumps of natural shape : hence the present mode is called the natural style. Architecture is not the imitation of any thing in nature or science—it is wholly artificial, hence improvements in it are more difficult, being *new intellectual creations.* This has rendered the styles various and numerous. Indeed for the number of styles, we might almost venture to multiply the number of civilized nations by the number of ages in which they have lived.

The construction of dwellings, is a department of enterprize and investment, which involves various considerations of vast moment. It should always be remembered that a dwelling is constructed *for the accommodation of a family.* Sound philosophy and good taste require that the site, form and character of a building should be suited to its use and expressive of its destination. The design of a dwelling should include in its basis, several very important considerations; such as the adaptation of the house to the site—to the necessities and conveniences of the family—to the healthful and economical appropriation of heat, light, air, water, &c. hence a variety of philosophical principles are to be consulted. To secure from all these principles, the greatest aggregate of convenience, comfort, pleasure and health, with symmetrical and ornamental structure, in a picturesque combination, with surrounding scenery, for a given sum, requires no small degree of practical skill and intelligence. In operations which are often repeated, a person acquires much knowledge and skill by practice and experiment: but the construction of a dwelling is an operation which thousands perform but once in a life-time; hence a mistake or error in the selection of a site—the formation of a plan, or in any other fundamental particular, brings a standing inconvenience upon the occupants. Such errors have often rendered expensive buildings comparatively valueless.

Much taste is manifested in this country, in the modern styles of Architecture, which many of our citizens have adopted, in providing themselves with convenient and, in many instances, elegant dwellings.

A well digested system of rural Architecture, adapted to the circumstances of our country, would greatly facilitate the construction of convenient and tasty buildings: but such a work is yet a desideratum. There are many valuable principles and suggestions scattered in various works, and the object of this work is to collect and systemize these principles, with such other instructions as experience has shown to be needful, and adapt them to general use in this country.

SITE AND ASPECTS.

A COTTAGE has just been erected according to Design I, which will accommodate a family of four to six persons. It is situated on a lot of something more than an acre, with a road on the east side, running in a southerly direction. Such a Cottage may be advantageously placed on a lot a hundred feet square.

The one here described, stands about fifty yards from the road, fronts east-north-east, and is nearly surrounded by fruit trees, which are preferred to forest trees by those who wish to combine utility with ornament, though for shade and ornament, the latter are generally chosen. A grove affords, to a house, a natural protection in both Summer and Winter.

One of the bay windows, affords a southerly view—of the garden and surrounding scenery for some distance ; and the other, a northern view—of part of the flower-garden, and the surrounding and distant scenery of a valley some fifteen miles wide, containing various forests and improvements, and a fine sheet of tide water. The green house has a south-south-west aspect, which is considered the best.

The rear of the lot is bounded by a brook, on the margin of which, there is a belt of fine forest trees. The bank is some ten feet high, and the declivity sufficiently steep to afford fine sites for an ice-house, poultry-house, stable &c.

In the composition of this Design, the object is to combine convenience, economy and elegance in such a manner, that neither shall predominate at the expense of the others. The exterior would be injured by more ornament—unless fully ornamented—and less, would destroy the general harmony. The windows, with diagonal sashes, and the ornamented peaks of the roof, are the prominent features of the Design.

The walks and carriage road are laid out in the natural style of Landscape Gardening. The borders are filled with a variety of shrubbery, producing a succession of flowers through the season, and a variety of delicate fruit trees are arranged in such order as to ornament the place nearly or quite as much as the standard shrubs, that produce only flowers.

SPECIFICATIONS,

Of the Materials and Labor required for the erection of a Cottage according to Design 1.

The divisions, heights, dimensions, and general arrangement, are to be found in Plates 3, 5 and 6.

MASON'S WORK AND MATERIALS.

EXCAVATIONS.—Three and a half feet below the surface, and the earth, graded properly around the foundations.

STONE WORK.—The cellar and kitchen walls, to be laid eight feet high—under the stairway six and a half feet, and dwarf walls three and a half feet—and eighteen inches thick, with quarry or bank stone, in suitable lime and sand mortar, blue stone steps and coping to outside, kitchen door—kitchen hearth, blue stone, two feet wide and six and a half feet long, and brown stone hearths and facings in the drawing and dining rooms.

BRICK WORK.—Three piers, three and a half feet high and twelve inches square, to support two girders under the main floor; a wall eight inches thick, one foot and six inches high, around the basement stairway; one chimney with four fire places—one, neatly plastered for a wood fire—one, for the kitchen, and two with neat ornamental sixteen inch grates, with blowers and fenders: the four flues well pargetted topped with hard brick, five feet above the peak of the roof. The outside walls between the weather=boarding and plastering to be strongly filled with brick, set on the edge, with lime and sand mortar, and bracketed.

PLASTERING.—All the rooms, halls, and closets, on the first and second floors, lathed, plastered, browned, and hard finished—the basement, lathed, and plastered with two coats, and whitewashed.

CARPENTER'S WORK AND MATERIALS.

FRAME.—To be made of good spruce or pine, square timber, framed and braced in every part, as drawn on plate No. 4—of the following dimensions :

Sills, ...	4 by 9.	First tier of beams, .	3 by 9—20 inches between centers.
Posts, ...	4 " 8.	Second " "	3 " 8—16 " "
Plates, . . .	4 " 8.	Collar beams, . .	3 " 6.
Framing beams, .	4 " 8.	Principal rafters, . .	3 " 5—2 feet 8 inches "
Interties, . . .	4 " 6.	Jack " . .	3 " 4.
Porch=posts and plates,	4 " 6.	Braces	3 " 4.
Window and door studs,	4 " 6.	Studding . .	3 " 4, 16 " "
Girders, . . .	4 " 7	Basemt. Sleepers, Chesnut,	4 " 6—2 feet 6 " apart.

SIDING.— Best Albany boards, clear of bad defects, planed, rebated and nailed strongly with 10ᵈ nails, and not over 8 inches to the weather ; the widest at the bottom—the water table to project two and a half inches —the corner boards, three inches wide by one and a quarter thick.

ROOFS.—The sheathing of the main roofs, of hemlock boards seven=eighths of an inch thick, edges laid close, covered with best split white pine shingles, three thick, and secured in the band with 4ᵈ nails—open two inches in the valleys. The lead in the valleys, to be sixteen inches wide, weighing three and a half pounds to the square foot, and the chimneys to be properly leaded. The octagon, porch, bay=windows and green=house, to be sheathed with milled plank, covered with best cross tin, put on in the most approved manner. All the roofs to be made perfectly tight.

TRIMMING AND GUTTERS.—The gutters to main roof and porch, to be made strong, of clear plank, one and a quarter inches thick, tongued and grooved, and properly moulded. The gutters on the green=house, bay win= dows and octagon, to be formed on the roof, by raising the front two inches—the parapets on the porch, bay win= dows and green=house, as drawn in Plate 6—the octagon with moulded embrasures.

On each side of the front entrance, a pine newel, turned, eight inches diameter, with a moulded rail, three by four and a half inches, supported by arch balusters, one and a half inches square—set diagonally.

WINDOWS.— All the windows in the first story, and four in the second, to be made with boxes, and all the sashes hung with weights and cords—three large windows in the gables of the second story—each to have two sashes hung with two and a half inch butts—the small window over the green=house, to slide—and the green= house sashes all hung with three inch butts—kitchen windows with two and a half inch butts. Best sash fastenings to all the first story windows, and three inch spring bolts, to all the sashes with butts. The glass in all the windows represented in the several elevations, to be Winslow brand, set in the sashes diagonally— all other glass, seven by nine, set perpendicular. The sashes in the bay windows to be one inch and five=eighths thick, and all others one and a quarter and one and three=eighths, thick. The inside shutters, to the three win= dows in kitchen and cellar, to be plain, cleted, hung by butts, and secured by metal bars.

BLINDS.—To all the first and second story windows made strong, with rolling slats—hung by welded hinges and secured by patent fastenings.

FLOORS.—To be of first quality of milled white pine plank, one and a quarter inches thick, laid in the best manner. The outside platforms, of narrow clear plank, laid in white lead and blind nailed.

PARTITIONS.—Set with joists three by four inches—sixteen inches between centers.

DOORS.—The front door, four feet wide and eight, high, in two parts—one and three=quarter inches thick. The passage doors in the first story one and a half inches thick, moulded on both sides. Two doors in the basement to have nine light sashes.

All the doors to be hung by best patent butts and screws, and fastened by good American locks. A rebated mortice lock to each of the other passage doors, in the first story—and five inch rim locks to the other doors—mineral knobs with bronze furniture to all the doors—two good bolts to the front doors and one to the back door.

BASE.—In first story to be one and a quarter inches thick and six inches high, moulded on the top edge—in second story and basement one inch thick and five inches high beveled on the top.

STAIRS.—From basement to first story to be enclosed with narrow tongued, grooved and beaded boards—one and one=quarter inch steps and three=quarter inch risers. The principal stairs, with winders—moulded steps, plain string—octagon newel—rail and balusters. The spandril to be paneled with one and one=quarter inch stiles and rails, a good scuttle to the roof of the octagon with a step ladder.

BELL.—To the front door to be hung with copper wire, in the best manner—mineral pull.

PRESSES AND CLOSETS.—The pantry in basement to have four good strong shelves on each of two sides; the two closets from drawing room to have five shelves neatly beaded on each of three sides—closet in dining room—to have four shelves—two dressing rooms, second story, to have a wardrobe in each, with shelf, hooks and pins, a wardrobe in the chamber, with shelves and hooks.

MANTLES.—Three wood mantles—one like the drawing in plate 5 and one the same, without trusses—and one neat plain mantle for chamber—borders to be put down to all the hearths.

MATERIALS.—All the trimmings for the exterior to be good and sound lumber, free from knots, shakes or sap—all the lumber for interior work, to be best clear and well seasoned—rails, newel and balusters, to main stairs, of best seasoned oak.

PAINTING.—All the wood work inside and outside (except shingle roof and interior floors) to have two good substantial coats of pure white lead and linseed oil—the tin roofs and leaders to be painted the same—the blinds to have three coats, the two last a bronze green; the work to be well done, and at proper times. The outside of the house may be shaded either drab, gray or brown, if required.

DESCRIPTION OF THE PLATES OF DESIGN I.

PLATE 1.—A perspective view of a half ornamented cottage, in the English style.

PLATE 2.—A protracted ground-plot, showing the several distances and dimensions, in sections of one square yard each. This plot, by its admeasurement of the ground, will guide to a ready location of the dwelling and out buildings, and a tasty arrangement of the trees, shrubbery, walks and alleys of the garden.

PLATE 3.—The plan and dimensions of the rooms, halls, closets, &c., on the first and second floors—all in the clear—with window and door openings. Scale,—8 feet to an inch.

PLATE 4.—Geometrical elevations, of the front and the side opposite the one in the perspective. Scale,—8 feet to an inch.

PLATE 5.—Framing plans of the front and side, with the distance between studs for window and door openings, and the hights of stories—in figures: also a profile section of a sill, post and plate, connected with rafter, gutter, beams, corner-board, water-table, stone wall, sleeper, floors, &c. And the basement: *a a*, dwarf-wall; *b b*, stone wall to the surface of the ground when graded; *c c*, the main wall; *d d*, blue stone steps and coping; *e e*, brick piers. Scale—of the basement and framing plan, ⅛ of an inch to the foot; of the profile, ¾ of an inch.

PLATE 6.—*A*, a profile section of a window frame and its connection with the floor and water table. Fig. 1, head of frame; *a*, hood moulding, 3½ by 3½; *b*, head casing, 1¼ by 5; *c*, sash rails; *d*, blind and sash stop, ⅝ by 2; *e*, check strip, ½ by 1; *f*, plastering, ¾ thick; *g*, interior casing, 1½ by 3; *h*, sash strip, ½ by 1½. Fig. 2; *k*, water sill 1¼ by 5; *m*, drip sill, 2 by 8½; *n*, siding, ¾ by 8; *o*, interior base, 1¼ by 6. Fig. 3; *p*, floor 1¼ thick; *r*, water table, 2½ by 10; *s*, main sill, 4 by 9.

B. Fig. 1, a front view of the several parapets. Fig. 2, a profile section of the same. Fig. 3, a profile section of the cornice of the porch; *a*, roof plank and tin; *b*, corner boards, 1¼ by 3; *c*, fascia and gutter back 1¼ by 10; *d*, moulded gutter front, 2 by 3; *e*, moulded gutter bottom, 1¼ by 5; *f*, bed mould with 1½ inch head; *g*, rafter 3 by 5; *h*, post 4 by 6.

C, a portion of the main gable. Fig. 1, face of the raking cornice. Fig. 2, a profile section of gutter, secured to the rafter; *a*, rafter, 3 by 5, planed below the plate; *b*, roof plank, 1¼ thick, planed, tongued, grooved, beaded, and laid face side down, below the plate—rough hemlock boards above; *c*, gutter back, 1¼ by 14; *d*, gutter bottom, 2 by 3½; *e*, gutter front, 1¼ by 7; *f*, gable bead returned in front of the gutter; *g*, shingles; *h*, gutter cap, 1 by 4.

D, a profile section of bay window cornice; *a*, fascia, 1¼ by 12; *b*, window head jamb, 1¼ by 4½; *c*, interior face casing, 1¼ by 8; *d*, cornice mould, 8½ inches high, and 4½ projection; *e*, gutter stop, 2 by 3; *ff*, sash rails; *g*, plastering of ceiling.

E, the parlor mantle. Fig. 1, a section of the front. Fig. 2, a profile. Fig. 3, ground section; *a*, the brick jamb; *b*, opened upright; *c*, jamb casing; *d*, fire mould; *e*, base.

F, the doors of the first story. Fig. 1, elevation of door and trimmings connected with the base. Fig. 2, ground section; *a*, jamb, 1¾ by 5½; *b*, cluster of beads or relief moulding, 1½ by 3; *c*, plinth, 2 by 3¾; *d*, stud, 3 by 4; *e*, plastering, ¾ thick; *f*, base· *g*, door step, 1 by 1; *h*, door stile, 1½ by 5; *k*, panel with cove moulding, or a plain bevel. Fig. 3, same as Fig. 2, except the relief moulding to be plain. Scale,—door plan ¾ of an inch to the foot, the others 1½.

ESTIMATE,

Of the Labor and Materials required for the erection of Design I.

MASON'S MATERIALS AND LABOR.

126 cubic yards of excavation	@ 10	$12 60	13 feet of kitchen hearth	@ 18	2 34
39 casks Thomaston lime	@ 1 00	39 00	2 sett brown stone hearths and jambs	@ 5 00	10 00
2 casks of lump lime	@ 1 75	3 50	2 16 in. ornamental grates, sett	@ 11 50	23 00
12000 plastering lath	@ 2 00	24 00	1 cask lath nails		6 50
2330 hard brick	@ 4 25	9 90	3 barrels white sand	@ 50	1 50
4190 salmon and soft	@ 3 00	12 57	49 days mason's labor	@ 1 75	85 75
15 bushels hair	@ 20	3 00	21 " laborer	@ 1 00	21 00
132 loads of stone	@ 75	99 00	carting		11 00
160 loads of sand	@ 25	40 00			———
31 feet of blue stone steps	@ 16½	5 12			$409 78

CARPENTER'S MATERIALS AND LABOR.

4727 feet of timber	$16 50 per m.	$78 00	14, 5 in. rim locks,	@ 83	11 62
12 chesnut sleepers	@ 37½	4 50	4 wardrobe and closet locks	@ 33	1 32
115 joists	@ 12½	14 38	4 closet knobs (mineral)	@ 8	32
25 wall strips	@ 10	2 50	8 rail screws	@ 9	72
265 floor planks	@ 27	71 55	3 shutter bars	@ 9	27
230 siding boards	@ 16	36 80	3 " knobs	@ 6	18
170 best planks	@ 27	45 90	3 " 7 in. spring bolts ⅝ square	@ 33	99
196 best boards	@ 18	35 28	24 pairs 4 by 4 butts	@ 21	5 04
400 feet of 2 in., 1½ in. and ⅝ in.	@ 3½	14 00	4 " 3 in. "	@ 7	28
110 hemlock boards	@ 12½	13 75	12 " 2½ in. "	@ 5	60
18 bunches shingles	@ 2 00	36 00	1 gross ¾ screws, No. 9		20
2 front newels	@ 1 00	2 00	1 " " No. 6		23
60 feet of oak	@ 6	3 60	1 " 1 in. " No. 9		31
1 oak newel		2 00	2 " 1¼ in. " No. 11	@ 41	82
30 oak balusters	@ 9	2 70	10/12 doz. sash fastenings	@ 3 38	2 80
377 feet of diagonal sash	@ 20	75 40	6 lbs. sash cord (patent)	@ 28	1 68
50 lights of 7 by 9 sash	@ 9	4 50	328 lbs. sash weight	@ 2	6 56
106 feet of rolling blinds	@ 75	79 50	4 doz. pullies (axle)	@ 62½	2 50
355 square feet of tin roofing	@ 9	31 95	1 doz. small spring bolts		50
70 feet 3 in. tin leader	@ 12½	8 75	1 front door bell		2 75
30 feet 2 in. tin leader	@ 10	3 00	1½ doz. hat hooks	@ 20	30
263 lbs. sheet lead	@ 6	15 78	4 carved finial heads	@ 1 00	4 00
6 casks of nails, 4d, 6d, 8d, 10 & 12d	@ 4 25	25 50	carting		14 00
10 lbs. fine finishing nails	@ 12½	1 25	134 days carpenter's labor	@ 1 50	201 00
1 rebated front door lock		3 50			———
8, 4 in. mortice locks	@ 1 40	11 20			$882 28

PAINTER'S MATERIALS AND LABOR.

300 lbs. white lead	@ $9 00	$27 00	½ lb. lamp black " "	@ 50	25
10 gallons linseed oil	@ 85	8 50	12 lbs. of putty	@ 6	72
5 " boiled "	@ 96	4 80	1 lb. glue		25
1½ " spirits of turpentine	@ 70	1 05	12 days painter's labor	@ 1 75	21 00
2 lbs. litharge	@ 12½	25			———
1 lb. chrome yellow, ground in oil		1 00			$64 82

RECAPITULATION.

Carpenter's bill	$882 28
Mason's "	409 78
Painter's "	64 82
	———
	$1356 88

PLATE 1.

DESIGN I.

W. H. Ranlett, Arch.

PERSPECTIVE VIEW.

Lith by F. & S. Palmer 43 Ann St.

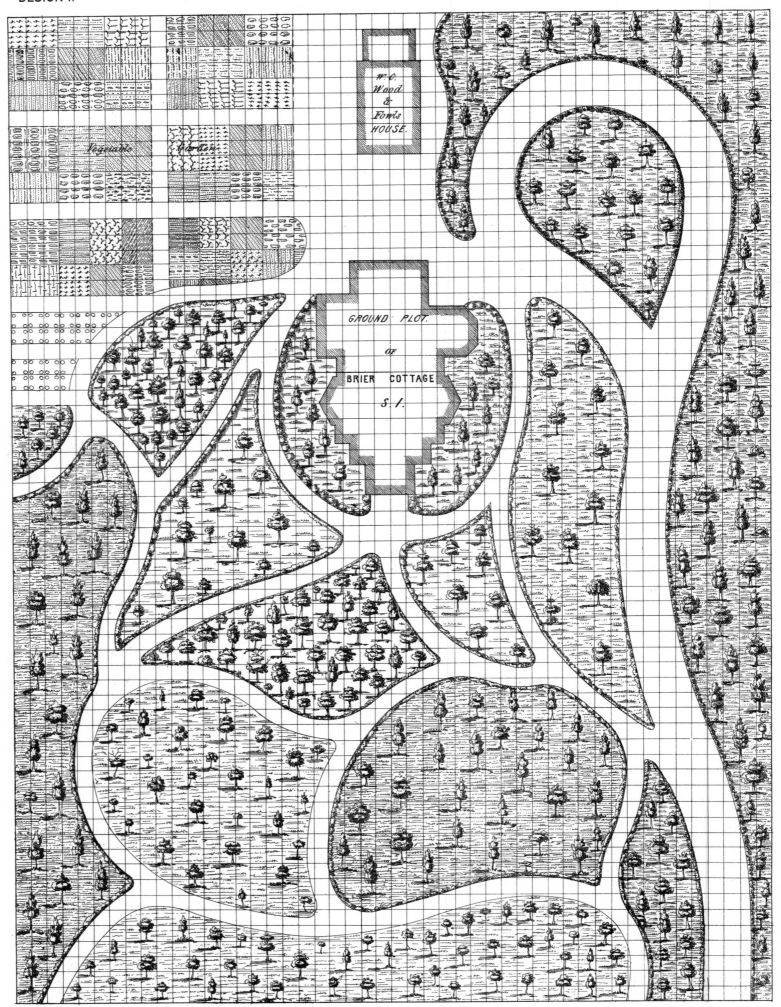

GROUND PLOT.
OF
BRIER COTTAGE
S. I.

W.^M. C.
Wood
&
Fowls
HOUSE.

Vegetable Garden.

PLATE 3.

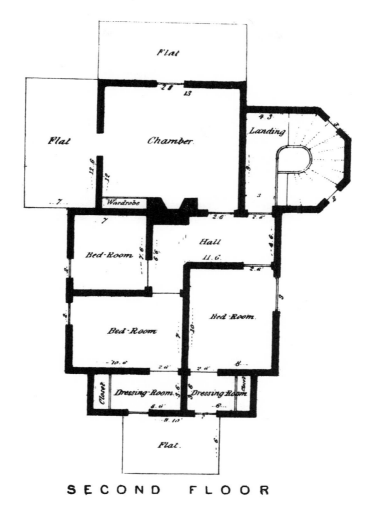

SECOND FLOOR

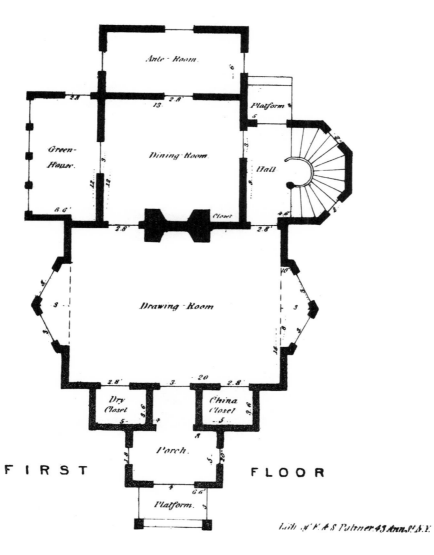

FIRST FLOOR

Lith of F. & S. Palmer 43 Ann St N.Y.

DESIGN I.   FRONT   ELEVATION.   **PLATE 4.**

SIDE   ELEVATION.

Lith. of F. & S. Palmer 13 Ann St. N.Y.

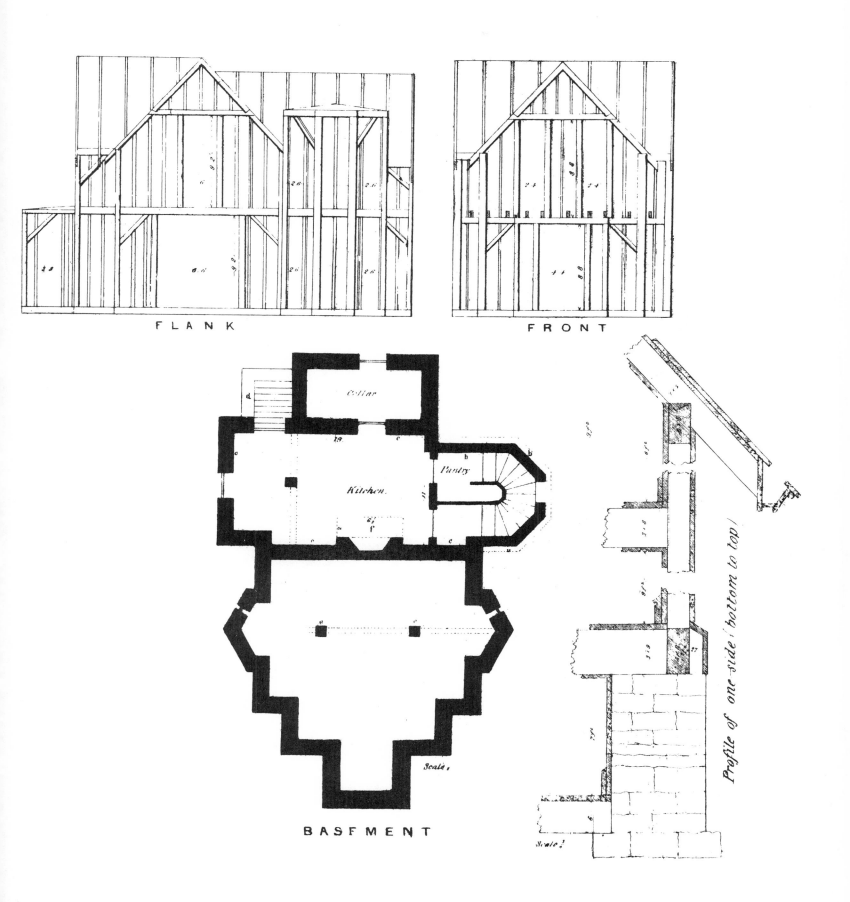

FLANK

FRONT

BASEMENT

Profile of one side (bottom to top)

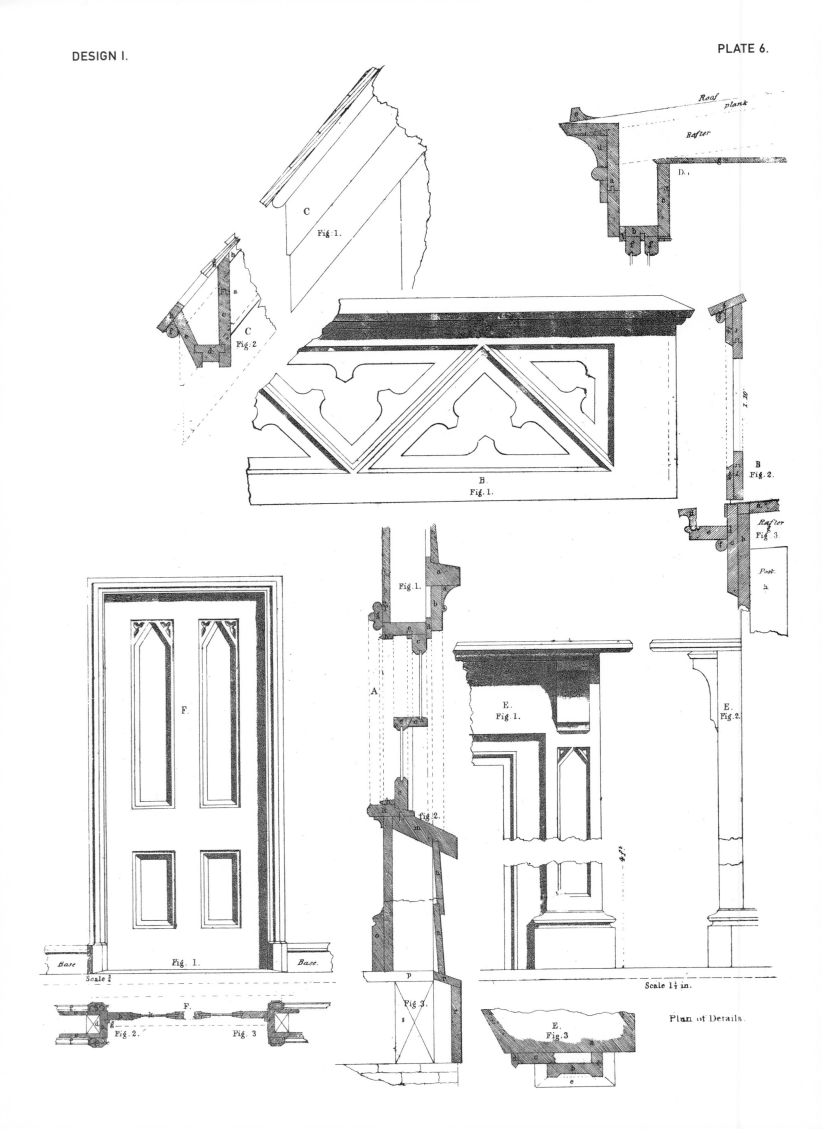

Roof plank

Rafter

Rafter

D.

C
Fig. 1

C
Fig: 2

B.
Fig. 1.

B
Fig. 2

Rafter
Fig. 3.

Post.

Fig. 1.

F.

A

Fig. 2

E.
Fig. 1

E.
Fig. 2.

Base

Scale ¾

Fig. 1.

Base.

Scale 1½ in.

Fig. 3

Plan of Details.

F.

Fig. 2.

Fig. 3.

E.
Fig. 3.

ARCHITECTURE.

THE ART of building naturally arose from the necessities of man, which required him to provide a place of defence for himself and his substance, from the effects of climate and weather. The conical hut or wigwam is deemed the original and simplest form of dwellings. An improvement on this, is believed to have resulted in the cubical hut; and the next step, probably is the tent or tabernacle of the wilderness, which was an obvious convenience to the wandering tribes of herdsmen, as were large portions of mankind in the early history of our race: hence a modern tent or marquee is a fit representation of the general characteristics of habitations of man, in the early ages of the world.

ARCHITECTURE as a Science, arose from the devotional feelings and tendencies of our nature. This is evident from the Architectural remains found in various parts of the earth; such as those in Egypt, India, Persia, Babylon, Phœnicia, Greece, Italy, Gaul, Britain, Central and South America, and other countries which are the only known records of the Architecture of those ages. Indeed the delineations of the classic architecture of Greece and Rome, have been of necessity gathered and systemized by admeasurement of the monuments of their Architectural taste and skill; for the wasting tooth of the dark ages, left to the world no other record of them. There are, in various countries, many remains of structures, evidently erected for devotional purposes, where there are no traces of the habitations of man in those ages. From these facts, it is plain that the ancients—as the moderns—had the greatest care and heaviest expense in their sacred edifices. King David was ashamed that " he dwelt in a house of cedar while the ark of God dwelt in curtains:" and on one occasion the Hebrews were reproved by Divine Inspiration for " dwelling in their ceiled houses while the house of the Lord was lying waste."

The earliest style of Architecture, recognized in ancient ruins, is the Egyptian, with which they more nearly harmonize than with any other now known; and there is not sufficient indication in them to warrant the conclusion that any other form obtain so far as to become a style of building. It is inferred that Solomon's Temple was constructed in the Egyptian style, from the general description and proportions of the edifice itself —from the fact that the Hebrews had much of Egyptian science and art, and from the additional fact that the foreign help which he employed in building it, was that of the Phœnicians, who built in the Egyptian style.

At the fall of the Roman Empire, the Egyptian, Grecian and Roman styles were in vogue and well understood. Indian and Persian architecture harmonizes so well with the Egyptian, that authorities generally refer them to a common origin, but they are not agreed as to which country is entitled to the credit of priority; the balance, however, is in favor of Egypt. All other styles are of later date, except perhaps the Chinese, which is scarcely entitled to the rank of a *style*. The rudeness, ignorance and barbarism of the dark ages produced the pointed style, which was prevailing in England in the commencement of the 16th century, when it began to be superceded by the

ITALIAN STYLE:

Which arose in Italy, in the early part of the 15th century, in an attempt to restore classic Roman architecture. The superiority of Rome over all the rest of Italy, before the decline of the Empire, and its being the great seat of learning, improvement, and power, gave to everything of importance, in that country, the style, "Roman:" hence "Roman Architecture." Since the Reformation, the country has had a much higher relative bearing upon the metropolis, which gives vogue to the style "Italian;" hence the modern architecture of that country is called the "Italian Style:" moreover it did not rise in Rome, but in other parts of Italy.

Brunelleschi, a Florentine architect, was the first who met with much success in attempting to restore Roman architecture. He fixed his eye upon the erection of a cupola on the cathedral, or Duomo, of his native city, as a favorite opportunity to display his architectural taste and skill. Cupolas had been erected in Constantinople, Venice, Pisa and some other places. The cathedral of Florence had been commenced a century before, but had not been finished; and Brunelleschi was thought to be wild in his professions of ability to erect a cupola upon it. He was even hissed from a convention of Italian and Ultramontane artists and the curators of the edifice, which had been assembled by himself in 1420 for the purpose of considering that subject. He was, however, employed the next year to undertake the enterprize, and it was successfully accomplished.

This splendid achievement of the taste and skill of Brunelleschi, established his reputation, settled the confidence of Italy in the practicability of his plans, and gave a decided impetus to the work of reform. This opportunity was improved by the leading Italian architects of that period, who professed to follow the example of Brunelleschi, which they did in all, except its most important feature—that of studying the classic remains of Roman architecture, instead of which they took for their guide, the indefinite, and, in many instances, incorrect writings of Vitruvius—a Latin author, so obscure that nothing is known of him except what he says of himself. The writings of Vitruvius have had great celebrity for four centuries, but we are fully satisfied that this has arisen more from their being deemed the earliest, on the subject, now extant, and the improper use made of them by the architects of the 15th century, than from any intrinsic merit that they possess. It is an imbecility of our nature, to venerate and lean upon hoary antiquity, when better guides are at hand.

The Italian architects of the 15th century are styled the "Cinquecento School." They found it necessary—from the traits to which we have referred—to explain or interpret the writings of Vitruvius, notwithstanding which, they were generally made the guide, and the classic examples of ancient Roman architecture, consulted only as frame-work on which to form models. This course resulted in a general formality and mannerism in the productions of those who adhered to their master, and a wild grotesqueness in the works of such as allowed themselves to depart from his rules: hence it appears that good taste was wanting in all of them; and they, moreover, perpetuated the worst qualities of the Roman school: such as the tasteless collocation of arches and columns—unequal inter-columinations—broken entablatures and heavy stylobates, which belonged alike to the productions of the best and worst architects of that school. Their productions were farther characterized by the constant attachment of columns and their appendages, to the front of buildings, and the infrequency of their use in insulated places, which are their proper positions in porticos and colonnades—also by the thinness of the smaller portions of the entablatures, and a bad proportion of their larger parts—by the general want of enrichment which fluting imparts to columns—by too great a projection of pilasters, which were often used as pro-columns or an apology for applying projecting entablatures—by the inconsistent practice of diminishing the pilasters, and sometimes fluting them—by the use of circular and twisted pediments, and the making of breaks in them to suit the projections: also other faults, such as windows like doors —the distyle arrangement of columns—the clustering of columns and pilasters—the cutting away of portions of the architrave and frize, and even of the *main bearing-beam*, to make an opening for a window—the alternation of circular and angular pediments, and the mutilating of them at the top or bottom; and sometimes the whole front was disfigured—as is often the case to this day, even in houses of no architectural pretentions—by that supreme vagary of bad taste, a prostyle portico or colonnade, suitable only for a public building, and infinitely better befitting a Grecian Temple than a private dwelling.

The first delineations and admeasurements of the remains of Roman architecture, published in Italy, were made by Palladio and Serlio, but the inaccuracies and—in many instances—misrepresentations of both works, prove the incompetency of the authors to their undertaking, and the toleration and perpetuation of their defects, equally prove the bad taste of the schools in which they are masters. The earliest delineations of those remains, on which reliance is placed by modern architects, were made by Stuart and Rivett.

In ancient architecture, only three orders were known—the Doric, Ionic, and Corinthian. Two others —the Tuscan and Composite—arose in Italy, in the architectural reform of the 15th century. Vitruvius describes—but without delineations, as usual with him—a fourth order which he calls Tuscan; which was, however, only a Roman debasement of the Doric. Some of the Cinquecento architects found some specimens of foliated columns which the ancient Romans had compounded of the foliated and voluted columns of the Greeks. These specimens they subjected to certain rules and gave them the rank and style of the fifth or Composite order. There are, therefore, five orders in this style, usually arranged thus: first, the Tuscan, which has no examples in antiquity, but owes its origin to a blunder of Vitruvius and the fancies of the " reformers." Second, the Doric, a poor and tasteless arrangement of that order on a Roman model. Third, the Ionic, which is nearly as great a debasement of the Grecian original, produced as the last. Fourth, the Corinthian, but quite unlike the ancient examples of both Greece and Rome, in beauty and expression; and fifth the Composite, an elegant variety of the Corinthian—a hybrid of the horned or angular Ionic volutes, with the deep necking and foliage of the Corinthian. The Italian style was introduced into England early in the 16th century, by Holbein, having prevailed in Italy nearly a century. Inigo Jones, coming after Holbein, had much greater success in giving it vogue; but it remained for Sir Christopher Wren to give it a flowing popularity, which he accomplished by the advantage afforded him by the burning of London in 1666. This style became established in England, after a severe contest with long settled usage and deep-rooted prejudices, supplanting the pointed style; and it produced a considerable change in the architectural aspect of the country, substituting the attic balustrade for the battlement—the cylindrical column for the clustered pillar—the pilaster for the buttress—the semi-circular arch for the pointed—the entabliture for the archivolt, &c.

A house in the Italian style, has neither gable, buttress nor pinnacle, yet the whole façade or front is greatly relieved and beautified by the agreeable variety in its composition; for in this respect, the style allows great latitude to the architect, admitting—besides the features of the accompanying design—porches, archivolt, window-heads, windows in triplets or qudruplications separated by mullions, projecting cornice, a ridged or furrowed roof, and the whole crowned by a graceful campanile. When the cornice is supported by brackets, the style is called the "Italian bracketed."

Design 2 is in the Anglo Italian style. It may have a terrace, or a concave slope of about four feet, or any other graceful connection with the ground. It has two piazzas, in the entrance and lawn fronts, which are north and east. There are also two balconies in the entrance front, a large bay-window, facing the south, the green-house, S. W., a projecting angular, lighted niche or oriel window in the lawn front, rectangular and semi-circular window heads without caps, and a flat roof supported by cantalevers and surmounted by an ornamental balustrade or blocking course—without pediments. The Anglo Italian admits of virandas which is not the case with "Paladian Italian."

DESCRIPTION OF THE PLATES OF DESIGN II.

PLATE 7.—A perspective view of an Anglo Italian villa, designed for General E——, and proposed to be erected (on a lot of ground 125 by 200 feet, bounded on three sides by streets), in the upper part of the City of New York.

PLATE 8.—The ground-plot of a portion of the lot, giving the position of the dwelling house, coach and wood houses, walks, carriage road, vegetable garden, &c., also a proper arrangement of the trees and shrubbery.

PLATE 9.—Plans of first and second floors with dimensions, &c.

PLATE 10.—Elevations of the lawn and entrance fronts.

PLATE 11.—Two frame elevations with dimensions of timber, stories and openings, also interior details. Fig. 1, ground section of front door frame and trimmings. Fig. 2, ground section of green house window frames. Fig 3, profile section of window frame. Fig. 4, ground section of a door and trimmings. Fig. 5, a profile section of second story base. Fig. 6, a profile section of first story base. Fig. 7, section of the face, and profile of mantle in the dining room.

PLATE 12.—Plan of basement and exterior details. Fig. 1, section of the framing and hights of stories. Fig. 2, face and profile sections of main and wing cornices. Fig. 3, front piazza cornice, pillar, caps, and base. Figs. 4 and 5, face sections of first and second story balconies. Fig. 6, section of chimney tops. Figs. 7 and 8, side piazza cornice, pillar, cap and base. Fig. 9, side and front of balcony brackets.

ESTIMATE,
Of the Labor and Materials required for Design II.

MASON'S MATERIALS AND LABOR.

163 cubic yards excavation	@ 10	$16 30	178 loads sand @ 31 — 55 18
157 loads stone	@ 75	117 75	30 bushels white sand @ 9 — 2 70
5628 hard brick	@ 3 50	19 70	40 bushels hair @ 19 — 7 60
17408 soft and salmon brick	@ 2 50	43 52	24000 plastering lath @ 3 00 — 72 00
60 ft. blue stone coping and steps	@ 16	9 60	2 casks lath nails @ 7 50 — 15 00
10 window sills	@ 50	5 00	3 grates @15 00 — 45 00
10 " lintels	@ 40	4 00	1 cooking range — 45 00
1 door sill		75	2 mantles each 35—70 — 105 00
12 ft. kitchen hearth	@ 19	2 28	73 lbs. sheet lead @ 6, carting @ 23 00 — 27 38
3 brown stone hearths and facings	@ 4 25	12 75	96 days mason's labor @ 1 75 — 168 00
101 casks lime	@ 94	94 94	67 " laborer @ 87½ — 58 62
10 casks lump lime	@ 1 50	15 00	
11 barrels Lubec plaster	@ 1 87	20 57	**$964 64**

CARPENTER'S MATERIALS AND LABOR.

11094 ft. timber	$15 75 per m.	$174 73	3 gross ¾ screws, No. 9 @ 29 — 87
289 joists	@ 14	40 46	2 " " " No. 6 @ 28 — 56
376 floor planks	@ 28	105 28	1 " 1 in. " No. 9 @ 31 — 31
270 spruce planks	@ 22	59 40	5 " 1¼ in. " No. 11 @ 42 — 2 10
85 narrow planks	@ 18	15 30	7 5 in. upright mortice locks @ 3 50 — 24 50
60 furring boards	@ 12	7 20	5 4½ in. " " @ 3 34 — 16 70
602 narrow siding boards	@ 18	108 36	10 4½ in. " " @ 2 34 — 23 40
185 piece planks	@ 30	55 50	7 rim locks @ 92 — 6 44
109 piece boards	@ 20	21 80	1 rebated front door lock — 10 50
1836 ft. 2, 1½ and 1¼ in. plank	@ 3½	64 26	2 flush bolts @ 75 — 1 50
2100 ft. 1 and ¾ in. boards	@ 3½	73 50	1 mortice latch — 3 50
880 ft. clear timber	@ 3	26 40	15 doz. axle pullies @ 62 — 9 30
251 ft. basement sleepers	@ 6	15 06	16 lbs. sash cord @ 31 — 4 96
38 ft. mahogany	@ 12	4 56	1428 lbs. sash weights @ 2 — 28 56
1 newel		5 50	1 9/12 doz. sash fastenings @ 3 50 — 6 12
43 balusters	@ 11	4 73	4 bells @ 4 25 — 17 00
2 caps and bases	@ 6 00	12 00	3 " @ 3 25 — 9 75
193 ft. blinds	@ 75	144 75	4 doz. cloak and hat hooks @ 25 — 1 00
2227 ft. metal roofing	@ 13	289 51	12 rail screws @ 9, 10 shutter bars @ 31 — 4 18
84 ft. 4 in. tin leader	@ 15	12 60	36 lights glass 11 by 17 @ 21, 84 lights 10 by 17, @ 21 — 25 20
32 ft. 3 in. "	@ 10	3 20	16 " 10 by 16 @ 20, 24 " 9 by 16, @ 20 — 8 00
32 ft. 2 in. "	@ 9	2 58	132 " 9 by 15 @ 19, 39 " 10 by 15, @ 19 — 32 49
7 casks of nails, 8, 10 & 12d	@ 4 00	28 00	216 " 9 by 13 @ 14, 36 " 9 by 14, @ 16 — 36 00
60 lbs. fine finishing nails	@ 7	4 20	120 " 9 by 11 @ 13, 16 " 12 by 24, @ 60 — 25 20
14 pairs 4 by 4 butts	@ 22	3 08	175 loads carting — 63 00
12 " 3½ by 3½ "	@ 15	1 80	390 days carpenter's labor @ 1 50 — 585 00
7 " 3½ in. "	@ 10	70	
24 " 3 in. "	@ 7	1 68	**$2232 28**

PAINTER'S MATERIALS AND LABOR.

750 lbs. white lead	@$6 50	$48 75	20 lbs. putty @ 4 — 80
30 gallons raw linseed oil	@ 65	19 50	3 lbs. glue @ 19 — 57
6 " boiled "	@ 75	4 50	40 days painter's labor @ 1 75 — 70 00
3 " spirits of turpentine	@ 60	1 80	
6 lbs. litharge	@ 6	36	**$146 28**

RECAPITULATION.

Carpenter's bill	$2232 28
Mason's "	964 64
Painter's "	146 28
	$3343 20

NOVEMBER 1st, 1846.

SPECIFICATIONS,

Of the Materials and Labor required for the erection of a Villa according to Design II.

For the divisions, hights, dimensions, and general arrangement, see Plates 9, 10 and 11.

MASON'S WORK AND MATERIALS.

EXCAVATION.——To be made three feet deep and the earth properly graded when the wall is finished.

STONE WORK.——All the walls to be formed of best quarry building stone, in good mortar, 18 inches thick, 8 feet high, on a foundation of flat stone 2 feet wide. The walls of the airie, to be based 20 inches below the paving; all the stone walls above the surface to be neatly pointed. Kitchen hearth, of blue stone, 2 feet by 6, well bedded in mortar——steps and coping in airie, 10 inches wide and 4 thick. The sills and lintels of all the basement windows and back door must be cut, of blue stone. A suitable slide to the coal cellar, covered with a flag. The hearths and facings, in the dining room and three chambers, of brown stone, rubbed——two mantles of white veined marble, for parlor and drawing room. See Fig. 7, plate 11, (without modillions.)

BRICK WORK.——An 8 inch wall one side of the basement stairway——8 piers 3 feet high, 1 foot square——2 chimneys with 7 fire places, suitable for the several rooms, with flues extending 6 feet above the roof. Outside walls, between weather boards and lathing, filled with brick, set on the edge in mortar and well bracketed. Pavement of the airie, two cellars and dairy. All the brick for the pavements, 8 inch wall, piers, chimney tops and in chimneys below first tier of beams——must be hard, smooth and sound. The brackets on chimney tops, of wood covered with sheet lead and secured with small iron anchors.

DEAFENING.——Two floors, suitably deafened with mortar 2 inches thick.

PLASTERING.——All the rooms, halls, closets, &c. in the first and second stories, must be lathed and plastered with two coats of brown mortar, and one of best hard finish. A lime and plaster moulded cornice in the hall, parlor, dining and drawing rooms. All the walls and ceilings in the kitchen, hall and kitchen pantry, the wood partitions and ceilings of all the remaining rooms in basement, to be lathed and plastered with two good coats of brown mortar——slipped and whitewashed.

GRATES.——The Parlor, Drawing and Dining rooms, each to have a 16 inch grate with ornamental cast frames, set complete with all the necessary trimmings for summer and winter, the style corresponding with that of the mantles.

"Pond's Union Range" set complete, with all the necessary furniture, in the kitchen.

16

CARPENTER'S LABOR AND MATERIALS.

HIGHT OF STORIES.—Basement, 7 ft. 6 inches—prin. story 11 ft.—second story 9 ft.—first story of wing 9 ft. second 8 ft.—all in the clear.

MATERIALS:—For the exterior trimmings and inside work to be of the very best seasoned clear white pine.

FRAME.—Of sound white pine square timber—well framed and braced—sills, framing beams and 6 main posts, 4 by 10—plates, girts, 4 rear posts, and 4 side posts 4 by 8, first and second tier of beams 3 by 10, 16 inches between centers—roof tier 3 by 8, 30 inches between centers—all trimmer beams 4 inches thick,—rafters 3 by 5, 30 inches between centers—window and door studs 4 by 6—braces 3 by 4—studding 3 by 4, 16 inches between centers—basement sleepers 4 by 6, of red cedar, or 3 by 5, of locust, 2 feet between centers—piazza floor timbers 3 by 8—sills 4 by 8—rafters 4 by 6, and purlins 3 by 5.

COVERING.—Narrow clear white pine boards 5=8 thick, planed and rebated and put on the sides with 8d nails.

ROOFS.—The main, green=house, bay and oriel window roofs to be covered with milled spruce plank, well nailed on—the piazza roofs with clear white pine milled plank, beaded and center beaded on the underside —a scuttle in the main roof strongly hung and secured.

TIN.—All the roofs to be overlaid with Moorewood's " Patent galvanised tinned plates," with ridged joints. Tin leaders, 4 in. to main roof, 3 in. to green=house roof, and 2 in. to the others.

CORNICES.—Composed of mouldings, and contalevers made and put up according to details in plate 10— all the cornices except side piazza, to be surmounted by ornamental blocking courses.

PIAZZAS.—The front piazza to have square pillars with bracketed caps and open skirting—the side piazza, square open pillars with plain moulded caps and lattice skirting, and the rafters and purlins of both, planed and beaded. The lower balcony to have moulded rail and vertical filling, and the upper one, supported by brackets, to have a moulded rail and cross filling with cut rosettes on the angles, as in plate 10.

FLOORS.—The first and second floors prepared for deafening by ledges and boards. All the interior floors of best milled pine plank, clear of defects and strongly nailed. Piazza and balcony floors of narrow, clear white pine plank, tongued and groved, put down with white lead, and blind nailed—that of upper balcony beaded on the under side.

PARTITIONS:—Set with 3 by 4 joists, 12 in. between centers in the first story, and 16 in. between centers in the basement and second story. Door studs 4 by 6. Partitions in first story center=bridged.

DOORS.—Front door 2 in. thick—folding. All the passage doors in first story 1 3=4 thick, 4 panels each, moulded on both sides. All other doors in the first and second stories 1 1=2 thick, 4 panels, moulded on both sides. Doors in basement 1 1=4 thick, 4 panels. Size of doors in first story. 3 ft. by 7 1=2—in second story, 2 ft. 10 by 7—in basement 3 ft. by 6 1=2.

ARCHITRAVES:—In first story, as in pl. 11, fig. 4, and moulded panel window backs, as in fig. 3. In second story, 5 in. casings and 3 1=2 in. mouldings, 1 1=4 thick, and 4 in. wide. In basement, plain moulded casings, 1 in. by 2 1=2. Two fluted Ionic columns with carved caps and turned bases, in the drawing room.

LOCKS AND HINGES.—The doors in first story, hung by butts 4 by 4—in second story, by butts 3 1=2 by 3 1=2—in basement, by 3 1=2 in. butts. Front door to have an upright rebated mortice lock with night key. The passage doors in first story to have 5 in. upright mortice locks, and all other doors in first and second stories, 4 1=2 in. mortice locks. Basement doors, 6 in. rim locks. All the lock furniture in first story to be porcelain, "blue drop pattern"—in second story, white porcelain—in basement, mineral. All the butts and locks of best American manufacture.

WINDOWS.—In basement, 10 w. 12 l. 9 by 11. In first story, 2 w. 18 l. 11 by 17—2 w. 12 l. 9 by 16—3 w. 12 l. 9 by 15—4 bay=w. 12. l. 10 by 17—2 do. 18 l. 10 by 17—2 oriel=w. 8 l. 10 by 16—6 green=house w. 36 l. 9 by 13. In second story, 8 w. 12 l. 9 by 15—3 w. 12 l. 9 by 14—one balcony double w. circular head, 22 l. 10 by 15—one circular w. head over the bay=w. 17 l. 10 by 15. Sashes in basement, 1 1=4 thick—in second story, 1 3=8—in first story, 1 1=2. All the windows to be double hung by weights and linen sash cord. Best patent sash fastings to all the windows in first story. A pair of sashes between drawing room and green=house, 18 lights 12 by 24, hung by butts and secured by flush bolts and a mortice knob latch. Winslow glass in all the sashes.

BASE:—In basement, 9 in. high and 7=8 thick—in first story, 7 in. high and 1 1=4 thick, moulded—in second story, 1 in. thick and 7 high, moulded. See figs. 5 and 6 in plate 11.

STAIRS.—From basement to first story enclosed by a door at top. Principal stairs with a moulded string and steps, brackets, carved newel, 2 in. fancy balusters and 4 in. moulded rail—newel, rail and balusters of best St. Domingo mahogany. A step=ladder to scuttle. Front steps wide and strong, with sides enclosed and paneled on the front. Steps to side piazza enclosed, plain. A platform and steps to green=house.

CLOSETS, &c.—Kitchen pantry to have 4 shelves 1 1=4 in. thick, on each of two sides—put up strong with uprights—3 closets in first story to have five shelves 1 in. thick, on each of 3 sides—closet in hall to have a strip and 1 doz. hat hooks—5 presses in second story, each to be fitted up with shelves, hooks, and pins.

BELLS;—In parlor, hall, drawing and dining rooms with porcelain lever knobs "blue drop pattern,"—3 bells in second story with white porcelain lever knobs.

MANTLES.——The dining room to have a wood mantle as in plate 11, fig. 7—3 neat wood mantles in second story without the modlions or openings in pilasters, but to have a bed moulding—a plain shelf and uprights to kitchen fire place—hearth borders to all the fire places.

BLINDS.—Rolling blinds, moulded on one side, hung by welded hinges and secured by best patent fastenings, to all the windows (except green=house) in first and second stories—inside panel shutters to the basement windows, hung by butts and secured by 10 in. metal bars.

PAINTING.——All the wood work outside (except blinds), tin leaders and the chimney tops, and all the wood work inside except floors, stair rail, balusters and newel, to have two coats of pure Saugerties white lead and American linseed oil, put on in the very best manner and at proper times—the blinds to have three coats of paint—the last two, bronze or Paris green.

PLATE 7.

DESIGN II.

PERSPECTIVE VIEW

Designed & del by Wm H Ranlett

Lith. of F. & S. Palmer 43 Ann St.

On Stone by Walmer.

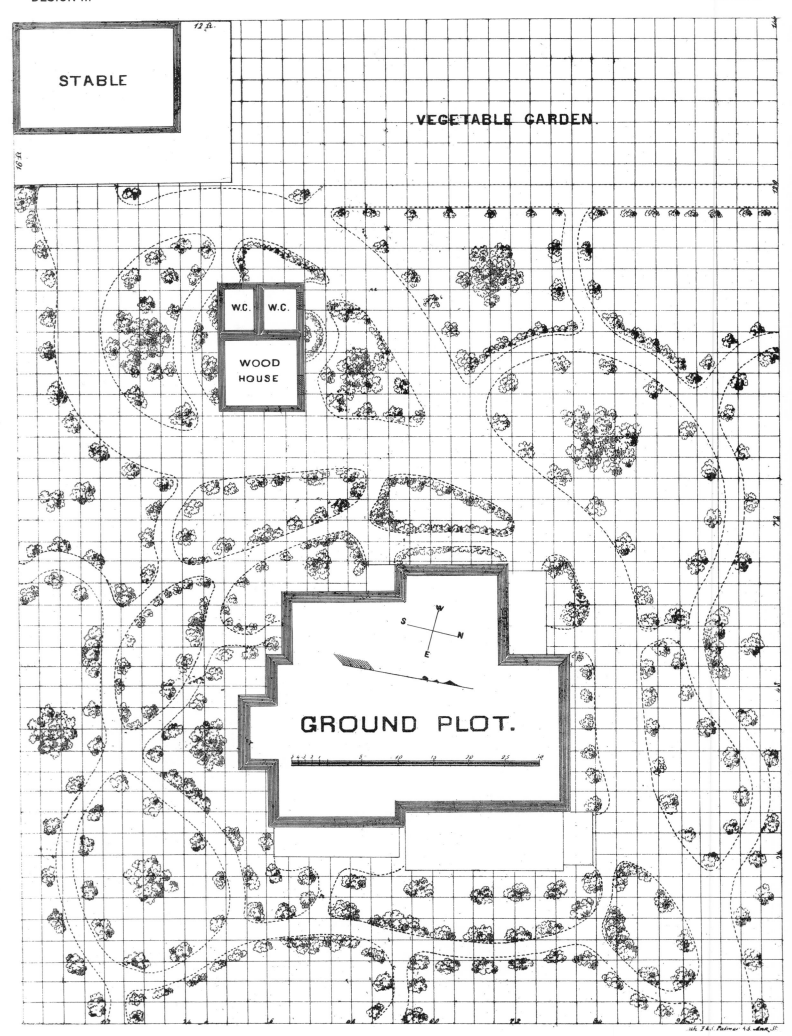

STABLE

12 ft.

16 ft.

VEGETABLE GARDEN.

W.C.

W.C.

WOOD
HOUSE

GROUND PLOT.

STABLE

Lith F&J Palmer 45 Ann St.

Press

Chamber

G.H.Roof

P.Roof

B.W.Roof

Entry

Hall

3½

7½

Bed Room

13½

Press
3½

Press

2½

Press

5

5

16

Chamber

13

Chamber

15

Bed Room

8

18

Balcony
6¼

3

P.Roof

SECOND FLOOR

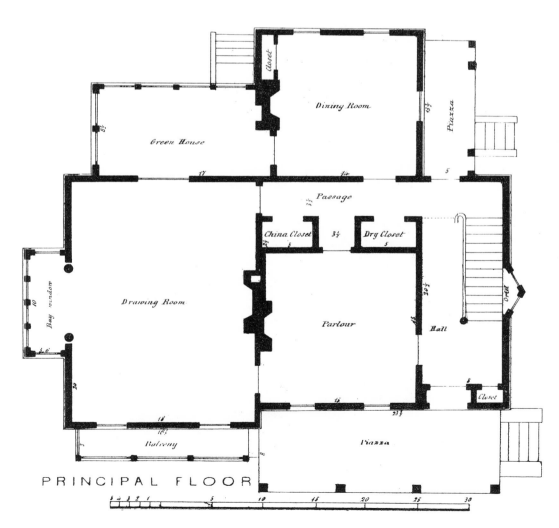

closet

Dining Room

16¾

Piazza

8½

Green House

17

14

5

3½   Passage

China Closet
5   5

3½

Dry Closet
5

10

Bay window

Drawing Room

20¾

Parlour

13

Hall

Closet

L.6

30

18

15

23½

16¾

Balcony

7

Piazza

8

PRINCIPAL FLOOR

5 4 3 2 1   5   10   15   20   25   30

PLATE 10.

GARDEN FRONT

ENTRANCE FRONT

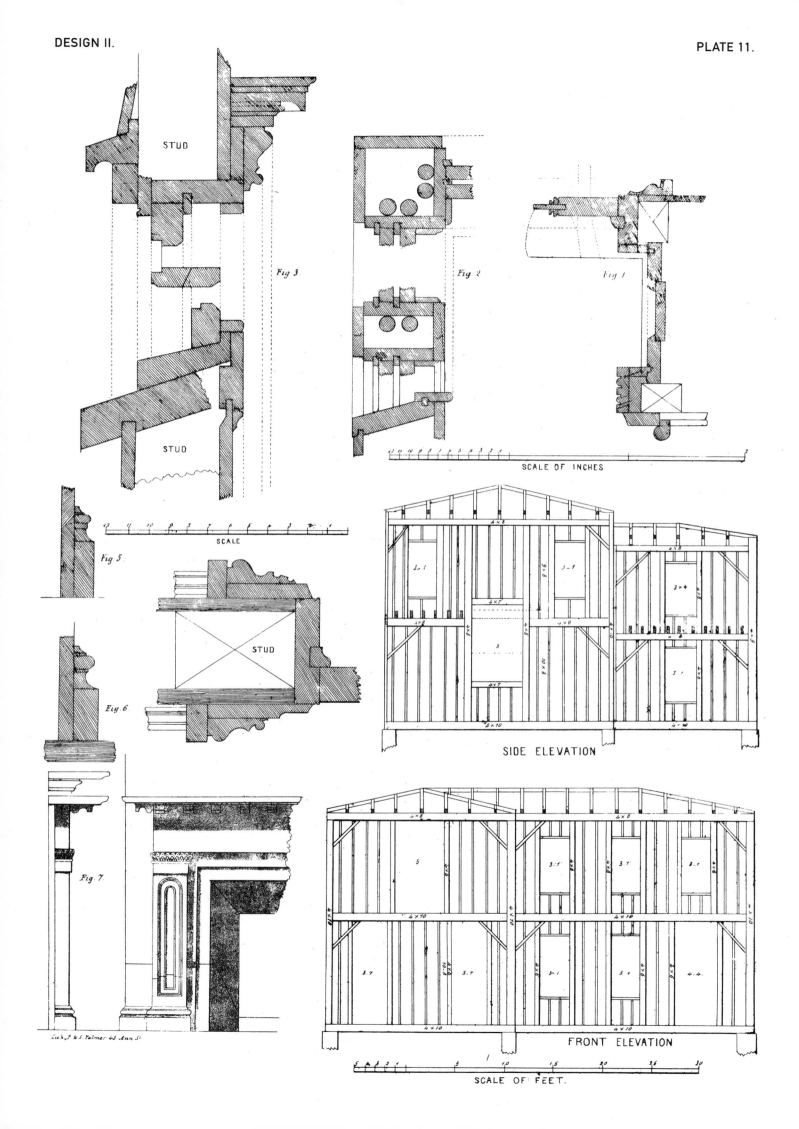

STUD

STUD

Fig 3

Fig 2

Fig 1

SCALE OF INCHES

SCALE

Fig 5

Fig 6

STUD

Fig 7

SIDE ELEVATION

FRONT ELEVATION

SCALE OF FEET.

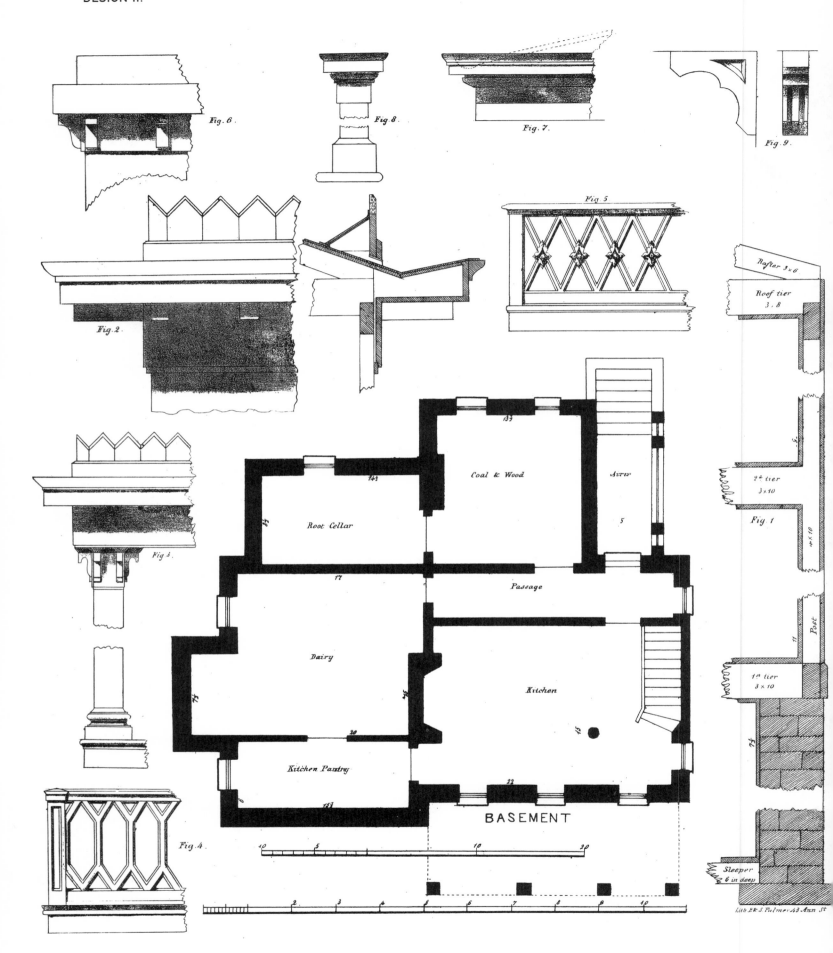

Fig. 6.

Fig. 8.

Fig. 7.

Fig. 9.

Fig. 5

Fig. 2.

Rafter 3×6

Roof tier 3.8

Fig 5

2ᵈ tier 3×10

Fig 1

4×10

Post

1ˢᵗ tier 3×10

Coal & Wood

Stairs

5

Root Cellar

Passage

Dairy

Kitchen

Kitchen Pantry

BASEMENT

Fig. 4.

Sleeper 6 in deep

Lith Bk S Palmer 43 Ann St

GARDEN FRONT.

Designed & del by Wm H. Ranlett.

Lith.F.&.S.Palmer 45 Ann St NY

ENTRANCE FRONT

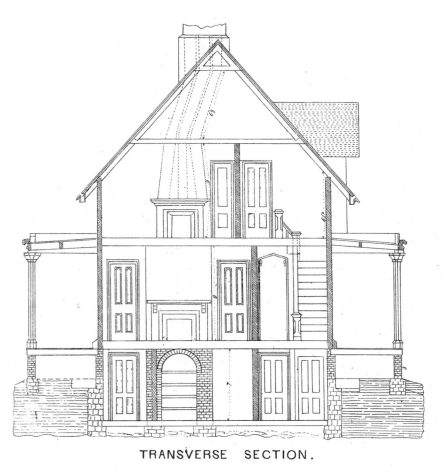

TRANSVERSE SECTION.

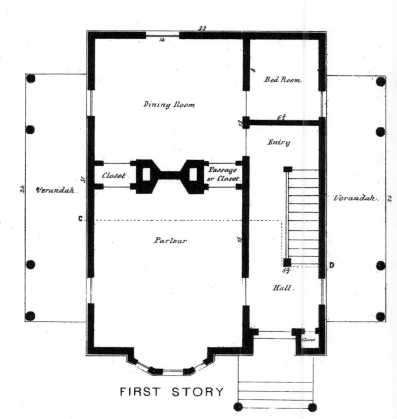

SECOND STORY.

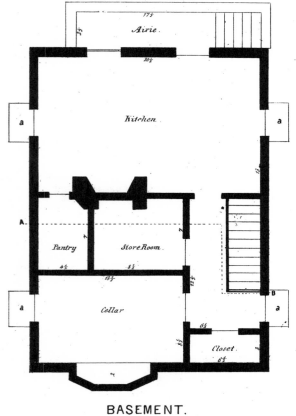

BASEMENT.

FIRST STORY

FRONT ELEVATION.

SIDE ELEVATION.

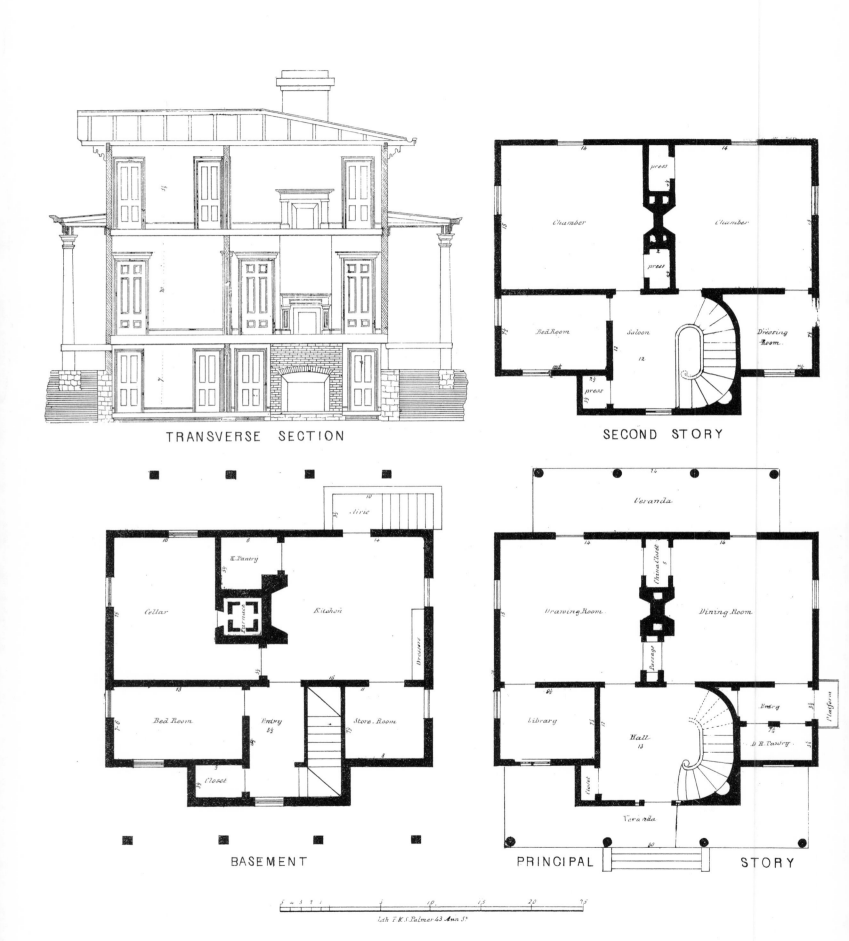

TRANSVERSE SECTION

SECOND STORY

BASEMENT

PRINCIPAL   STORY

Lith F.K.S.Palmer 43 Ann St.

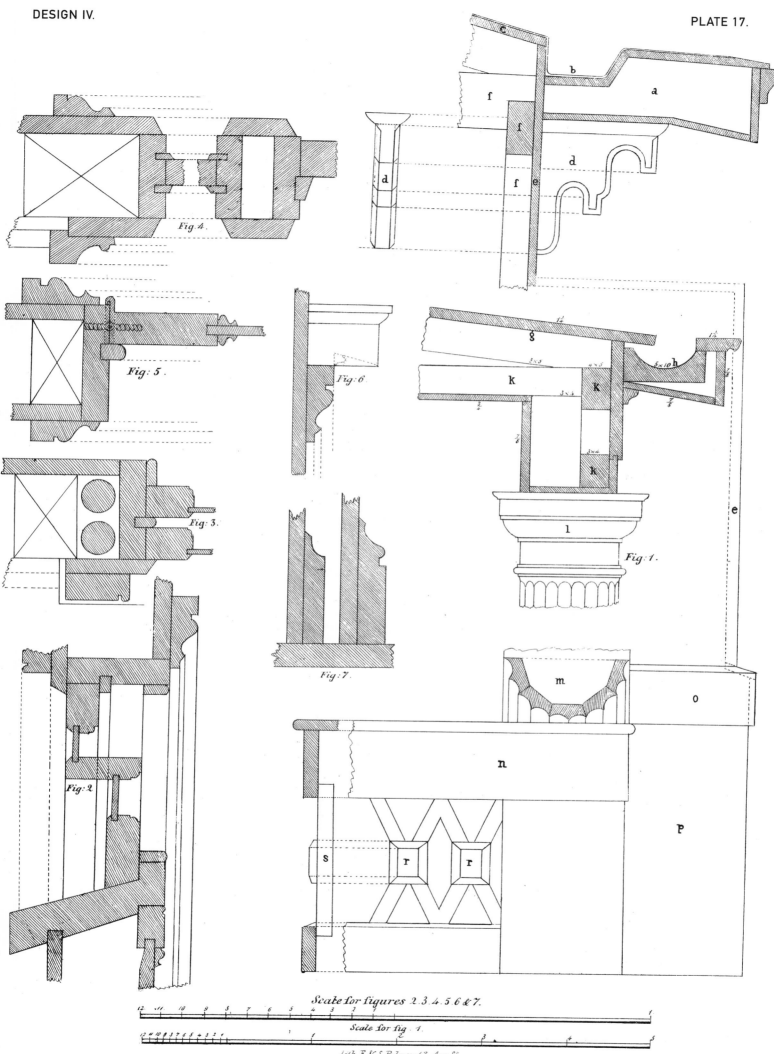

Fig. 4.

Fig: 5.

Fig: 6.

Fig: 3.

Fig: 2.

Fig: 7.

Fig: 1.

Scale for figures 2. 3. 4. 5. 6 & 7.

Scale for fig. 1.

Lith F. & S Palmer 43 Ann St.

PLATE 18.

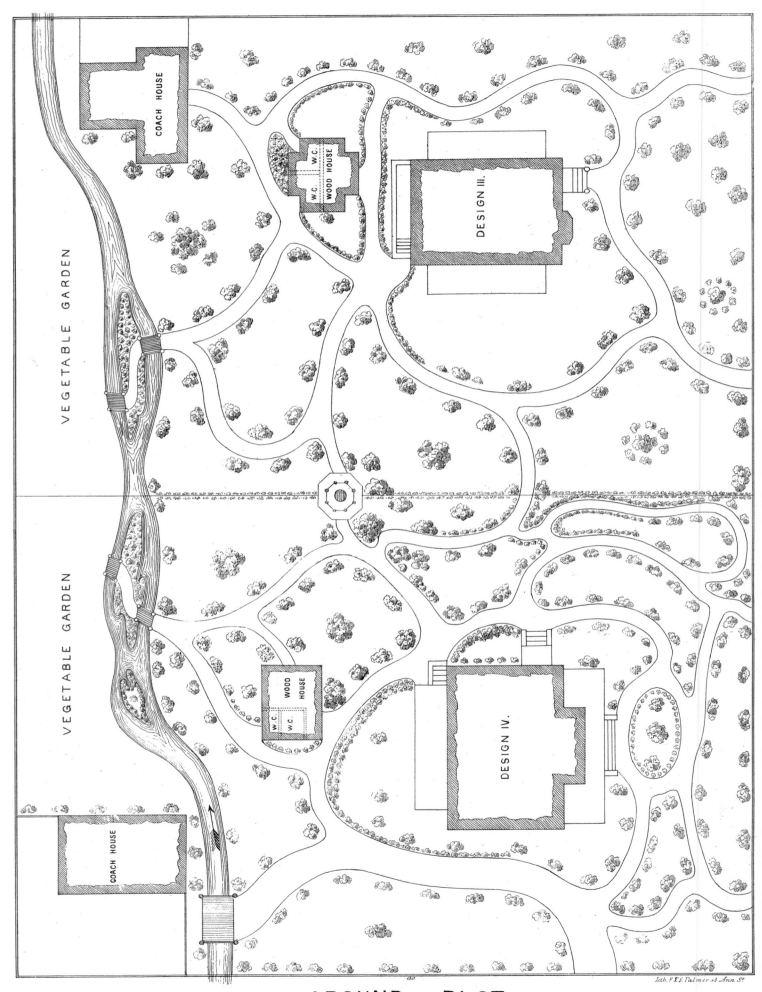

COACH HOUSE

W.C. W.C. WOOD HOUSE

DESIGN III.

VEGETABLE GARDEN

VEGETABLE GARDEN

WOOD HOUSE W.C. W.C.

DESIGN IV.

COACH HOUSE

Lith. F & S. Palmer 13 Ann St.

GROUND PLOT

RURAL ARCHITECTURE.

In providing a dwelling, several considerations are important and should be allowed to have their proper influence on all conclusions touching the enterprize. This topic includes suburban, and country residences.

1. SITUATION.

A suburban residence combines, to some extent, the advantages and pleasures of city, and country life, but does not contain those of either to the full. A country residence affords, to the intelligent mind and diligent hand, pleasures and profits which are unknown in exclusive city life. A situation should be selected with due respect to the employment of the proprietor, and the intended style of architecture, if it has previously been determined.

Probably no portion of the globe, offers a greater variety of beautiful country seats than the vicinity of New-York. No man who has any taste for the retired tranquillity of a suburban retreat, or the lovely beauty of a picturesque scene, or the romantic grandeur of an enchanting landscape of cities, towns and country; rivers, bays and ocean, could fail to be suited with some of the numerous situations on the undulated shores, gentle declivities or towering heights of Staten Island, Long Island or the banks of the noble Hudson. Much might be said in commendation of these delightful places. Their contiguity to the great commercial emporium of the western world, and their proverbially salubrious character are sufficient to render them peculiarly desirable.

Health is the most important consideration in the selection of a situation. In a country like ours, affording every variety of surface, soil and climate, different principles are brought into action in different parts. In all climates, currents and eddies of air, excessive heat of the sun, and the *malaria* of swamps, marshes and impure ponds and streams, should be avoided or guarded against, though they are less hurtful in some latitudes than they are in others. A current or draft of air often produces "colds" when the wind unconstrained is perfectly salubrious: to avoid such effects therefore, a dwelling should not be placed in a narrow vale nor at the head of a hollow. To avoid the injurious gases which often accumulate in eddies of air, a residence should not be situated to the leeward of abrupt hills or copses; and to avoid malaria, a dwelling which is necessarily in the vicinity of its source, should be to the windward; considering the prevailing course of the wind in the warm season, which is generally from the westward, in this country, unless varied by local causes. Low situations should be avoided on account of fogs and humidity; and very high ones, relatively considered, are found to be less salubrious than those of medium elevation.

Soil is an item of some importance, especially where gardens and pleasure-grounds are contemplated; but a good *sub-soil* is more important, being essential to the vigorous growth of trees, and incapable of improvement, while the soil may be improved to any extent by artificial means.

A farm house should be accessible to all parts of the farm, if health will allow it. On this depends much of the convenience of carrying on the farming operations; hence a want of it often costs much sacrifice. It should also be convenient to the rôad; but there is a very great lack of taste and propriety in placing it in immediate contiguity to the line of the road, or separated by only a very small yard, as is often done. A large yard should be the least space allowed to intervene; and if the house could be approached by a wide, well improved avenue, either straight or curved, or through a graceful campus, it would be still better taste.

Aspects affect, considerably, the general comfort of a dwelling. A southern aspect has the greatest amount of sunshine, hence the most heat, but snows melt away, and the soil dries more readily than in any other. The north never has full sunshine, hence it is the coldest, snows lie the longest, and the soil requires the longest time in drying. In all these respects, eastern and western aspects have a medium between the north and south. The view has, in the morning, objects to the east, in the shade, to the west, in the light, to the north and south, in a combination of light and shade ; but in the evening, the light and shade are reversed. At mid-day the objects to the south, are in the shade, and in the light to the north, and to the east and west, in light and shade combined. And a view is always greatly beautified by a stream or sheet of water.

The seaside is much resorted to for the benefit of sea-air and sea-bathing, also for the luxuries of the sea. It generally has a milder temperature, than regions distant from water. The shores of a lake or river afford most of the advantages of the seaside. There are great conveniences in being near a creek or brook, if no larger water can be attained ; and in the absence of all these, an artificial pond may be formed in almost any place where the qualities of the earth are such as to retain water, which most earths will do. A pond is easily formed by excavating to the desired extent and depth, across any place where the water flows in a stream after a shower, and throwing a dam across, by the earth which is removed. The sediment will soon enable it to retain a good supply of water in most kinds of earth.

A good supply of pure water is very important to health and comfort; and should in all cases, be secured in the selection of a site or the construction of the buildings. In the absence of springs and common wells, a tolerable supply of the purest water—except distilled—may be obtained by good cisterns. A cistern, well constructed and properly protected by a house and other shade, and filled only in cold weather—in part with snow and ice if convenient—affords very good water for drinking through the summer even without ice. It is estimated that 100 square yards of roof will afford 18,700 gallons of water annually. If water cannot be obtained by the ordinary process of digging, or if it should be bad, a good supply can often be obtained by an Artesian well, i. e., a shaft or tube of metal sunk to any necessary depth by boring, even through strata containing water ; through which the water will rise to the surface, if the source of its supply should be sufficiently high, which is often the case.

The scenery around a dwelling is well worthy of particular attention. It is important that a situation should have as much of natural beauty as possible—a natural scene may, however, be greatly improved by art, and materially changed by much time and expense. Trees are very desirable for their shade and the beauty of their composition with the architectural feature of the scene ; but they should not be so thick as to produce dampness, nor so situated as to prevent a distinct view of the edifice.   In distant views, tastes differ; some preferring them to be visible from the dwelling, and others wishing them to be seen only by a short walk from the house, which may be rendered pleasant by any improvement and interesting by changing the scene.

II. CLASSES OF DWELLINGS.

The general characteristics of a residence must be determined by the tastes, habits and circumstances of the family who are to occupy it.   There is, very properly, a great variety in the styles and dimensions of Rural Residences.   The moderate means, plain manners and industrial habits of a large portion of our citizens, render *cottages* and small villas the most appropriate dwellings for those who aim at competence and comfort in the simple independence of American country life.   Cottages or houses, one story or a story and a half high, may be erected in any style, and possess all the desired accessories, such as porches, verandas, balconies, pediments, gables, &c.   A cottage indicates a disposition in the proprietor to live within his income, and to appropriate his means rather for the convenience and comfort of his family, than for show which he is ill prepared to sustain.   The style and finish of any house, denote the intelligence and taste of the proprietor.   The general information, and distribution of property in this country, render cottages and small villas the most appropriate class of dwellings for the mass of citizens in the country; and the practice of erecting such buildings will become more general in the progress of other improvements and the diffusion of information.

III. EXPRESSION OF PURPOSE.

The form and character of a building, should be expressive of its use and destination, while particular features indicate its purpose in a marked degree.   Thus, very large plain doors and the absence of chimneys, denote a stable or barn—very high chimneys indicate a factory—a spire designates a church, and heavy columns *should* denote a public building, but in the tasteless use that is often made of them, it is difficult to distinguish a bank from a church—a town hall or even sometimes a private dwelling.   Verandas, piazzas and porches are very expressive of purpose, and a dwelling should always have one or more of them ; and balconies, which are decidedly ornamental and not without use.   Windows are among the most expressive features that denote purpose.   They should be well proportioned to the size and style. Bay and oriel windows are highly expressive of purpose and are very ornamental and useful features. Chimney tops denote the use of an edifice, and they should be so elevated as to prevent the wind from interfering with the smoke, by the influence of the roof or gables.   They may, with great propriety, be ornamented and made pleasing to the eye, rendering them important features in the scene.   The front door is highly expressive of purpose, and may be made an important part of the scene by a graceful porch or campanile.   Color is another expressive feature.   A stable or barn should have an unobtrusive tint, while the cottage or villa has a pleasing mellow hue, harmonizing with the verdure of the surrounding scenery. The dazzling white so common on wooden buildings in this country, is in decidedly bad taste, and should be avoided in all cases.

IV. EXPRESSION OF STYLE.

Taste, in civilized society, demands gratification from surrounding objects, especially those produced by art; and that arising from the beauty of *form*, is the most general, and the most subject to the control of man : hence taste has much influence on the production of the means of its own pleasure. This principle of action, modified by convenience and interest, is the basis of all *fashions*, in forms; hence, for example, the buildings of the Greeks, in their classical refinement, were constructed in certain *classes of forms*, which are, collectively, called the *Grecian Style ;* and the *classes* of forms, the *orders* of the style. These, they developed in their highest perfection, in the construction of their temples, which gave them grandeur, influence, and permanence. In a similar way, other *styles* of building arose in different countries. These styles were employed in suppressed developments of their forms, in the construction of dwellings, and thus diffused through their respective countries.

They were intimately connected with the most important characteristics and interests of the nations in which they arose; hence they are monuments of their intelligence and tastes, as well as of their greatest refinement and highest artistical skill. This renders the various styles of architecture expressive of certain *sentiments*, which are as legible to the intelligent eye, as the written productions of the poets, statesmen, and sages of those times. The indication of these sentiments, with the varied beauty of the forms, is the expression of style. It is manifest from these considerations, that an expensive building, in which no particular style of architecture is recognized, may be compared—in an æsthetic view—to a fine book in which no particular language is perceived; and one containing a combination of styles, to such a book in a confused mixture of languages.

From the foregoing view, it is plain that if the proprietor of an edifice, values his reputation for taste and refinement, he must necessarily have it in some specific style ; as the mere consideration of *room* may be attained to the fullest extent, by the form of a Chinese tea chest, and wealth may be indicated by a mass of chaos, while neither denotes any claim to polished intelligence. We cannot, therefore, too strongly urge upon our fellow-citizens, the importance of building in some particular style ; and of preserving uniformity of style throughout their establishments, that their homesteads may not be disfigured by erecting the mansion in one style, the coach house in another, and the stable in a third; which is a very absurd exhibition, and a certain indication that the proprietor attempted a work of taste, which he lacked the intelligence to complete.

The accompanying designs exemplify two styles which are well adapted to the United States. Design 3, is particularly adapted to this latitude, as also Design 1 ; and Design 4 is peculiarly appropriate to the warmer climate of the Southern States.

SPECIFICATIONS,

Of the Materials and Labor required for the erection of a Cottage according to Design III,

MASON'S WORK AND MATERIALS.

EXCAVATION:——*According to plate 14—and completely graded.*

STONE WORK.——*Walls of quarry stone and good mortar, 18 in. thick and 4 ft. 6 in. high, on good foundations. Kitchen hearth of blue stone, 20 in. wide and 5 ft. long. Steps and coping of airie, of blue stone, 10 in. wide. Window sills in basement, of blue stone. Brown stone hearths in parlor and dining room.*

BRICK WORK.——*Walls from the stone work, 8 in. thick and 3 1-2 ft. high. Piers, 8 in. square. A chimney with five fire-places—3 of them finished—the shaft above the roof to be cemented according to plate 13. Brick filling between the exterior studs. Paving in the airie. A cistern, 6 by 8 ft. arched and cemented.*

PLASTERING.——*All the rooms, halls and closets in first and second stories, to be lathed plastered, and hard finished—in the basement and attic, lathed plastered and whitewashed.*

GRATES:——*In the parlor and dining room, and a crane and hooks in the kitchen fire place.*

CARPENTER'S LABOR AND MATERIALS.

FRAME;——*Of sound square timber, strongly framed and braced, sills, framing beams, posts and plates 4 by 8 in.—girts, and door and window studs 4 by 6—beams in first and second stories 3 by 8, 16 in. between centers—trimmers 4 in. thick—rafters 3 by 6, 30 in. apart—collar beams 3 by 6—studding 3 by 4, 16 in. between centers—basement sleepers of chestnut, 6 in. thick and 30 in. apart—veranda floor timbers 3 by 8—rafters 4 by 7—purlins 3 by 6.*

COVERING.——*The sides with clear boards, planed, rebated and put on 7 1-2 or 8 in. to the weather.*

ROOF.——*Of hemlock boards and best split white pine shingles, 3 thick. The dormer valleys lined with sheet lead, 15 in. wide. Veranda roofs of narrow seasoned white pine plank, tongued, grooved and put together with white lead. Bay window roof of plank and tin. Three 3 in. tin water leaders.*

CORNICE.——*Of 1 1-4 in. plank, moulded and strongly secured, with lead in the joints. The gable to project 20 in., with moulded drapery 2 in. thick.*

VERANDA;——*With octagon columns 6 1-2 in. diameter, with moulded caps and bases. Rafters and purlins planed and beaded.*

FLOORS;——*Of sound milled white pine plank, strongly nailed down.*

PARTITIONS;——*Set with 3 by 4 joists, 16 in. between centers.*

DOORS.—Front door 1 3=4 in. thick, with head light. First story passage doors 1 1=2 in. thick, with 4 panels, each moulded on both sides. All other doors 1 1=4 in. thick, with 4 panels.

WINDOWS.—In first story, 5 w. 8 lights, 11 by 17—bay w. 30 lts. 11 by 17. In second story, 4 w. 8 lts. 10 by 15—1 w. 12 lts. 10 by 15—2 w. 4 lts. 11 by 17. Two attic w. 3 lts. 11 by 15. In basement, 4 w. 9 lts. 10 by 12—1 w. 12 lts. 10 by 12. Winslow glass, single thickness. All the windows in first and second stories, and one in basement, double hung by cords and weights—all other sashes hung by 3 in. butts and secured by bolts—sashes 1 1=2 in. thick in first story, and all others 1 1=4 in. thick. Panels, hung by butts to two of the windows in first story.

LOCKS, &c.—Six 4 1=2 in. mortice locks, first story, and all others 5 in. rim—mineral knobs to all other doors—first story doors, hung by 4 by 4 butts, all others by 3 1=2 in.

ARCHITRAVES, &c.—In the first story, a single oval bead, 1 1=4 in. thick and 2 in. wide. In second story, cove moulding, 1 in. by 2 1=2—plinths to the doors, and stop sills to the windows. Plain band mouldings, 3=4 in. thick, to all the doors and windows in the basement and attic.

BLINDS:—All the windows above the basement, to have rolling blinds—and panel shutters to those in the basement.

BASE.—In the first and second stories, 5 and 6 in. high, 1 1=4 thick and moulded. In basement and attic, 6 in. and 3=4 thick.

STAIRS:—From basement to first story, enclosed—first to second story, open, with moulded steps, rail, newel and turned balusters, and close stairway to attic.

PRESSES, &c.—All to be properly fitted up with shelves, hooks and pins.

MANTLES:—Of wood to all the fire places in first and second stories, with hearth borders.

PLANS:—Of gutters, bay window cornice, window frames, first story doors and mantles, as in plate 6, design 1.

MATERIALS:—Of best quality, well seasoned, and clear, for all the interior work.

PAINTING.—All the wood work, except the interior floors and shingle roofs, to have two coats of white lead and linseed oil, and shaded on the outside with a light brown or drab. The blinds to have 3 coats of best bronze green paint.

SPECIFICATIONS FOR DESIGN IV.

MASON'S WORK AND MATERIALS.

Excavation, stone work, brick work, and plastering as for design 3.

MANTLES, &c.—Veined marble mantles in the dining room and parlor—"Walker's patent improved hot air Furnace" in the cellar, with 5 registers.

CARPENTER'S LABOR AND MATERIALS.

FRAME:—Of good pine timber well seasoned. Posts 4 by 9. Plates, sills and framing beams 4 by 8. Girts 4 by 6. Rafters 3 by 5. First and second tiers of beams 3 by 8—16 inches between centers. Roof tier, 3 by 8—4 ft. between centers. Veranda sills, 3 by 8. Rafters and purlins 3 by 6. Basement sleepers of cedar 5 in. thick and 30 in. apart.

ROOFS.—The main roof of milled plank covered with galvanized tinned plates. Veranda roofs, as for

Design 3. *The cornice as in Plate 17.* *Two three inch tin leaders, to convey water from the roof to the cistern.*

COVERING.—*Narrow clear white pine clap-boards, 5=8 thick, rebated and firmly put on the sides.*

VERANDA, *Columns, cornice, steps, &c. as in Plate 17.* *The underside of the roof, paneled and beaded, with mouldings in the angles of the panels.* *Projecting roof and brackets over the side door.*

FLOORS.—*As for Design 3.*

WINDOWS.—*In basement, 7 w. 6 lts. 12 by 14, hung by butts and secured by 4 in. bolts.* *In first story, 2 w. 10 lts. 12 by 18—5 w. 8 lts. 12 by 18.* *In second story, 8 w. 8 lts. 12 by 15—1 w. 30 lts. 9 by 12, with circular head.* *Sashes 1 1=2 inch and double hung, in both stories.*

DOORS.—*The front door, 1 3=4 thick, with head and side lights—side door, 1 3=4 thick, with head lights.* *All the passage doors in the first story, 1 1=2 thick—6 panels double faced.* *Closet doors 1 1=4, single faced.* *All other doors 1 1=4 thick, 4 panels, moulded on one side*

ARCHITRAVES, &c.—*Panel backs to first story windows.* *All the jambs, casings and base, as in Plate 17.*

LOCKS, &c.—*The first story to have 6 in. upright mortice locks to front and side doors—all the other locks in the house 5 in. rim—mortice locks to have porcelain knobs and drops, " star pattern,"—rim locks to have mineral knobs.* *Best patent 4=4 butts in first story, and 3 1=2 butts to all other doors.*

PRESSES AND CLOSETS:—*To be fitted with shelves, hooks, &c. appropriate to their use.*

MANTLES.—*Two neat wood mantles in the second story, and borders to all the hearths.*

BLINDS:—*Moulded on one side, to all windows in first and second stories, and shutters to basement windows.*

PAINTING.—*The blinds to have three coats bronze green.* *The stair rail and balusters to have three coats of varnish.* *All other wood work—except interior floors—and the tin leaders to have two coats of best paint— the last coat on the exterior may be shaded.*

DESCRIPTION OF THE PLATES OF DESIGNS III. & IV.

PLATE 13.—Design III. Two geometrical elevations of a Rural Cottage, containing 11 rooms with a high roof, and ornamented gables.

PLATE 14.—Three floor plans and a transverse section, showing the several rooms, &c.—through the basement, from A. to B.; first story, C. to D.; and second story, E. to F.—Design III.

PLATE 15.—Two elevations of a small Villa in the bracketed style, containing 10 rooms, besides pantries, closets, &c.

PLATE 16.—A transverse section showing the rooms, doors, &c., with the plans and dimensions of the floors—Design IV.

PLATE 17.—Details of design IV., Fig. 1.—Sections of main cornice, piazza cornice, column and base : a, cornice bracket; b, gutter; c, rafter, planking and tin; d, exterior bracket; e, corner board and covering; f, post, plate and beam; g, rafter and plank of veranda; h, gutter; k, plates, and ceiling beam; l, cap of column; m, section of the shaft; n, floor and base of veranda; o, water table; p, brick wall; r, ornamental skirting of veranda; s, a profile section of it. Fig. 2.—Side section of window frame. Fig. 3.—Ground do. Fig. 4.—Ground section of front door and frame. Fig. 5.—Ground section of interior casings, doors, &c. Fig. 6.—Section of door caps of first story. Fig. 7.—Base of first and second stories.

PLATE 18.—Ground plot, for Designs III. and IV., of houses, proposed to be erected near the shore, at Clifton, Staten Island, 100 ft. by 150 each, showing the locations of the house and other buildings, with the walks, carriage way, shrubbery, &c., also a stream of water between the lawn and vegetable garden.

ESTIMATES,

Of the Labor and Materials required for Designs III. & IV.

DESIGN 3.

MASON'S BILL.

155 yds. excvation, 11 cts. ; 82 loads stone, 75 cts.	78 55
10350 hard brick, $4 25 ; 8650 soft brick, $2 75	67 78
133 loads sand, 31 cts. ; 12 bush. sand, 12 cts.	42 67
55 casks Tho. lime, 95 cts. ; 4 casks lump lime, $1 50	58 25
3 casks plaster, $1 75 ; 27 bush. hair, 20 cts.	10 65
15000 lath, $3 50 ; 135 lbs. nails, 7 cts.	61 95
2 brown stone hrths. $2 25 ; 9 ft. kitchen hrth. 16 cts.	5 94
2 grates, $9 00 ; 44 ft. coping, 14 cts.	24 16
6 win. and door sills, 50 cts. ; 81 lds. carting, 31 cts.	28 11
2 casks hydraulic cement, $1 75 ; cistern neck, $5 00	8 50
59 days mason's labor, $1 65 ; 45 days labor, 90 cts.	137 85

CARPENTER'S BILL.

5025 ft. timber, $1 50 ; 172 joists, 14 cts.	99 46
225 ft. bas't. sleepers, 3 cts. ; 244 floor planks, 26 cts.	70 19
137 narrow planks, 17 cts. ; 166 piece planks, 27 cts.	68 11
418 piece boards, 18 cts. ; 200 hmlk. boards, 12 cts.	99 24
590 ft. 2 in. clear plank, 3¼ ; 540 ft. 1½ and 1¼ in. 3¼ cts.	36 73
21 bunches shingles, $2 50 ; 25 wall strips, 12 cts.	55 50
94 ft. blinds, 70 cts. ; 24 ft. sheet lead, 18 cts.	70 12
22 ft. tin roof, 10 cts. ; 60 ft. tin leader, 10 cts.	8 20
78 lts. glass, 11 by 17, 22 cts. ; 4 lts. gls. 11 by 14, 20c.	17 96
50 lts. " 10 by 15, 20 cts. ; 48 " 10 by 12, 14 cts.	16 72
6 lbs. sash cord, 31 cts. ; 352 lbs. sash weights, 2 cts.	8 90
600 lbs. nails, $4 00 ; 25 lbs. fine nails, 7 cts.	25 75
6 mortice locks, $1 40 ; 16 5 in. rim locks, 83 cts.	21 68
8 pair 4 by 4 butts, 22 cts. ; 16 prs. 3½ in. butts 10 cts.	3 36
19 pairs 3 in. butts, 7 cts. ; 9 4 in. bolts, 14 cts.	2 59
56 pullies, 5½ cts. ; 8 sash fastenings, 29 cts.	5 40
2 gross 1¼ screws, No. 11, 42c. ; 1 grs. 1 in. No. 9, 31c.	1 15
1 " ¾ " " 9, 29 cts. ; 1 " ¾ " 7, 28 cts.	57
3 doz. hat hooks, 25 cts. ; 49 lds. carting, 35 cts.	17 90
191 days carpenter's labor, $1 50	286 50

PAINTER'S BILL.

400 lbs. white lead, $6 50 ; 4 lbs. litharge, 6 cts.	26 24
20 galls. oil, 65 cts. ; 2 gall. spirits, 70 cts.	14 40
20 lbs. putty, 5 cts. ; 2 lbs. glue, 25 cts.	1 25
2 lbs. chrome yellow, 75 cts. ; 1 lb. black, 50 cts.	2 00
Carting, $2 50 ; 16 days painter's labor, $1 75	30 50

RECAPITULATION.

Mason's	bill,	-	-	-	524 41
Carpenter's	"	-	-	-	916 03
Painter's	"	-	-	-	74 39
					$1514 83

Design 3 may be built with brick, 12 in. walls, for $1804 83 ; and with stone, 18 in. walls, for $1909 83 : and Design 4, with brick, for $2475 43 ; and with stone, for $2584 43—plastering put on, in all cases by furring.

DECEMBER, 1st, 1846.

DESIGN 4.

MASON'S BILL.

152 yds. excavation, 11 cts. ; 92 lds. stone, 75 cts.	$95 72
40 ft. coping, 14 cts. ; 8 window sills, 50 cts.	9 60
9 ft. flagging, 16 cts. ; 2 marble mantles, $30 00	61 44
9993 hard bricks, $4 25 ; 13940 soft bricks, $2 75	80 80
68 cks. Thos. lime, 95 cts. ; 4 cks. lump lime, $1 50	70 60
3 " plaster, $1 75 ; 16000 lath, $3 50	61 25
144 lbs. lath nails, 7 cts. ; 30 bushels hair, 20 cts.	16 08
164 lds. sand, 30 cts. ; 12 bush. white sand, 12 cts.	50 64
1 csk. cement, $2 00 ; cistern neck, $5 50	7 50
92 lds. carting, 25 cts. ; furnace , $130 00	153 00
75 days mason's lab. $1 65 ; 62 days labor, 90 cts.	179 55

CARPENTER'S BILL.

6370 ft. timber, $1 50 ; 242 ft. bas't. sleepers, 3 cts.	102 81
241 joist, 14 cts. ; 71 wall strips, 12 cts.	42 26
175 roof planks, 19 cts. ; 236 floor planks, 26 cts.	94 61
152 narrow plks. 17 cts. ; 232 piece plks. 27 cts.	88 48
300 ft. 3 in. plk. 3½ cts. ; 690 ft. 2 in. 1½ and 1¼ in. 3¼ cts.	32 93
257 piece boards, 18 cts. ; 60 hlk. boards, 12 cts.	53 46
436 narrow siding, 17 cts. ; 34 ft. mahogany, 12 cts.	78 20
33 balusters, 13 cts. ; 1 newel, $3 00	7 29
60 lts. gls. 12 by 18, 27 c. ; 64 lts. gls. 12 by 15, 23 cts.	30 92
42 " " 12 by 15, 20 c. ; 6 " " 11 by 13, 16 cts.	9 36
10 " " 6 by 17, 22 c. ; 20 " " 9 by 12, 13 cts.	4 80
1228 ft. metal roof, 13 cts. ; 70 ft. tin leader, 10 cts.	166 64
369 lbs. sash weights, 2 cts. ; 6 lbs. sash cord, 30 cts.	9 18
6 doz. pullies, 63 cts. ; 7 sash fastenings, 29 cts.	5 81
12 prs. 4 by 4 butts, 22 c.; 15 prs. 3½ in. butts, 10 cts.	4 14
21 " 3 in. " 7 cts. ; 7 flush bolts, 19 cts.	2 80
3 grs. 1¼ screws, No. 11, 42c. ; 2 grs. 1 in. No. 9, 31 cts.	1 88
1 " ¾ " " 9, 29 cts. ; 1 " ¾ " 7, 28 cts.	57
2 upright m. locks, $3 50 ; 5 4½ in. m. locks, $3 34	23 70
20 5 in. rim locks, 92 cts. ; 7 shutter bolts, 15 cts.	19 45
700 lbs. nails, $4 00 ; 30 lbs. fine nails, 7 cts.	30 10
3 doz. coat hooks, 25 cts. ; 8 rail screws, 11 cts.	1 63
105 ft. blinds, 70 cts. ; carting 56 loads, 35 cts.	93 10
243 days carpenter's labor, $1 50	364 50

PAINTER'S BILL.

550 lbs. pure white lead, $6 50 ; 4 lbs. litharge, 6 cts.	35 75
20 galls. linseed oil, 65 cts. ; 2½ galls. spirits, 70 cts.	14 75
6 " boiled oil, 78 cts. ; 3 lbs. color, 65 cts.	6 63
20 lbs. putty, 5 cts. ; 2 lbs. glue, 25 cts.	1 50
22 days painter's labor, $1 75 ; carting, $2 50	41 00

RECAPITULATION.

Mason's	bill,	-	-	-	776 18
Carpenter's	"	-	-	-	1268 62
Painter's	"	-	-	-	99 63
					$2144 43

APPROPRIATION OF HEAT.

"If we could always keep in one temperature of warmth, we should always keep in health."—*Swift*.

THERE are various means and methods of warming the different apartments of dwellings. The old fashion is a cheerful wood fire in an open fire-place, which is still in extensive use in many parts of the United States.

The construction of chimneys, is a department of building which has received much less attention than its importance demands. The *very common complaint* of "smoking chimneys"—even in portions of our country where mechanical skill is at high-tide, in other departments of architecture—indicates a deplorable lack of attention to elementary principles. Various causes operate to prevent chimneys from drawing, the most common of which is, *too large a throat*. A transverse section of a flue should contain at least 144 square inches, and the square form is the best; and each fire-place should have a separate flue to the top of the shaft, which should always extend above the highest portions of the roof, sufficient to prevent the wind from being thrown down the flue by their influence. A general principle touching the throat, is, the *smaller* it is, the better will be the draft of the flue. The patent cast iron throat, which was invented for the flues of chimneys, is considered a certain remedy for a defective draft.

Where grates are used, the most convenient plan is a flue of nearly uniform size from the foundation to the top of the chimney, and the grate set in front of it, and the flue of the grate running back into it. Such a flue can be swept without interfering with the apartment, for the soot will fall to the base whence it can be removed by an aperture that must be kept closed by a piece of sheet iron to preserve the draft. A chimney that smokes by the influence of a hill or higher house adjoining, may usually be remedied by an arch, raised tile or a "smoke fan."

Air is not heated by the passage of rays of heat through it, but by receiving the heat of other bodies with which it is in contact: hence a fire in an open fire-place or grate, warms the apartment mainly by radiating the heat to various parts of the room, where it is absorbed in part, and partly reflected by the walls and furniture, and its tendency toward an equilibrium raises the temperature of the apartment. A stove or iron pipe heats, by radiation, and by imparting heat to the air in contact with it, which becomes specifically lighter by being heated, and is immediately displaced by the cold air, which, being heavier, rushes into the place of the warmer air, thus keeping up a circulation, that is, from the heating body to other portions of the apartment. If the fire in a grate or open fire-place is directly under the throat of the flue, it will be found very difficult to warm the room, for a large portion of the heat will escape up the chimney.

The use of water and steam in heating edifices, is a modern invention, and it has been brought to great

27

perfection in heating green-houses, factories, &c. and there is no good reason why they may not be used in warming dwellings. It is done by conducting the hot water or steam through metal pipes to all parts of the edifice, from a boiler in the basement or some other convenient place, which may be outside of the building, if desirable. Heating by hot air furnaces, is an ancient method. The Dioclesian Palace at Rome was warmed by this means, according to Gibbon, in the time of the Roman Empire. It has latterly come into extensive use in this and other countries. Air which is heated by a heating surface above 212 degrees, Fahrenheit, is deprived of its vapor, which is an essential part of atmospheric air, and it cannot sustain a heat above the boiling point. It is this that produces the depressing dryness that has been so often experienced in rooms warmed by hot stoves. This has been the principal difficulty in the use of the hot air furnaces. The remedy, in such cases, is the restoration of vapor to the air by the evaporation of water, which is easily done in connection with stoves, and is coming into use in hot air furnaces. These are considered economical, by warming all the apartments of a dwelling with one fire; and pleasant on account of the freedom from the dust usual to stoves, grates, and fire-places. The best, of which we have any knowledge, is "Walker's patent improved hot air furnace." It is one of great economy in point of fuel; and its simplicity renders it easily managed; but its great excellence consists in its evaporating apparatus, by which the air, with its natural qualities preserved or restored, is sent into the apartments, mellow, moist, and pleasant.

VENTILATION.

THE necessity of air to animal life, is known to all, but the great importance of *pure air* is understood by only a very small proportion of the community; and it was indeed unknown to the learned till the modern discoveries of pneumatic chemistry.

Atmospheric air is a compound substance, consisting of oxygen, 20 per cent., nitrogen, 79 per cent. and carbonic acid gas, 1 or 2 per cent.—sometimes more—combined with aqueous vapor. The proportion of oxygen and nitrogen is nearly the same in all countries, but that of carbonic acid gas, varies in different places; and if it should amount to twenty per cent. it would be fatal to animal life.

Air which is expired from the lungs, is found to be deprived of a large portion of the oxygen, and to possess increased proportions of carbonic acid gas and vapor; and if it should be repeatedly respired without being renewed, the oxygen would soon be entirely exhausted; and if a person or animal were confined in it in this state, death would be the immediate result. These positions are well known chemical facts; and it is equally well known that it is the oxygen of the atmosphere, which supports combustion. It is evident from these considerations that the oxygen is the main ingredient of the air, which is employed in the support of animal life, and the production of heat and light; and that it is therefore rapidly consumed from the air, in a living apartment, by the respiration of the inmates, and the burning of the fire and lights.

Much of the air which is rendered impure by the fire, escapes by the draft of the chimney, but that which is rendered so by the burning of lights and respiration, is naturally confined within the apartment. The specific gravity of nitrogen is less than that of atmospheric air, hence it rises to the ceiling. The proportion of carbonic acid gas is increased by combustion as well as respiration, and it is a very poisonous gas, often producing death by the burning of charcoal in close rooms. It has a greater specific gravity than atmospheric air, which, with varied degrees of heat forces it into all parts of the room.

Ventilation consists in discharging the impure air from apartments, and supplying its place with *pure atmospheric air*, and the rapidity with which the change should take place, may be inferred from the following estimate. A person consumes, on an average, the oxygen of five cubic feet of air, and vitiates 50 feet in an hour; hence, a room containing four persons, must receive and discharge air at the rate of 200 cubic feet per hour to retain a healthy state of the air. Add to this consumption of oxygen, that by the burning of a fire and lights, and the change must be at a much greater rate.

It is plain from what has been said, that ventilation should proceed by discharging the impure air at the top of the apartment, and admitting atmospheric air at the base, and this will be found to accord with nature—as all such operations should—by holding a lighted candle to a crevice at the top of a door, and another to one at the base, when it will be found that the blaze at the top will be forced outward, and that at the base, inward.

The chief ventilator of an apartment, is the chimney; hence, it is manifestly improper to stop their draft by close " fire-boards," or summer pieces to grates as is often done. Summer pieces should always be constructed open, or with registers, so as to allow a draft. The impure air in the upper part of rooms can escape only by the windows, which should, therefore, extend as near the ceiling as may be, and be " double hung," so as to allow the impure air to escape at top, and admit atmospheric air at the base. Open stairways allow the impure air to rise from the lower parts of a dwelling to the upper rooms, where it is too often confined to the sleeping apartments of children and others, greatly to their injury. The effect of the impure air that rises in such stairways, is often experienced in ascending to the third or fourth story of a large house where the way is closed above the stairs. It is very perceptible at the top, even where there is an opening at the base of the upper flight of stairs. It is therefore very important, that there should be some mode of conveying the vitiated air from the upper portions of such stairways without allowing it to pass into the rooms, which may be easily done by ventilators in the roof. A better method, however, is by flues in the walls, with registers near the ceiling, that shall discharge the impure air at the top of the wall. Another good mode of ventilating such places,—indeed any part of a house—is by tin tubes with registers running through the floors into the flues of the chimneys which will give effective drafts, and greatly facilitate the process of ventilation.

To be continued on page 35.

THE TUDOR STYLE

Arose in England by the authority and auspices of Henry VII. who built extensively himself, and promoted Architecture among his subjects, by depressing the nobility and elevating members of other families who would be more dependant on him for their rank and privileges. The spirit of improvement and a desire to distinguish his reign, induced that monarch to produce and patronize a new modification of Gothic Architecture which had long been one of the most fashionable styles throughout Europe. This modification was gaining credit through the reign of Henry VII. and was improved and established, as the leading style of the country by Cardinal Woolsey, in the erection of his princely palace at Hampton Court, about 1525, in the reign of Henry VIII. and it prevailed till it was supplanted by another modification of the Gothic, about the middle of the 16th century, in the time of Elizabeth. It is called by modern architects, the " Tudor Style," after the royal family then in possession of the throne. If the English have ever had any style of architecture that may be called national, it was the Tudor style which arose and prevailed in that country but never found much favor anywhere else; it is beginning, however, to come into use in this country, being well adapted to building with wood—a principal material with us—and harmonizing well with our scenery.

This style was characterized by very broken outlines of the plans and elevations. The principal entrance was ornamented by turrets, and often the gaudy embellishments of heraldry. Windows were usually made with right lines and cross transoms, divided by mullions; the separate bays, however, were often finished with the low pointed arch, which was substituted in this style for the high-pointed, of the Gothic. Projecting oriel windows, supported by clustered mouldings, high roofs, with many acute angled gables, and pediments over the attic windows, were prominent features. The pediments and gables were often kneed and moulded, and surmounted by pinnacles, finials, and crockets, and the roofs embattled. The chimney tops were a highly ornamental feature, often resembling groups of small columns, with pedestals, plinths, bases and capitals, and highly ornamented by fleur de lis, zig-zag, moulding, twisted reeds and lozenge-work, forming, on the whole, a curious and picturesque feature.

There were three modifications of palatial architecture in this style—that of Henry VII.—characterized by bay-windows and turrets, crowned with bulbous domes—for this monarch erected his palace in a style peculiarly his own; second, that of the time of Henry VIII. distinguished by oriel windows, turrets and gables with pinnacles, established by Cardinal Woolsey in the splendid palace at Hampton Court, which he presented to his monarch, and lastly, that of the time of Elizabeth; with only gables and pinnacles.

30

SPECIFICATIONS,

Of the Materials and Labor required for the erection of a Cottage according to Design V.

EXCAVATION: Four ft. deep, and the earth graded around the building, and sodded.

STONE WALLS: Eighteen in. thick and eight feet high, of best quarry stone, laid in mortar of 2=7 Thomaston lime, and 5=7 sharp bank sand, on foundations of wide, flat stones. Walls of the airie, 2 feet below the paving, and coped with 10 in. blue stone. Steps of airie of the same.

BRICK WORK.—An 8 in. wall, 3 ft. high, on two sides of the basement stairway. Two chimneys with five fire places. The kitchen fire=place of face=brick—the two in first story with grates and the two in the second story fitted for wood fires. All the flues at least 12 by 12 in. extending 7 feet above the top of the roof, and capped with cut brown stone, as in elevations. The airies paved with brick. All the outer walls filled between the studs with brick set on the edge, and secured by brackets every sixth corner. Mortar for chimneys, 1=4 lime and 3=4 sand—for filling, 1=5 lime and 4=5 sand—for basement walls, piers and chimney tops 1=3 lime and 2=3 sand. All the brick exposed by dampness, must be hard and smooth—all others, salmon and soft.

PLASTERING.—All the rooms, halls and closets of first and second stories, lathed and plastered with two coats of brown mortar and hard finished—the basement and attic, lathed, and plastered with two coats of brown mortar, and slipped. Plaster cornice, 10 in. wide in the three principal rooms in the first story. Mortar of best Thomaston lime and clean sharp sand. "Walker's Furnace" sett complete in the basement, with registers in four rooms and hall.

FRAME,—Of best white pine timber, strongly framed, and secured by white oak or locust pins. The sills, framing beams and trimmers, 4 by 9. Posts, plates and girts, 4 by 8. First and second tier of beams, 3 by 9, 16 in. between centers. Rafters, 3 by 6, 30 in. between centers. Collar beams, 3 by 6, and 4 by 6. Door and window studs, 4 by 6. Basement sleepers, of red cedar, 5 in. thick and 2 ft. between centers.

SIDES,—Of clear white pine clap=boards, 5=8 thick, planed and rebated, and put on with 8d nails. The water table to project 1 in. and the corner boards 1 1=2.

ROOFS.—The main roof of best split white pine shingles, laid three thick on hemlock boards, with close joints, the valleys open 3 in. and lined with sheet lead 16 in. wide. All the under side of the projections, of 1 1=4 in. milled plank, beaded and center=beaded, and rafters projecting, planed and beaded. All the main gutters and gables made as in Plate 22, Fig. 1. The finials to be octagon 10 in. diameter with carved heads and moulded pendants. Veranda roof, of 1 1=4 in. plank, 3 in. wide, grooved and the tongues put in with white lead, and made tight where it joins the house. Bay window roof best tin, on milled plank.

31

VERANDA COLUMNS,——*Octagon, 9 in. with moulded caps and bases, moulded cornice and gutter, open fascia and parapet as in Plate 22, Fig. 2.   Steps to the sides of veranda; and steps, platform and rail to rear door.*

FLOORS,——*Of the veranda, narrow clear white pine plank, tongued and grooved, put down with white lead and blind nailed—interior floor of best milled 1 1=4 plank, laid in courses—the first and second tiers of beams bridged and prepared for deafening, by boards and strips.*

WINDOWS,——*In the basement, 3 windows, 12 lights, 10 by 14—3 w. 6 lts. 10 by 15—two w. 12 lts. 8 by 12—sashes, 1 1=4 thick.   In first story 6 w. 20 lts. 8 by 16—3 w. 16 lts. 8 by 16—3 w. 16 lts. 7 by 16—sashes, 1 3=4 thick.   In second story, two w. 16 lts. 8 by 15—two w. 16 lts. 7 by 15—sashes, 1 3=8.   Under the eaves, 4 w. 8 lts. 8 by 13, and 2 w. 8 lts. 7 by 13—sashes 1 1=4 thick.   In the attic, 3 w. 4 lts. 11 by 14—sashes 1 1=4 thick.   Winslow glass of single thickness in the basement, second story and attic, and of double thickness in the first story.   All the frames to be made of plank, with strong grooved stops and outside casings, and 9 w. to have moulded hoods.   The bay window cornice and parapets as in Plate 22, Fig. 3.   Six windows under the eaves to have ornamental screens.*

BASE,——*In the first story, 1 3=4 thick and 9 in. high, moulded.   In second story 1 1=4 thick and 7 in. high, moulded at top.   In basement and attic 3=4 thick and 6 in. high.*

STAIRS,——*From the basement, enclosed by boards 7=8 thick, tongued and grooved, and a door at the bottom. From the first story to the second, 3 feet 4 in. wide, with moulded steps and strings, return brackets to the risers. Newels, 6 in. square, paneled, with moulded cap and base—a moulded rail 3 by 5 in. and balusters, turned in the middle, with four in. of each end two in. square.   From second story to attic two ft. wide, with moulded steps and strings, newel four in. square, octagon balusters 1 1=4 inch, and moulded rail two by three inch.*

MANTLES,——*Two of wood, in first story, as in Plate 22, Fig. 4.   Two in second story without the brackets. Three inch borders to all the hearths.*

DOORS,——*In the first story 6, to be 1 3=4 thick, and 6 to be 1 1=2 thick.   Front doors to fold, two in. thick, four panels, moulded on both sides.   The heads arched as in Plate 22, Fig. 6.   In second story, 3 passage doors, 1 1=2 thick, four panels, moulded on both sides, and 5 doors, 1 1=4 thick, moulded on one side.   All other doors 1 1=4 thick, four panels, "bead and butt."*

ARCHITRAVES,——*In the first story, of two in. plank, four and a half in. wide, beaded as in Plate 22, Fig. 6. In second story, one and a quarter by three and a half, plain cove and bead—all sett on plinths 7 in. high. All other casings one and a quarter thick and two and a half wide.*

HARDWARE,——*All the doors in the first and second stories, to be hung by patent butts 4 1=2 by 4 1=2 in. and those in the basement and attic, by butts 3 1=2 by 3 1=2 in.   A 6 in. upright rebated mortice lock to the front doors, with night key, double furniture and two 5=8 flush bolts.   All other doors in first story, to have 4 1=2 in. mortice locks, with porcelain knobs and drops, "star pattern."   In second story, passage doors to have four and a half in. mortice locks, and all others 5 in. rim locks with mineral knobs and bronze drops.   All the sashes in first story and four windows in second, to be hung by "parlament hinges," two and a half by five inches, and secured by French bolts. The sashes in the basement, hung by cord and weights—all other sashes by 3 in. butts, and fastened by spring bolts. Blinds hung by welded straps and hooks and secured by best patent metal fastenings—shutters by 3 in. butts, and secured by hooks and drops.*

CLOSETS AND WARDROBES,—To be fitted up with beaded shelves, 3 in. beaded strips, glazed hat and cloak hooks, each appropriate to its use.

BELLS.—A front door, and three room bells, with porcelain lever knobs, in first story, and four bells with mineral lever knobs in the second story.

BLINDS.—Heavy moulded moving blinds hung to all the windows in first and second stories—moulded panel outside shutters to all the windows in basement.

PAINTING.—The blinds to have three coats of dark bronze green. All the other wood work, outside and inside, except shingles and the interior floors, to have two coats of pure Bellville white lead and American linseed oil—the interior of first story to have a third or ground coat of oil color and painted in imitation of heavy oak in shades—the exterior to have a third coat of lead and oil, shaded with chrome yellow and lamp black, making a light or dark drab—the chimney tops to be painted a brown stone color.

DESCRIPTION OF PLATES.

Design V.—Elevations, plans, details, ground plot and scenic view of a cottage in the Tudor style, designed for a country residence on the bank of the Bronx river, in Weschester County, N. Y. The tenement comprises ten acres of ground, lying on both sides of the river, and mostly covered by forest trees. The premises will contain a gardener's lodge, summer-house, stone bridge, coach-house, bath-house, and out-buildings, screened by ornamental shrubbery.

PLATE 19.—Dimensions and arrangement of rooms, &c. on the first and second floors. (The attic is divided into three rooms.)

PLATE 20.—Geometrical elevations of the lawn and entrance fronts.

PLATE 21.—Plan of the basement and dimensions of timbers, and other particulars relative to the framing.

PLATE 22.—Details. Fig. 1.—Section of cornice—a, moulded barge board; b, transverse section of the same; c, section of gutter, roof boards, shingles and plate connected with the rafter and post. Fig. 2.—Veranda; d, open parapet; e, cornice; f, open facia; g, cap of column; h, transverse section of shaft; i, base. Fig. 3.—Bay window; j, open parapet; k, cornice. Fig. 4.—Section of mantle in first story; l, front section; m, profile section; n, ground section. Fig. 5.—Section of a window-frame—connecting the interior and exterior finish, the sashes to hang by butts; o, interior head casing, head jamb and hood moulding; p, sash transom rebated; q, drip and stop sills; r, base in the rooms; s, water table and main sill. Fig. 6.—Elevation of a door, and sections; t, architrave, mouldings, and face of door; u, ground section, for first and second stories; v, section, for basement and attic. Scale $\frac{3}{4}$ of an inch to a foot.

PLATE 23.—Ground plot, showing the location of the house, walks, roads, &c. in the natural style, with hedge and shrub borders.

PLATE 24.—Scenic view, presenting the entrance and river fronts, with the gardener's lodge, summer house; and the bridge in the distance.

ESTIMATE,

Of the Labor and Materials required for Design V.

MASON'S BILL.

163 yds. excavation, 18 cts.; 156 lds. stone, 60 cts.	$122 94	6 casks plaster, $2 00; 40 bushels hair, 25 cts.	22 00
3700 hard brick, $4 25 ; 14000 salmon brick, $2 50	50 72	20,000 lath, $3 75 ; 180 lbs. nails 7 cts.	87 60
500 face brick, $8 00 ; 21 ft. flagging 18 cts.	7 78	Crane and hooks, $2 40 ; 2 grates, $12 00.	26 40
8 window sills, 50 cts. ; 46 ft. coping 14 cts.	10 44	Furnace, $130 00 ; 107 loads carting, 31 cts.	163 17
2 brown stone hrths. $4 50 ; 2 bn. stone chy. tops, 8 00	25 00	95 days mason's labor, $1 65 ; 73 days laborer, 90 cts.	222 45
186 loads sand, 35 cts. ; 25 bush. white sand, 10 cts.	67 60		
83 casks lime, $1 00 ; 8 casks lump lime, $1 50	95 00		$901 10

CARPENTER'S BILL.

7796 ft. timber, $15 00 ; 320 joists, 14 cts.	161 74	700 lbs. nails, $4 00 ; 50 lbs. fine nails, 10 cts.	33 00
364 ft. bas't. sleepers, 3 cts. ; 404 floor planks, 26 cts.	115 96	188 lbs. sash weights, 2 cts. ; 4 lbs. sash cord, 30 cts.	4 96
186 narrow planks, 16 cts. ; 291 piece planks, 28 cts.	111 24	32 axle pulleys, 6 cts. ; 3½ doz. cloak hooks, 31 cts.	3 01
243 piece boards, 18 cts. ; 325 hmlk. boards, 13 cts.	85 99	21 pair 4½ by 4½ butts, 25 c. ; 12 prs. 3½ by 3½ in. butts 14 c.	6 93
5750 ft. clear plank, 2 in. 1½ 1¼ and ¾ in. 3½ cts.	201 25	20 pairs 2½ by 5 in. butts, 8 cts. ; 35 prs. 3 in. " 7 cts.	4 05
32 bunches shingles, $2 25 ; 26 wall strips, 11 cts.	74 86	8 gross 1¼ screws, 42 cts. ; 2 gross ¾ screws, 28 cts.	3 92
431 narrow siding, 16 cts. ; 4 finial heads $2 00.	76 96	16 lever sash bolts, $2 50 ; 2 flush bolts, 75 cts.	41 50
103 ft. blinds, 75 cts. ; 23 stair balusters, 15 cts.	80 70	2 8 in. flat bolts, 44 cts. ; 7 4 in. flat bolts, 15 cts.	1 93
168 lts. glass, 8 by 16, 28 cts.; 48 lts. gls. 7 by 16, 28 c.	60 48	1 front door lock, $14 50 ; 11 4½ mortice locks, $3 34,	51 24
18 lts. glass, 10 by 15, 20 cts. ; 32 " 8 by 15, 18 cts.	9 36	3 4½ mortice locks, $1 80 ; 17 5 in. rim locks, $1 31,	27 67
32 lts. gls. 7 by 15, 16 c. ; 12 lts. gls. 11 by 14, 18 cts.	7 28	8 hooks and drops, 10 cts. ; 3 closet locks, 50 cts.	2 30
36 " " 10 by 14, 16 c. ; 32 " " 8 by 13, 13 cts.	9 92	4 bells, $4 00 ; 4 bells, $2 25,	25 00
16 " " 7 by 13, 12 c. ; 24 " " 8 by 12, 11 cts.	4 56	402 ds. carpenter's labor, $1 50 ; 70 lds. carting, 31c.	624 70
96 ft. sheet lead, 18 cts. ; 70 ft. tin roof, 13 cts.	26 38		
72 ft. 4 in. leader, 15 cts. ; 25 ft. 3 in. leader, 10 cts.	13 30		$1970 19

PAINTER'S BILL.

900 lbs. white lead, $7 00 ; 7 lbs. litharge, 6 cts.	63 42	1 lb. burnt umber $1 00 ; 1 lb. venetian red, 30 cts.	1 30
39 galls. oil, 75 cts. ; 9 gall. boiled oil, 87 cts.	37 08	Graining first story,	40 00
4 galls. spirits, 75 cts. ; 20 lbs. putty, 5 cts.	4 00	Carting, $2 00 ; 44 days painter's labor, $1 75	79 00
2 lbs. glue, 25 cts. ; 11 lbs. yellow ochre, 20 cts.	2 70		
4 lbs. chrome yellow, 75 cts. ; 2 lbs. black, 50 cts.	4 00		$231 50

RECAPITULATION.

Mason's bill	-	-	-	-	-	-	$901 10
Carpenter's "	-	-	-	-	-	-	1970 19
Painter's "	-	-	-	-	-	-	231 50
							$3102 79

Items additional to the above Estimate.—The walls of stone in rubble work—basement, 2 ft. thick—first story, 20 inches—second story and gables, 18 inches thick. The following, of hammered stone—the quoins, 10 in. high—water table, 8 in. high—window sills, 6 in.—lintels, 12 in. high—$590. The excess of area will be 250 square ft. Glass set diagonally, $45 00—diamond, $75 00. A drain should be made to the basement, with a run 3 in. wide and 4 deep, which will require 9 bricks to a foot ; hence for 100 ft. 900 bricks $3 83—1 cask of cement, 2 00—mason, 1 day, 1 65—laborer 1 day, 90 cts. —Total for drain, $8 38, or 8¼ cts. per ft.—exclusive of excavation.

JANUARY 1ST, 1847.

PLATE 19.

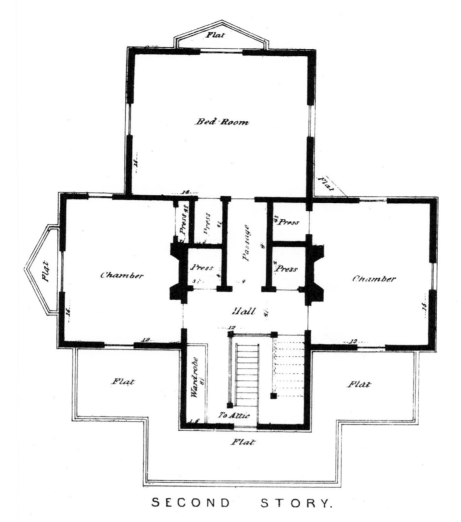

SECOND STORY.

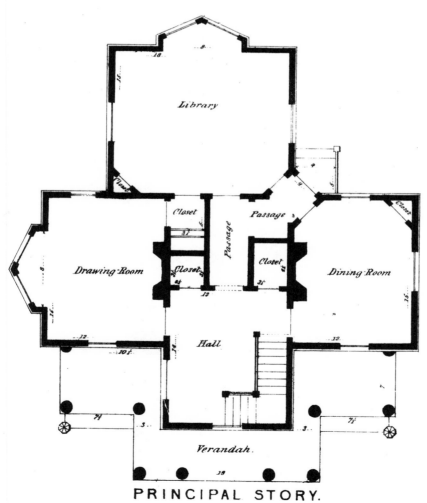

PRINCIPAL STORY.

Scale of 40 feet.

LAWN FRONT.

Del & desg. by Wm H. Ranlett.

Lith of F. & S. Palmer, 34 Ann St.

ENTRANCE FRONT.

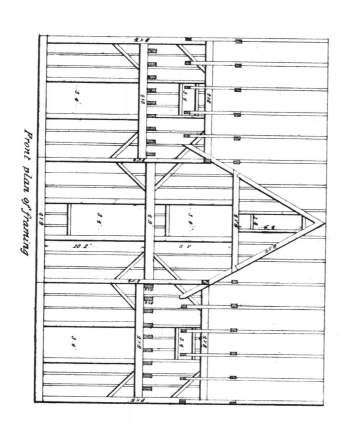

Front plan of framing

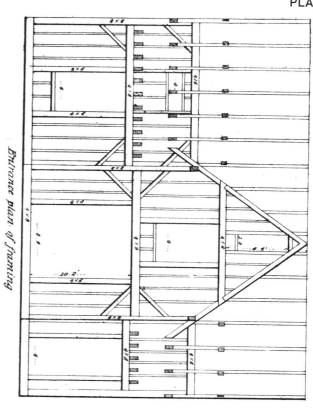

Entrance plan of framing

Design V.

Scale of 40 feet.

Plate 21.

Bed-Room

Bed-Room

Entry

Area

Cellar

Store Room

Kitchen

Area

Kitchen Pantry

Hall

Area

BASEMENT

PLATE 22.

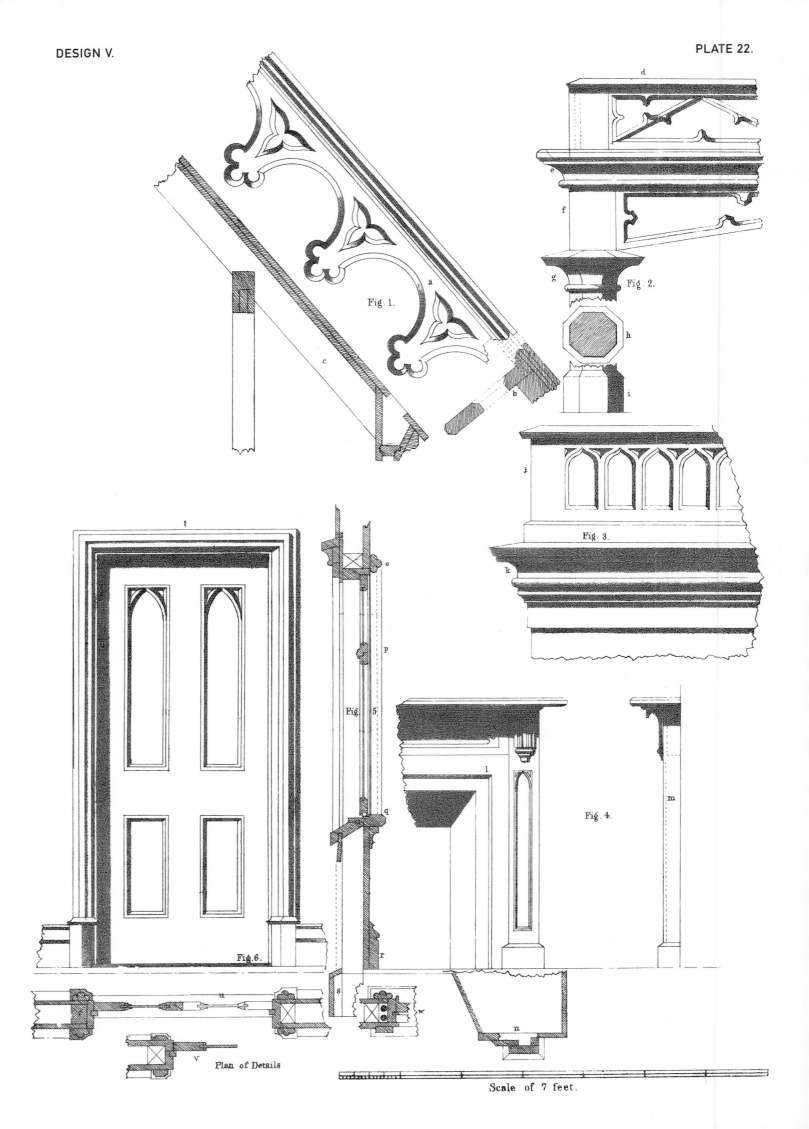

Fig. 1.

Fig. 2.

Fig. 3.

Fig. 4.

Fig. 5.

Fig. 6.

Plan of Details.

Scale of 7 feet.

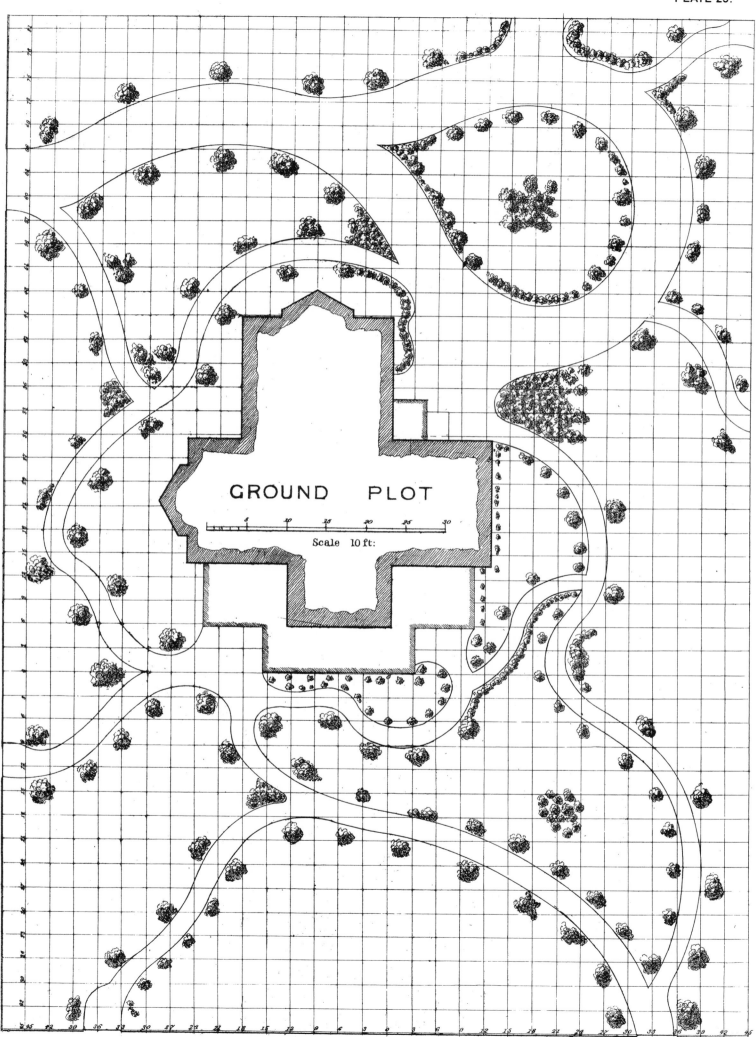

GROUND PLOT

Scale 10 ft:

THE ELIZABETHAN STYLE.

THE reign of Queen Elizabeth was distinguished by a new era in architecture, by a modification of the Tudor, which rendered it more plain and simple, and added a considerable admixture of the Italian, imported by Holbein—the Tudor prevailing without and the Italian within. This hybrid has been christened the "Elizabethan Style"—often called also "Old English;" this title, however, belongs more particularly to the Tudor of the four preceding reigns.

The outlines, in this style, were quite irregular, though less so than in the earlier Tudor. Porches were often within the outline of the plan, instead of projecting. The windows were wider and divided by more mullions, and had rectangular heads instead of the low-pointed arch, and were sometimes extended through the first and second stories. Oriel windows were common and various; and dormer windows were constructed with acute angled, projecting gables, finished with pendants, pinnacles, ornamented barge boards, &c. The chimney shafts were continued in groups but made plain, except a moulding at the base and a projection at the top. This style afforded convenient interior arrangements, though their beauty was often marred by grotesque carvings and other "scientific deformities." It harmonizes well with much of the scenery in this country, and costs but little more than the *box style* so common with us; but it lacks one important feature of a comfortable country or suburban residence—verandas—which may, however, be added with great propriety.

The Gothic was restricted to ecclesiastical edifices till the time of Henry VII. who applied it to dwellings in the Tudor or Old English, which was perfected in the time of Henry VIII. and modified, as above, in the reign of Elizabeth, and wholly supplanted by the Byzantine or Stuart's Style, when the Stuart family succeeded to the British throne, in the person of James I.

VENTILATION.

Continued from page 29.

THE admission of cold air at the base of a room—the natural and usual place for admitting it—is attended by one inconvenience—the distribution of it on, and near the floor—the very place where we least want it. This is obviated by the use of hot air furnaces, by supplying warm air instead of cold. Another mode of preventing this evil, is by admitting atmospheric air at the top of the apartment, by a register, and allowing the impure air to escape through a flue, at the top of the wall or side, under the

35

roof. Atmospheric air will enter through a horizontal opening at the ceiling, if the lighter air within is allowed to escape at a higher opening, which a flue will afford, besides giving a draft upon the lighter air. Such an opening and flue are easily made in the walls; and it is not difficult in a frame building, to admit air at the top of the room by an opening properly plastered and prepared between a pair of studs, that will conduct the air from the base of the weather-boarding, between it and the filling, to the desired point; and a similar flue above for the escape of the impure air. A still better method of admitting cold air, is to distribute it into various portions of the room by a tube in the ceiling, and discharge the impure air by a register in the chimney at the ceiling.

Another point that should be well understood and properly guarded, is the draft of chimneys. A high chimney of good draft, has a tendency to rarify the air in the room, by extracting it very rapidly; and it draws into the apartment, all the impure air that is accessible to it, from crevices in the walls, basement, cellars, sewers, &c., thus doing injury in two ways—depressing the spirits and muscular systems of the inmates, by the rarification of the air, and exposing them to disease by bringing into contact with them, the most impure air about the place. These points should be strictly controled, by having proper guards to the draft of the chimney, and carefully closing, about the base and walls of the dwelling, all avenues of malaria.

In further estimating the rate of ventilation, it is found that a moulded tallow candle, six to the pound, will consume the oxygen of fourteen cubic feet of air, at the temperature of 62 degrees Fahrenheit, in an hour, and vitiate about 30 feet in the same time; hence a room containing four persons, with two such candles burning, must receive atmospheric air and discharge the impure, at the rate of 260 feet per hour, to retain a healthful state of atmosphere. A fire which consumes three pounds of coal per hour, consumes about seventy-four times as much oxygen as a moulded candle, but it does not vitiate so large a proportion as respiration and the burning of lights, because the deleterious gas and vapor produced by the fire, are mainly carried off in the draft. Such a fire would consume the oxygen of 1036 feet of atmospheric air per hour, and vitiate about 1500 feet: hence a room containing four persons, two lights and such a fire, should receive and discharge air at the rate of 1760 feet per hour.

A chapel of sufficient capacity to contain 1500 persons in the auditory and galleries, is a good basis of an estimate for illustration. Suppose it filled, warmed by stoves, and lighted. The respiration of such an audience, would consume the oxygen of 7500 feet of air, and vitiate 75000 feet per hour. The lights, consuming 100 feet of gas, equal to the consumption of 200 moulded candles in an hour, would consume the oxygen of 2800 feet of air per hour, and vitiate 6000 feet in the same time. The fires, consuming coal at the rate of 15 pounds per hour, would consume the oxygen of 5180 feet of atmospheric air and vitiate 7500 feet per hour; hence atmospheric air must be admitted and the vitiated air discharged at the rate of 88500 cubic feet per hour, to preserve an atmosphere that would be agreeable and safe, to the audience. This exchange of air amounts to near three-fourths of the whole contents of the edifice in an hour, supposing it to be 60 by 80 feet, and 25 feet high. If such a chapel, thus filled, lighted and warmed, were kept air tight two hours, it would be fatal to many of the audience.

The most disastrous instance of the fatal effects of bad ventillation, or rather of the want of ventillation, on record, occurred in 1756 in Calcutta, in the case of 146 Englishmen who were imprisoned in a small prison only eighteen feet square, called the "Black Hole of Calcutta." It had only two small windows, both on one side, and so situated that the room could not be ventillated by them.* Soon after the door was closed, the prisoners began to experience an oppressive heat and intense thirst, many soon became delirious, and in six hours 96 of them were relieved by death from their torments. Only 23 survived the next morning, and but few of these recovered. There can be no rational doubt in the intelligent mind, that thousands of lives are the forfeit of bad ventilation, even in the enlightened cities of New York, Paris and London, notwithstanding the boasted "march of intellect" and improved practical applications of scientific principles.† There is really more necessity in cities, for municipal interference to prevent or expel the impure air which is produced in our midst, destroying by night and noon, with insidiousness and certainty, thousands of our fellow-beings, than there is of quarantine regulations to prevent yellow fever or Asiatic cholera, which are only occasional visitants to our shores.

* In small dwellings, certain and thorough ventillation is of still more importance than in large ones, for large apartments contain so much more air, that it requires a much longer time to vitiate it by respiration, &c. therefore the inmates inhale air which is much less impure, than that of a small room similarly situated. Low ceilings are a very common, and highly improper feature of small houses, for they do not allow the impure air to rise above the heads of the inmates, sufficient to prevent them from constantly inhaling it. The first story of a cottage in a country situation should be at least nine feet, in a city, from ten to fourteen, and attic rooms nine feet, and if no better method of ventillating is at command, a door or window should be left a little open, or frequently opened; for it will be found that if a warm room should be suddenly filled with cold air, it would produce a very temporary inconvenience, because the warm walls, furniture, &c. would quickly warm it. Small close bed-rooms are a very mischievous feature, which is by far too common in cottages and other small dwellings. Some—as if they intended to reach the climax of absurdity in such matters—place a bed in a recess about five by seven feet, closed by doors or curtains in front. Such a place is utterly unfit for a sleeping apartment unless it is for the sleep of strangulation. Close curtains about a bed, are highly improper, if it is designed to sleep in : for if a bird were kept through the night in the valance of open curtains above a bed where a person sleeps, it would be found dead in the morning. The air in a close bed-room, as small as they are often made, containing two persons, cannot retain a healthful state more than three hours, yet how often are children, domestics and others shut closely in such rooms from seven to ten hours, acquiring stupor by sleeping in bad air and then sleeping in it because they are stupid! What wonder then that so many children, who commence life with highly promising muscular constitutions, should become the early prey of disease, and be doomed by the very hand of care, to premature graves, or to linger out a few years in weakness and pain, with impaired constitutions, and to find themselves in the imbecility and decrepitude of age ere they see the noon of life! What wonder that the wealthy and refined parent has so often endured the pain of comparing the wan countenance and feeble frame of his care-burdened child, with the ruddy face and vigorous muscles of a hutted urchin by the way-side, and wondered " why Providence did not allow the blessing of health to rest upon the more important child of His care, and dispense weakness and disease—if send them He must—to the less valuable member of society;" never even dreaming that his own ignorant and misguided hand had planted most deeply the withering blight of which he complains, in the very vitals of the object of his solicitude.

† It is gratifying to witness an increasing interest among our countrymen, in architectural improvements; and a growing taste for good style in them. Small cottages in good taste, are becoming more common, and are found to be very appropriate, for many a mechanic or tradesman is able, by a little retrenchment besides the amount of his rent bills in a few years, to erect a tasty cottage on a pleasant country or suburban lot; which will soon be accompanied by the convenience of a vegetable garden, and all the decorations of bowers, shrubs and flowers, that his means and the taste and industry of nimself and family may enable them to accumulate. This number contains four designs of cottages in approved styles, that would cost from 975 to 1050 dollars. These designs are accompanied by the necessary specifications and estimates to guide the proprietor in contracting, and the builder in their construction.

THE ENGLISH COTTAGE STYLE.

HENRY VII. was the first to employ, in domestic architecture, the Ecclesiastical style called Gothic. This enterprize was followed by different modifications of the same original, and out of these modifications has arisen the style so extensively employed in England, called the "English Cottage Style." The classical improvement and refinement of taste that have characterized the English, had a chastening influence on their Architecture, which has cleared this modification of the Gothic, of many of the incongruities and absurdities which debased the earlier modifications, and produced a style of Cottage architecture, which is well adapted to the purposes of domestic edifices and harmonizes in great beauty with much of their scenery.

The great number of cottages which have been erected in the suburbs of London in latter years, has afforded the finest opportunity for the application of improved taste and skill in Cottage Architecture, and the result is a vast amount of rural scenery, comprising, in great harmony, the most chaste and tasteful Architecture, and highly improved gardens and yards with their exquisite flowers, shrubs and vines, constituting views which are admired by visitors from all countries. One of the chief sources of the beauty of those rural residences, is the positions of the houses on the lots, which is back sufficient to afford front yards for the cultivation of plants and vines which are arranged and trained in graceful combinations with the architectural features, thus hightening the general effect by promoting the influence of the various parts. This style is well adapted to a large portion of the surface and scenery of the United States, especially those portions in the higher latitudes.

The improved taste of modern times, has repudiated the monotony of regular houses—i. e. houses in which the parts produced by a central line, have a similar appearance—so common in the several classical styles, in the favor bestowed upon the several modifications of the Gothic. The extensive relish for irregular or picturesque dwellings, is one of the principal causes that produced this style—and most admirably does it meet this demand of good taste. This feature, as developed in the English Cottage Style, affords an opportunity of enlarging a dwelling, or of constructing a part of it at a time, without giving the different portions, the appearance of addenda of various dates; and this characteristic is very important to us, inasmuch as many of our countrymen have to build in that way, whose taste and associations lead them to desire dwellings of respectable style and accommodations, whose means, however, require them to attain such homes by degrees. When this method of constructing an edifice is adopted, the original plan should comprehend, or at least contemplate the enlargement.

The selection of a situation, is a matter of deep and lasting—and sometimes of fatal interest to the occupant. Many places are utterly unfit to be occupied by human beings. Whoever selects a situation with any view to health and only a tolerable degree of comfort, should carefully avoid marshes, low grounds, ravines and mountain peaks as decidedly unfavorable to both. It is also important to attain scenery that may be made useful in the improvements by harmonizing with the architectural features to be placed in combination with it. Design VII. in the Grecian style, is appropriate to a site somewhat elevated, with an even surface, without much inequality of trees, &c. Then in improving the ground, care must be taken to have round topped trees prevail so that they may harmonize with the prevailing horizontal lines and flat roof, for different designs may be formed for the same place, that would require very different classes of trees to harmonize with them. Designs VI., VIII. and IX., in the English cottage style, with high roofs, acute angled gables, and generally prevailing perpendicular lines, require that pointed trees prevail, to give harmony to the scene.

It often happens that after a man has determined on his general arrangement and plans, he finds much difficulty in informing his architect or builder what style would be most agreeable to his wishes, which might indeed be expected, since it requires a painter's imagination and eye to perceive all the elements of beauty that may be employed, and a skillful intellect to combine them. To accomplish all this requires a high degree of taste and skill in the architect. He should have a well balanced taste for rural scenery—nature improved and dressed by art—a knowledge of landscape-painting, landscape-gardening, and a high relish for the arts in general; without which he is unqualified to design, with success, small houses. Climate must have an important influence on the architect in designing a house, for the parts should be arranged and combined according to the latitude and general character of the place; 'i. e. its exposure to the rays of the sun and the more direct influence of storms. If, for instance, there were an unpropitious view to the north-east, that quarter would hold no inducement to place a drawing-room, parlor or dining-room in that part of the house, for it would combine all the unfavorable traits —a forbidding view, bad aspect, and exposure to the severest storms; and such a position is fit only for a sleeping apartment, which should never have a western aspect, where the house is much exposed to the sun. The arrangement should be such that the rays of the sun may be admitted or excluded at pleasure, and protect the inmates from the cold as much as possible.

The connection of a house with the ground is an important consideration. In all situations, the edifice should be above the ground sufficient to afford thorough ventilation between the ground and the first floor, for which purpose, openings should be left in the foundation. This will prevent the accumulation of impure air, and the decay of the timbers in or near the base of the building. In a low or level situation, the foundation should rise from three to four feet above the natural surface. A proper medium should always be observed between spreading a cottage out too much on the surface, and contracting it into too small a space by piling one part upon another, both which have a very bad effect in the landscape.

A small house is more difficult to design than a large one; and an irregular one is more difficult than a uniform one. In the last, the architect is restricted in point of variety, and in a small one he can indulge no ideas of grandeur: hence in cottages, he must rely on the good proportions of the edifice, the best accommodations of the family that the space will allow, and a picturesque scene in its combination with the ground and surrounding scenery.

SPECIFICATIONS

Of the Materials and Labor required for the erection of Cottages according to Designs VIII. & IX.

EXCAVATIONS.—The cellar, foundation, cistern and sink, and the proper grading around the buildings.

STONE WORK.—Cellar walls, 18 in. thick and 5 ft. high—other foundation walls, 30 in. below the surface and 18 in. thick—chimney piers to the floor beams—all of quarry stone, laid in good lime and sand mortar—sink, 4 ft. by 5, 8 ft. deep, with a stone wall, 6 ft. dry and 2 ft. in mortar—a stone cess=pool to the cistern—parlor hearth of brown stone, 4 ft. by 20 in.—kitchen hearth of blue stone, 3 by 4 ft. 2 in. thick, laid in mortar on the floor—3 blue stone sills in the cellar windows—the cistern covered with blue flagging, laid on locust supporters.

BRICK WORK.—Walls 8 in. thick and 16 high, on the foundation and cellar walls—bricks set on the edge in mortar, secured by wood brackets, between all the exterior studs—Designs 8 and 9, each to have a chimney of good bricks, with one fire=place and two flues, one commencing in the cellar, with a branch extending to the dead space behind the cellar for ventilating. (In Designs 6 and 7, the chimneys each to have four fire=places, two of them with brown stone hearths)—all the chimney shafts, as in the perspective views.

PLASTERING.—The first and second stories to be lathed and plastered with one heavy coat of brown mortar, floated off and hard finished—the kitchens all to be slipped and whitewashed, and the privies, hard finished.

FRAME,—Of sound spruce or pine, square timber. The sills, trimmers, posts and framing beams, 4 by 8—girts and window studs, 4 by 6—rafters and collar beams, 3 by 6—first and second tiers of beams 3 by 8, 16 in. between centers—braces, 3 by 4—studding for outside and partitions, 3 by 4, and set 16 inches between centers.

COVERING,—Of the side, clear boards 3=4 thick and 8 1=2 in. wide, rebated, and lapped 1 1=4 in. and put on with 10d nails. The water tables, corner boards, gutters and other exterior trimmings, of clear seasoned plank.

ROOFS,—Of hemlock or spruce boards, covered with best white pine shingles, three thick—valleys open three in. and lined with sheet lead 15 in. wide. The bay=window roof of tin, on milled plank, the porch roof with shingles on milled plank, face downward, beaded and center=beaded. Four 3 in. tin leaders.

CORNICE.—Design 8, with plain moulded projections, supported by brackets 4 by 5 in., with moulded steps and caps: Design 9, the cornices moulded and project 20 in.—the gutters of plank, put together with white lead.

FLOORS,—Of good milled plank, put down with 12d nails.

WINDOWS,—For Design 8, with square heads. In first story, 7 windows, 8 lts. 10 by 16—one double w. 16 lts. 8 by 15. In second story, two w. 8 lts. 10 by 15—two w. 12 lts. 9 by 15. In cellar, 3 w. 3 lts. each, 10 by 14, the sashes hung by butts on the tops. All the sashes 1 1=4 in. thick, and double hung with weights and cord,—all the windows in first story secured by best patent sash fastenings. Windows the same in Design 9, with the addition of angular heads—all the glass to be good American, single thickness.

BLINDS.——Square, moulded, moving blinds to all the windows in first and second stories, hung by welded straps and hooks, and secured by patent fastenings. The angular heads in design 9 to be stationary.

BASE.——Of clear plank, 1 1=4 thick in first story, and 7=8 in the second, put down in the usual manner.

DOORS.——The front door 1 3=4 thick, moulded both sides, hung by 5 in. butts, and fastened by a seven in. rim lock. All other doors 1 1=4 thick, four panels moulded on one side, hung by 4 by 4 butts, and secured by 5 in. rim locks with mineral knobs. All the casings made and put on as in plates 29 and 30.

STAIRS.——To the cellar, an open step ladder, with sides two in. thick, and wide steps 1 1=4 thick. From the first story to the second, in Design 8, an open stair=case, a wrought and capped newel, square balusters, a moulded rail and string, as in Fig. 4, Plate 29—in Design 9, enclosed by narrow tongued and grooved clear boards, extending 3 ft. above second floor, capped and moulded.

CLOSETS, &c.——China closet, with ten shelves on two sides. Kitchen pantry with four shelves on each of three sides. A sliding sash between the closets. Presses, each to have a shelf and 1 1=2 doz. clothes hooks. The linen closet to have 3 shelves 1 1=4 thick, and 2 ft. wide, with uprights in the center.

MANTLES,——In the parlor, with moulded and open uprights, ogee bed mould and bead, and 1 1=2 in. shelf. A three in. border to the hearth. Materials for the interior trimmings well seasoned and clear.

CISTERN.——To have a neck, with a rack and, lid hung by butts, and a good wood pump.

WOODHOUSE, &c.——Seven ft. by 11,—posts 7 ft.— the roof and sides covered as the dwelling. One part, 4 by 6 ft. finished with a floor, base, seats with lids hung by butts a panel door hung by butts, and fastened by a latch bolt,—a four light window with a stationary blind. The other part of the building to be open in front.

PAINTING.——All the exterior trimmings and sides to have two good coats of pure lead and best linseed oil, put on at proper times. The last coat may be shaded a light brown or drab. The interior trimmings all to have two coats of white lead, neatly put on. The blinds to have three coats, the last two, a substantial green.

DESCRIPTION OF PLATES.

PLATE 25.—Perspective views of two cottages—Design VI. in the English style, and VII. in the Grecian style.

PLATE 26.—Cellar, foundation, first and second story plans, and framing sections for Designs VI. and VII.

PLATE 27.—Perspective view of two cottages, Designs VIII. and IX., in the rural or English cottage style.

PLATE 28.—Ground plan of the two stories and cellar of Designs VIII. and IX. and a framing plan for Design VIII.

PLATE 29.—Details for Design VIII. Fig. 1.—A section of the main cornice and gutter, the face and profile of front and gable brackets—the dotted lines show the width of the front and gable fascia. Fig. 2.—Sections of the columns, fascia, rail and balusters of the porch. Fig. 3.—Cornice, sill and water table of the bay-window. Fig. 4.—Interior stair rail, newel, balusters, string and skirting. Fig. 5.—A transverse section and elevation of the chimney-shaft, scale 1½ in. to the foot. Fig. 6.—Front door and window casings in first story, made ¼ full size. Fig. 7.—Section of first story door with the casings, &c.

PLATE 30.—Details of Design IX. Fig. 1.—Barge boards and mouldings to the main roof, with the gutters in dotted lines. Fig. 2.—Base and cornice of bay-windows. Fig. 3.—Ground section of the bay-window—(inside shutters may be hung and folded in the box, if required). Fig. 4.—Roof, columns, barge board and moulding of porch. Fig. 5.—Profile of the gable of the porch. Fig. 6.—A window with the sashes in, showing the weather-boards fitted on the cap. Fig. 7.—Ground section of a window. Fig. 8.—Section of an interior door and casings. Fig. 9.—Ground section of the door. Fig. 10.—Section of chimney shaft for Design VI. Fig. 11.—Sections of the base in the two stories.

ESTIMATE,

Of the Labor and Materials required for Design VIII.

MASON'S BILL.

37 yds. excavation, 10 cts.; 77 lds. stone, 75 cts.	$66 45
5800 hard brick, $4 50 ; 4300 salmon brick, $3 00	39 00
12 ft. hearth, 16 cts. ; 40 ft. flagging, 12 cts.	6 72
3 window sills, 50 cts. ; 1 brown stone hearth, $2 00	3 50
69 loads sand, 35 cts.; 6 bush. white sand, 10 cts.	24 75
31 casks lime, $1 00 ; 2 casks lump lime, $1 38	33 76
2 casks plaster, $1 75 ; 1 cask cement, $1 50	5 00
12 bushels hair, 20 cts.; 6500 plastering lath, $3 00	21 90
58 lbs. nails, 7 cts. ; 4 stove pipe rings, 30 cts.	5 26
4 ventilation registers, $1 00 ; 12 loads carting, 40 cts.	8 80
32 days mason's labor, $1 50 ; 28 days laborer, 90 cts.	73 20
	$288 34

CARPENTER'S BILL.

3986 ft. timber, $16 25 ; 135 joists, 14 cts.	83 66
43 ft. locust, 10 cts. ; 120 hmlk. boards, 13 cts.	19 90
291 piece planks, 29 cts. ; 318 piece boards, 19 cts.	144 81
16 bunches shingles, $2 50 ; 144 floor planks, 25 cts.	76 00
170 ft. 2 and 1½ in. clear pk. 3½ cts. ; cistern pump, $6 00	11 95
75 ft. blinds, 70 cts. ; 61 ft. tin roof, 11 cts.	59 21
56 lts. glass, 10 by 16, 20 cts.; 16 lts. gls. 9 by 16, 20 cts.	14 40
16 " " 10 by 15, 19c.; 24 " " 9 by 15, 19 cts.	7 60
9 " " 10 by 14, 16c. ; 4 " " 9 by 12, 15 cts.	2 04
65 ft. leader, 10 cts. ; 260 lbs. sheet lead, 6 cts.	22 10
400 lbs. nails, 4, 8, 10 and 12d. ; 52 axle pulleys, 6 cts.	20 12
290 lbs. sash weights, 2 cts.; 6 lbs. sash cord, 31 cts.	7 66
2 gr. ¾ screws, Nos. 7 and 9, 20c.; 2 gr. 1¼ No. 11, 41c.	1 22
1 front door lock, $1 50 ; 13 5 in. rim locks, $1 31	18 53
2 latch bolts, 60 cts. ; 15 prs. 4 by 4 butts, 22 cts.	4 50
3 prs. 3 in. butts, 10 cts. ; 3 sash bolts, 20 cts.	90
127 ds. carpenter's labor, $1 40 ; 30 lds. carting, 40c.	189 80
	$684 40

PAINTER'S BILL.

275 lbs. white lead, $7 00 ; 14 galls. linseed oil, 65 cts.	28 35
1 gal. sp. turpentine, 70 cts. ; 3 lbs. litharge, 6 cts.	88
10 lbs. putty, 5 cts. ; 1 lb. glue, 25 cts.	75
Carting, $2 00 ; 13 days painter's labor, $1 60	22 80
	$52 78

RECAPITULATION.

Mason's bill - - - - - -	$288 34
Carpenter's " - - - - - -	684 40
Painter's " - - - - - -	52 78
	$1025 52

Each of the four cottages in this number will cost about the same sum. The interior arrangements of Designs VI. and VII. will probably be considered less convenient than the other two, yet they are larger. In Design VI. the gables are ornamented, the drapery open, the finials plain, the roof high, and other corresponding features; and Design VII. has a flat roof of best galvanized tin roofing, and the trimmings plain, all the principal features of the above two, such as mason work, frame, sides, floors, doors and windows, to be constructed according to the specification for Designs VIII. and IX. Either of these cottages may be placed on a lot 50 feet by 150, with flower and vegetable gardens, shrubbery, fruit trees, &c. If the lot should be well situated to the road or street, and require but little grading, the whole cost of the improvements will be :—

Cottage and out buildings, - - -	$1025 52	Making garden and walks, - - -	50 00
Front fence, painted, 50 feet, 32 cts. - -	16 00	Furnishing trees and shrubs, and planting, -	45 00
Common pale fence, 100 ft., white-washed, 17 cts.	17 00	Manure and sodding, - - - -	25 00
Common tight fence, 250 ft., 5 ft. high, 18 cts. -	45 00		
			$1223 52

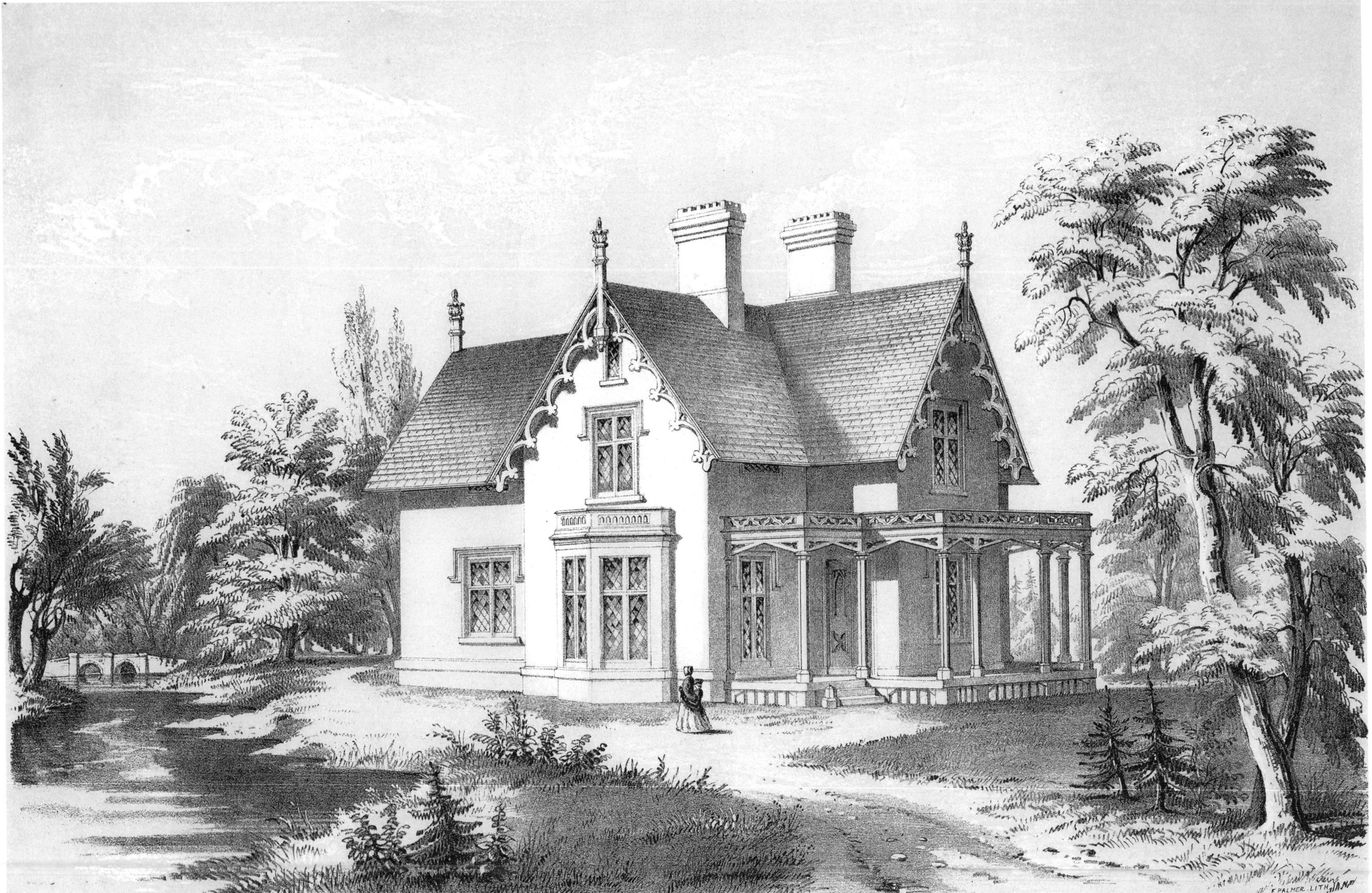

PLATE 24.

DESIGN V.

PERSPECTIVE VIEW.

Lith. of F. & S. Palmer, 34, Ann St.

PERSPECTIVE VIEW

in the English Style .

Lith. F. & S. Palmer 43 Ann St.

Designed by W.ᵐ H. Ranlet.

PERSPECTIVE VIEW.

in the Grecian Style .

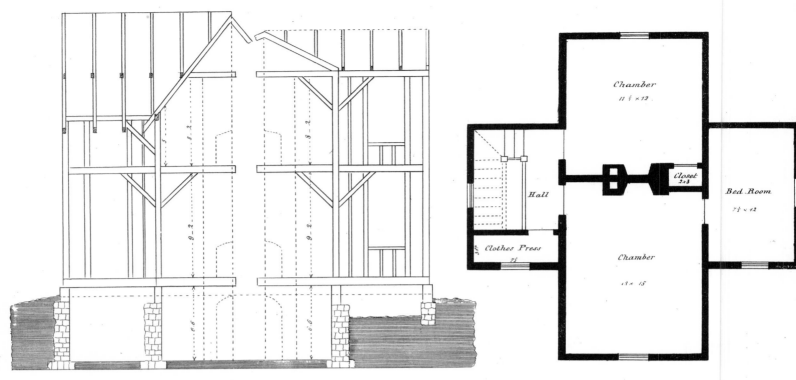

FRAMING SECTIONS FOR DESIGNS VI & VII.

SECOND STORY

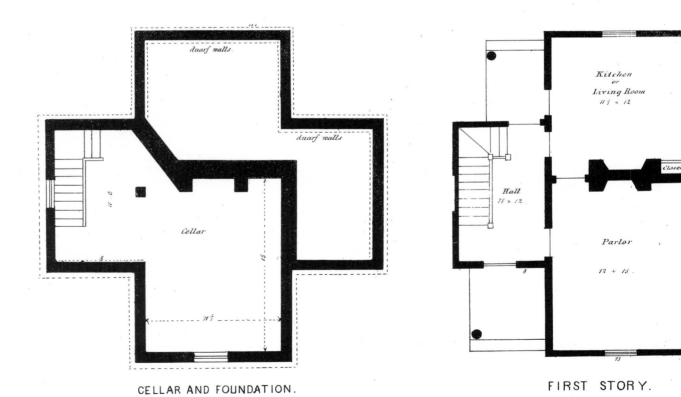

CELLAR AND FOUNDATION.

FIRST STORY.

ENGLISH COTTAGE STYLE.

ENGLISH COTTAGE STYLE.

PLATE 28.

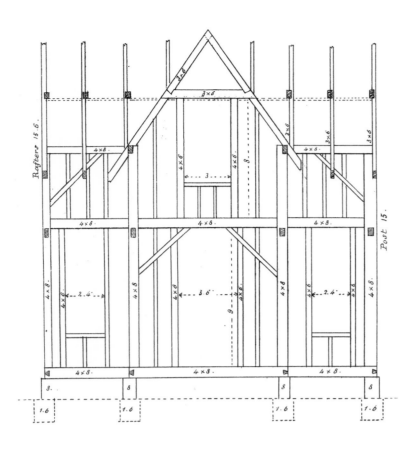

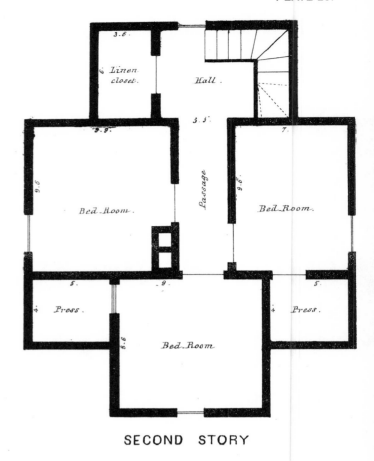

SECOND STORY

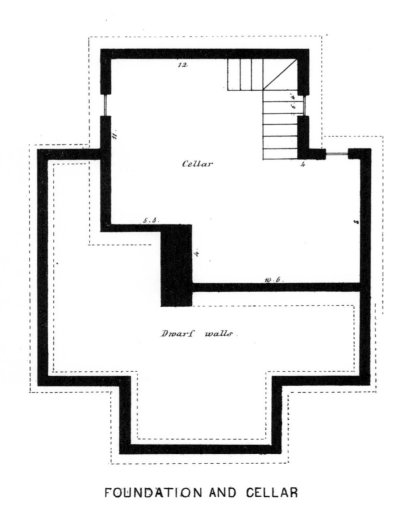

FOUNDATION AND CELLAR

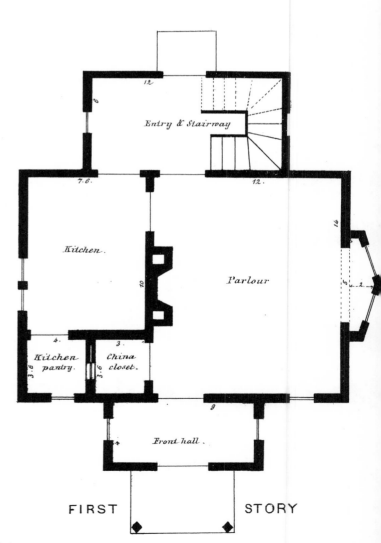

FIRST STORY

Lith. F & S. Palmer 43 Ann St. N.Y.

Fig. 1.

rafter

guter

Bracket

Fig. 5.

⅛ in to the ft

¼ full size

Fig. 6.

Fig. 2.

Fig. 4.

Fig. 7.

Fig. 2.

Lith. F. & S. Palmer 43 Ann St

Scale of feet

PLATE 30.

Fig. 10.

Scale of inches.

Fig. 5.

Fig. 4.

5. feet.

Fig. 1.

Fig. 2.

8. feet.

Fig. 6.

Fig. 8.

Fig. 11.

Fig. 9.

Fig. 7.

Fig. 3.

Lith. F. & S. Palmer 43 Ann. St.

Scale of feet.

GRECIAN ARCHITECTURE.

WHEN the Greeks produced their style of Architecture, their country was rugged and abounded with forests, and their dwellings were rude huts of wood. They were contiguous to Egypt and Persia, and not remote from India, where Architecture had reached a high state of improvement; and from these countries the Grecian philosophers and artists drew their materials to a great extent; but their national ambition and independence of spirit induced in them, great efforts to produce a national character in their arts and sciences. Another important consideration is the strong probability that several of the colonies which formed the Grecian States, were from Persia, Phœnicia, India and especially Egypt; and with the last named country, the Greeks were in such intimate relations when Grecian Architecture commenced its most rapid advance, 400 years B. C. in the reign of Psammaticus, King of Egypt, that he induced them to plant colonies on the Nile.

The Egyptians had no wood, but they possessed extensive quarries of granite, porphyry and marble, therefore their edifices were constructed of the most durable material, which was a strong inducement to their artists to make the greatest possible improvement in their Architecture, as their productions would continue for ages to be monuments of their artistical skill as well as of national grandeur.

The columns, entablatures, and peculiar ornaments of the magnificent temples of ancient Egypt, Persia and India, would afford hints quite sufficient for a people less ingenious and inventive than the Greeks. The Doric column, which is the earliest order of Grecian Architecture, is the most natural imitation in wood, of the ancient Egyptian marble column, and their entablatures were a modification of the Egyptian, equally as appropriate to their material and circumstance, and above all the pointed roofs and pediments of the Greeks, which were original with them, were the most natural variation from the flat marble roofs of the Egyptians: and indeed the general form of Grecian edifices—parallelograms with regular outlines and without arches or any other curved lines—is the most appropriate and convenient for wood, the material with which they began to build.

In decorating their edifices, they aimed at the ornamenting of the essential parts, rather than the production of addenda for the purposes of decoration, in which their attention was confined almost exclusively to the exterior. Many features of the style of the Greeks, were peculiarly their own, for they made valuable improvements on Egyptian Architecture. So great indeed were their improvements, that their earliest edifices of any considerable importance, displayed a degree of judgment, taste and skill that placed the Architecture of the Egyptians, Persians and Indians, in the infancy of the fine arts.

The Greeks produced three *orders* of Architecture in the course of their improvements—the Doric, Ionic and Corinthian.

43

THE DORIC ORDER.

This is the earliest Order of Grecian Architecture, and it is named from the country of Greece in which it rose. In the earliest examples, the proportion of the hight of the column to its diameter, bears a striking resemblance to that of some of the Egyptian temples; but the arrangement of the triglyphs, metopes and mutules, indicates the disposition of wooden beams and the ends of the rafters in the construction of their sloping roofs, for the log houses of the Grecian colonies, were evidently the models of the Doric order, which was developed in fine proportions and established in the affections of the Greeks, in the construction of the temple of Juno at Argos in the District of Argolis, which was the cradle of Grecian civilization. After this, the Doric order was employed in many temples—in the splendid triple portico in the city of Elis, and above all in the memorable temple of Minerva Parthenon.

The Grecian temples were of an oblong form, with porticos at the ends: some, however, had porticos at the sides also, and some had single ranges of columns, and others double rows; and some had colonnades through the centers of the edifices. The buildings were placed on platforms, three steps from the ground on all sides, on which the columns were placed without bases. In the early examples of Doric columns their hight was four or five diameters; they afterwards were made more delicate in their proportions, until they came to be constructed six and a half diameters high, and always with small plain capitals. The finest marble was used and the best artists employed in the construction of the temples of the Greeks, on which they placed so high an estimate that they would not allow the name of the greatest conqueror to be inscribed on one of them, even if he would pay the whole cost of the edifice as the reward for such an honor: and moreover they were constructed under the strongest impulses of rivalship. Such were the circumstances, influences, talents, taste and artistical skill, that produced the chaste and severe Doric order which prevailed, almost exclusively in Greece and its European colonies in Sicily and Italy, until after the Macedonian conquest by the Romans, B. C. 168.

This order produced the highest effects of simplicity and grandeur, when employed on the grand and imposing scale of some of the Grecian temples. These magnificent colonnades were the chief ornaments of their cities and common resorts for protection from the sun and rain, and for social business and pastime.

THE IONIC ORDER.

Ionia was a portion of Asiatic coast occupied by Grecian colonies. They possessed a fertile country with many cities well situated for commerce; hence they became numerous, rich and intelligent. The arts and sciences flourished among them to so great an extent, that they have been considered more eminent than any district of the mother country, even in the zenith of her glory. It is said that the final adjustment and refinement of the Doric order, was by the Ionians; but that refined people were not satisfied with the simplicity of the Doric, therefore they invented another order and called it Ionic after their country. In this order, the hight of the column is greater in proportion to the diameter than in the Doric. The capitals were formed on different principles, and ornamented by four spiral projections, called volutes, so arranged as to present a flat face on the two opposite sides. They also invented an entablature of parts and proportions different from that of the Doric, and added a base to the column. These are the chief characteristics of the Ionic order, the most distinctive of which, is the capital. The Greeks erected, in this order, many temples of great magnificence—one of the most splendid was that of Diana of the Ephesians, which was produced by the contributions of all Asia. It was 425 feet long, 220 wide and 70 high, and was 400 years in building.

THE CORINTHIAN ORDER.

The success of the Ionians in their attempt to depart from the simplicity of the Doric, and produce a more delicate and refined order, encouraged the artists of Grecia proper, to make an effort to produce an order still more refined than that of the Ionians. The attempt was entirely successful, and the new order was styled Corinthian, and its invention accredited to Callimachus, an Athenian sculptor.

This order has a greater hight of column in proportion to its diameter than the Ionic, and it is decidedly more delicate and elegant in its proportions and finish, its whole fabric being constructed with exquisite taste, which gives it a highly ornamental character, and renders it very expressive of the refinement and excellence of Grecian taste and skill in architecture. Of this Order, the great distinction is the capital of the column. It is more than a diameter in hight, and has much of the shape of an inverted bell. Its whole surface is richly wrought into acanthus leaves with eight volutes.

The entablature is composed of the architrave, four sixths of a diameter high, the frieze, of the same dimension, and the cornice nearly a diameter—each richly ornamented; the whole constituting a splendid production of noble proportions, amounting to two-ninths of the hight of the column; while the column, including the base and capital, is ten diameters high. The Greeks had a very thorough school of architecture in the three orders which they produced, yet the dwellings of the common people were poor and mean, while the villas of a few were excellent, and their temples magnificent.

The accompanying Design X. is for an Anglo-Grecian Villa, in the *Ionic* Order, to be constructed of brick, for a gentleman's residence at New Brighton, on Staten Island. The situation is elevated and uneven, containing oak, elm, chestnut, and other trees with a forest in the background; to which the broken outline of the edifice renders it highly appropriate. The plan allows four principal rooms on each floor, so arranged that each has three distinct and full views. The drawing-room affords a view of New York city; the parlor, of the ocean, Narrows, bay, and Long Island; the dining-room, of the "Kills" and the Jersey shore, and mountains in the distance; and the view from the library comprises a forest.

DESCRIPTION OF PLATES.

PLATE 31.—Design X. A scenic view of an Anglo Grecian Villa, with an irregular outline, in the Ionic Order of that style of Architecture.

PLATE 32.—Ground plans of the first and second stories of the same.

PLATE 33.—Details of Design X. Fig. 1, Section of main cornice and pediment, with the lines for the raking mouldings. Fig. 2, Veranda cornice and sections of a column—A, entablature; B, face, profile, and side view of the capital; C, C, plan and face section of the base. Fig. 3, Mantles for the principal story—M, section of face; N, profile. Fig. 4, Section of the architraves in the first story—I, face; J, profile; K, section of ground plan; L, ground section of the architraves in second story. Fig. 5, H, face section of circular window head for the second story; G,G, ground section, of the same. Fig. 6, Profile section of bases—D, of first story; E, of second do.; F, of attic and basement.

PLATE 34.—Details of Design X. Fig. 1, Profile section of the cupola cornice. Fig. 2, Projecting window cornice. Fig. 3, The green house cornice—A, face section; B, section of ground plan. Fig. 4, Section of principal stairs—C, string; D, profile of string; F, face and section of rails; G, balusters; H, bracket. Fig. 5, Architraves of the principal story made one half the size required. Fig. 6, The same for the second story. Ground plans of the basement and attic by putting windows in the four pedaments.

PLATE 35.—Front elevation and ground plan of a wood-house, to be built of wood, with narrow siding and metal roof; coal and wood rooms lined with boards, and all others plastered; two coats of paint on the exterior—A, apartments for wood and coal; B, work room; C, gardener's bed-room; D, gardener's lock-up; E, principal privy; F, servants' do. Hight of rooms 8 ft.

Elevations and ground plans of coach-house, stables, &c.—the walls of hard brick, 8 in. thick; foundation of stone, 18 in. thick; stories, 10 ft. in coach room, 8 ft. above; in wings 9 ft. and 7 ft. above, all in the clear. Beams, 3 by 10; rafters, 3 by 6. Stable floors double, of 2 in. plank—all other floors of milled spruce plank; roofs of milled plank, covered with galvanized tinned plates; cornices of clear, seasoned white pine; windows, shutters, doors, &c. as in the elevations.

Three yards, with suitable houses well covered with metal roofs, for cows, pigs and poultry, are connected with the coach-house. The piggery to be excavated 2 feet, a wall 18 in. thick, sunk 3 feet below the surface when graded; and coped with blue stone clamped with iron—the enclosure 3 feet high; of 2 in. upright plank, capped. All the exterior wood work and brick, painted with two coats of dark brown stone color, and interior of first story finished with planed, tongued and grooved boards. a, coach-room, sufficient for four carriages; b, stalls, three single and one double, the divisions and feed-boxes of 2 in. spruce plank, ironed on top edge; c, feed-room; d, harness-room; f, farmer's room; e, coachman's bed-room; h, stairway to; v, fowls' roosting-room, and w, their laying-room; i, stairway to; s, hay-loft, sufficient to hold four tons of hay; j, entry to; k, covered and laticed fowl yard; l, ladder for fowls; m and n, piggeries; o, stable manure, open to m; p, passage to cow and manure yard; r, cow-house; t, grain room; x, boxes for hay and grain slides. G, e, and u, to be plastered.

PLATE 36.—A perspective view of the east or garden front of a villa in a style partaking of the Gothic and Tudor, now erecting for Dr. S. M. Elliott, at Elliottville, Staten Island. The entrance from the street, in the west front. Two parlors, a library, and dining-room on the first floor; two chambers and two bed-rooms on the second; two sleeping-rooms in the attic, and the kitchen in the basement.

SPECIFICATIONS,

Of the Materials and Labor required for the erection of a Villa according to Design X.

BASEMENT.——Walls 20 in. thick and 8 ft. 6 in. high, of quarry stone laid in best mortar, on a wide foundation; the door and window sills of cut stone; airie walls of blue stone, 18 in. thick and 5 ft. 6 in. high, and stone steps, coped and flagged with blue stone; kitchen hearth of blue stone 3 by 8 feet; two chimneys on 16 in. piers and two with fire-places; Pond's large range set in one, and a boiler of 36 gallons in the other. Also one of Walker's large size furnaces, set complete with registers.

SUPERSTRUCTURE.——Walls 12 in. thick, of hard brick, laid close, with flush joints, and rubbed for painting; the door and window sills and lintels of brown stone plain tooled; water table of brown stone 9 in. high and 3 in. wash; the chimney shafts in panel work, with tops of brown stone—brick piers to all the columns.

MANTLES AND GRATES.——In the first story 4 mantles of statuary marble, as in Plate 33 and 4 ornamented grates, and in second story, 4 mantles of veined marble, and two plain grates.

PLASTERING.——All the rooms, halls, closets, &c. lathed and plastered with two coats of brown mortar, and hard finished in the first and second stories, and all others slipped and whitewashed; two plain, and three decorated cornices in the first story, and a neat 10 in. cornice in all the rooms and hall in the second story, and two floors deafened.

TIMBER.——All of best white pine: the first and second tiers of beams 3 by 12, 16 in. between centers and bridged—roof tier 3 by 9, 2 ft. 4 in. between centers; all trimmers 4 in. thick; plates 5 by 8: rafters 3 by 8, 28 in. between centers: cupola frame of timber 4 by 8, and 4 by 10, substantially braced by timber 4 by 6: basement sleepers of red cedar 6 in. thick. 28 in. between centers: studding 3 by 4, 12 in. between centers and bridged in first and second stories, and 16 in. between centers in basement and attic.

ROOFS.——Of good milled plank, covered with Moorewood's tinned plates, the joints ridged and clamped: the veranda roofs flat and soldered—four 4 in. leaders, and eight 2 in. leaders of tin.

CORNICES,——All of best clear plank, firmly put up as in Plate 33.

VERANDA.——Columns of best clear plank put together with white lead—the ceiling of each, of narrow clear plank tongued, grooved and beaded—front steps with buttress sides—and rear steps with 10 in. newels, 5 in. rails and 3 in. balusters—the extension of the rear porch over the carriage road, resting on two square pillars —ceiling, cornice and roof as on the veranda, and the green-house and projecting roofs and cornices the same.

FLOORS.——In the basement and attic, of good milled white pine plank—in the first and second stories and veranda, of best clear, narrow white pine, milled plank, blind nailed—two to be prepared for deafening.

STAIRS,——From basement to first story, close with a door at the bottom and a rail newel and balusters at the head; principal stairs with a moulded rail 2 1=2 by 5 in. continued to the attic—a scroll on a curtail step, secured by a turned iron newel—balusters 2 1=4, fancy turned with two members cut in leaves—rail and balusters of best seasoned St. Domingo wood—the steps 1 1=2 in. thick with coves, and the risers return with brackets, and continue around both galleries.

WINDOWS,—In the basement with box frames and inside shutters; in the principal and second stories, sashes 1 1=2 in. thick—all the windows in the second story and cupola to have circular heads—all the windows glazed with French glass, of single thickness in the green=house, basement, attic and cupola, and of double thickness in all others in the first story—sashes double hung, and fitted with all necessary trimmings of the best kind—Venetian rolling blinds to all the windows above the basement—two Ionic columns with carved caps and bases and enriched entablatures to each recess in the rooms of the principal story.   Panel backs to all the windows in the first and second stories, with elbows and seats.

BASE,—Of clear lumber, in all the rooms, halls and closets as in Plate 33.

DOORS,—In the first story, 2 in. thick, double faced and moulded—in the second story 1 5=8 thick, double faced and moulded, all others 1 1=4 in. single faced, moulded and hung by patent butts—mortice locks to all the doors in the first and second stories; porcelain knobs and furniture of Victoria pattern, in the first story, and plain white, in the second—6 in. rim locks with mineral knobs in basement and attic.

ARCHITRAVES,—As in Plate 33, Fig. 4—I, in first story, and L, in second—a single 1 1=4 in. band moulding 3 in. wide in basement and attic.

FURRING,—All the outside walls for lathing, furred with 2 by 4 wall strips 16 in. between centers—the ceilings all to be tight furred, 12 in. between centers.

PRESSES AND CLOSETS—Fitted up with drawers, doors, shelves, hooks and pins suitable for their several uses.

BELLS,—Twelve bells hung in the several rooms as required—the pulls and levers corresponding with the lock furniture.

HIGHTS OF STORIES,—Basement, 8 ft.—principal story, 12 ft.—second story 10 ft.—attic 7 ft., all in the clear.

PAINTING,—All the outside walls of brick and stone—chimney tops and tin leaders to have two good coats of pale straw colored paint—all the wood=work (except blinds, interior floor and mahogany) to have three good substantial coats of pure white lead and best linseed oil—the blinds, three coats of Paris green—all the mahogany rails, &c.—to have six coats of varnish, rubbed and polished.

*** For specifications for wood=house, &c. see Description of Plate 35.

ESTIMATING.

CORRECT estimating requires the exercise of considerable intelligence, skill and candor, being based on different classes of data, and requiring many minute computations that involve interests which are important to the builder and proprietor.

MENSURATION.—A good knowledge of this art in many of its applications is absolutely necessary to enable a man to compute the number of yards in excavations and grading—the number of bricks, or of feet of stone, requisite for walls, foundation, &c.—the quantities of various kinds and qualities of lumber—also of nails, glass, putty, lime, sand, oil, paint, &c. necessary for a specified building. How, for example, can a man give the quantity of nails for the floors of a house, unless he is able to compute the number that they will require, and the number in a hundred pounds, of a specified size? Similar ability is requisite for estimating other parcels of the materials and the amounts of labor.

PRICES.—A distinct knowledge of the market prices of the various materials at the time of making the estimate, is necessary; also a knowledge of the expense of collecting the materials and of the labor of mechanics and common laborers, which will be requisite in the erection of the edifice, for on these data all the others depend.

PERCENTAGE.—A builder is entitled to a reasonable percentage on the funds he expends in advance, also on the amount of the cost of the materials and erection, as his own remuneration. This is a very correct method of computing the allowance to a builder and it has received the sanction of long continued usage.

CANDOR.—To produce a reliable estimate, it is necessary that a man should possess, in addition to the above specified knowledge, a reasonable share of *candor*, or what is commonly called HONESTY! On this depends the faithfulness of the applications of all the above prerequisites.

The following practical occurrences of recent date, will illustrate this subject. Of a few proposals for the labor of a small mechanical job, the highest was found to be more than double the amount of the lowest. In another instance, eight proposals were received for the erection of two dwellings and a coach-house, which varied in amounts, from $8,000 to $18,000; and in another instance, eighteen proposals for two brick edifices, varied upward of $4,000 on each. The above proposals were all from responsible sources: seven of the last being from builders among the most reliable and competent in the city of New York, who varied in their estimates, to the amount of $3,000, *on each house.* In each of the above instances, the estimates were made from the same specifications and plans.

Now is it not perfectly manifest that some of the builders who made such variant proposals, lacked some one or more of the necessary qualifications of a trust-worthy contractor? Where then, it may be asked, is the safety of an employer? We answer, in enlightening the public mind on the subject, so that citizens will become qualified to understand their own wants and interests in relation to it, and thereby be able, not only to prevent others from imposing on them, but also to direct, to better advantage, their own means and efforts. The subject of Architecture should be placed in the reach of the common people, and we shall miss our object, if the " ARCHITECT " does not do much toward that desirable improvement in our country, and we hope to see the time when the science will be a branch of common school education, for it is intimately connected with the general and elementary interests of the people; and if it were inculcated upon the youth of the country at large, it would do more than any other branch of science towards cultivating the public taste, and elevating the general style and grace of improvements, public and private.

ESTIMATE.

Materials required for Design X.

MASON'S.

360 yds. excavation, 12 cts. ; 330 lds. building stone, 75 cts. ;
17 blue stone door and window sills, 60 cts. ;
17 blue stone lintels, 60 cts. ; 242 ft. flagging, 10 cts. ;
40 ft. hearth, 13 cts. ; 70 ft. steps and coping, 14 cts. ;
279 ft. of brown stone water table, 42 cts. ;
31 brown stone sills, 139 ft. 42 cts. ;
19 brown stone lintels, 87 ft. 42 cts. ;
147,000 hard brick, $4 50 ; 14,000 salmon brick, $3 25 ;
265 casks Thomaston lime, $1 00 ;

14 cks. Glens Falls lime, $1 50 ; 8 casks Lubec plaster, $1 75 ;
6 casks marble dust, $1 25 ; 60 bush. white sand, 10 cts. ;
611 loads brown sand, 42 cts. ; 42,000 plastering lath, $2 75 ;
375 lbs. lath nails, $7 00 ; 84 bush. hair, 20 cts. ;
Cooking range, $68 00 ; copper boiler, $42 00 ;
4 marble mantles, $75 00 ea.; 4 marble mantles, $35 00 ea.;
4 grates, $28 00 each ; 2 grates, $17 00 each ;
Walker's furnace, $180 00 ;
Mason's wages, $1 75 ; laborer's wages, $1 00.

CARPENTER'S.

13200 ft. timber $1 60 cts. ; 175 joists, 14 cts. ;
522 wall strips, 11 cts. ; 800 lineal ft. basement sleepers, 6c. ;
787 milled plank, 27 cts. ; 1080 narrow clear planks, 18 cts. ;
590 hemlock boards, 13 cts. ; 1200 ft. 3 in. plank, 3½ cts. ;
2400 ft. 2 in. plank, 3½ cts. ; 1600 ft. 1½ in. " 3½ cts. ;
4500 ft. 1¼ in. " 3½ cts. ; 8900 ft. 1 in. and ¾ in. " 3½ cts. ;
280 ft. mahogany, 11cts. ; 185 balusters, 32 cts. ;
224 lts. of gls. 8 by 13, 13 cts.; 88 lts. gls. 12 by 16, 26 cts.;
32 " " 8 by 12, 13 cts. ; 148 " " 9 by 12, 13 cts. ;
180 " " 10 by 18, 42 cts.; 124 " " 12 by 18, 44 cts. ;
186 " " 10 by 16, 42 cts.; 72 " " 12 by 16, 45 cts. ;

224 ft. blinds, $1 00 ; 1 iron newel, $6 50 ;
36 lbs. cord, 31 cts. ; 2260 lbs. sash weights, 2 cts. ;
4 doz. sash fastenings, $3 50 ; 27 doz. pullies, 62 cts. ;
4324 ft. roofing, 13c. ; 80 ft. 4 in. ldrs. 15 cts. ; 90 ft. 3 in. 10c.;
30 pair butts, 5 by 5, 30 cts.; 15 pair butts, 4 by 4, 22 cts. ;
40 " " 3 in. 70 cts. ; 16 gross screws, ¾, 1, 1¼, 35 cts. ;
700 lbs. nails, $4 25 ; 100 lbs. finishing nails, $7 50 ;
14 mortice locks, $3 50 ; 9 mortice locks, $3 34 ;
16 rim locks, $1 50 ; 10 flush bolts, 50 cts. ;
Carpenter's wages, $1 50.

PAINTER'S.

1700 lbs. white lead, in oil, $7 50 ; 80 galls. linseed oil, 82c.;
8 galls. spirits turpentine, 48 cts. ; 25 lbs. putty, 4 cts. ;

3 lbs. glue, 20 cts. ; 4 lbs. chrome yellow, 35 cts.
Painter's wages, $1 75.

Design X. will cost $8,500. Coach-house, &c. $1200. Wood-house, $450.

Prices of Building Materials, March 10th, 1847.

MASON'S MATERIALS.		CARPENTER'S MATERIALS.			
Baltimore front brick, per m.	$— a 35	Mill cut timber per m.	$— a 20	Spruce plank, 2 in.	$24 a 25
Philadelphia do. do.	18 a 22	Yard do. do.	— a 16	Do. do. 1¼	16 a 17
Poughkeepsie do. do.	12 a 16	Joist,	14c a —	Indian gutter,	— a 10
Newburgh do. do.	— a 8	Wall strips,	10c a —	Fence palings,	9 a 10
Newburgh pavers,	— a 6	Shingles, per bunch,	— a 2½		
N. R. Common hard brick,	4 a 4½	Cedar shingles, 3 feet, 1st quality,	26 a 27	PAINTER'S MATERIALS.	
Salmon do.	3 a 3½	Do. do. 3 " 2d "	23 a 24	Pure white lead, in oil,	—c a 7¼
Blue stone flagging, per ft.	7c a 10	Do. do. 2 " 1st "	17 a 18	Extra,	—c a 6½
Large size do. do.	12c a 13	Do. do. 2 " 2d "	15 a 17	No. 1.	—c a 7
Roman cement, per bbl.	— a 6	Do. (Comp'y) 2½ "	28 a 30	No. 2.	—c a 5½
Hydraulic do. do.	— a 1½	Cypress shingles, 2 "	13 a 14	Chrome yellow,	—c a 35
R. Island lime, do.	— a 3	Do. do. 2½ "	20 a —	Yellow ochre,	—c a 6
Glens Falls, do.	— a 1½	Clear plank and board, per m.	35 a —	Chrome green,	—c a 35
Thomaston, do.	— a 1	Best piece plank,	— a 27	Paris do.	40c a 45
North River, do.	87c a —	Do. boards,	— a 18	Spanish brown,	—c a 6
Lubec plaster, do.	— a 1⅜	Narrow siding	— a 17	Venetian red,	—c a 5½
Brown sand, per load,	35c a 50	Pine milled floor plank	26 a 27	Linseed oil,	—c a 82
White do. do.	— a 1	Spruce do. do.	20 a 21	Spirits turpentine,	—c a 48
1¼ in. plastering lath, per m.	— a 2¾	Narrow clear do.	17 a 18	Putty,	—c a 4
Plastering hair, per bush.	20c a —	Hemlock boards	12 a 13	Litharge,	—c a 6

DESIGN X.

PLATE 31.

ANGLO GRECIAN VILLA.

Designed by A. H. Ranlett.

Litn. of A.S. Palmer 43 Ann St N.Y.

PLATE 32.

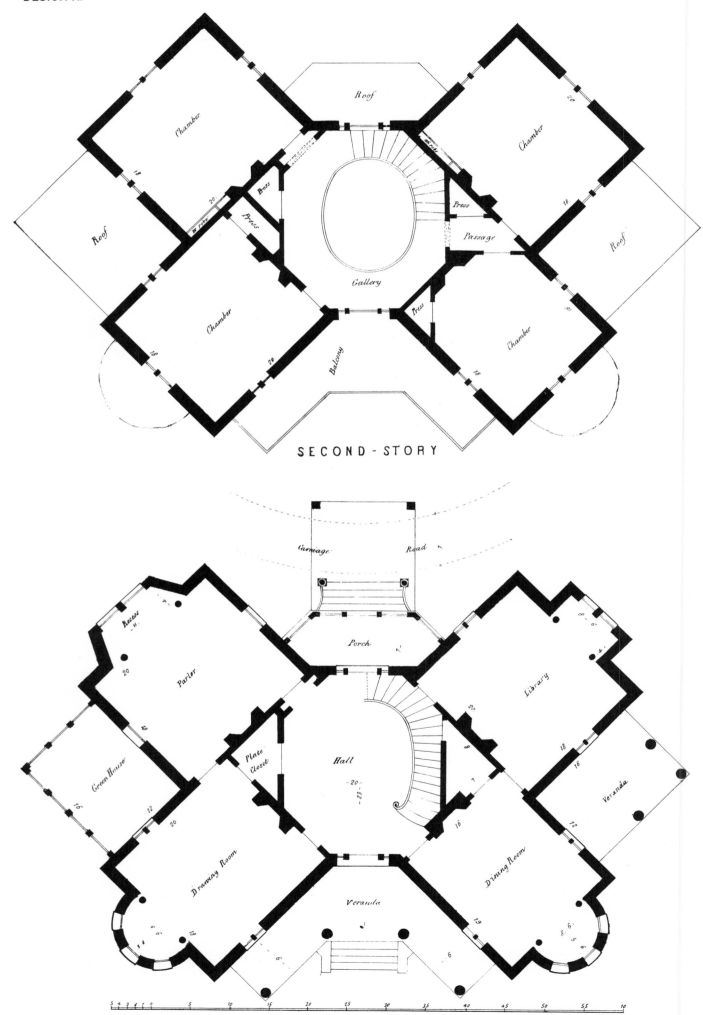

SECOND-STORY

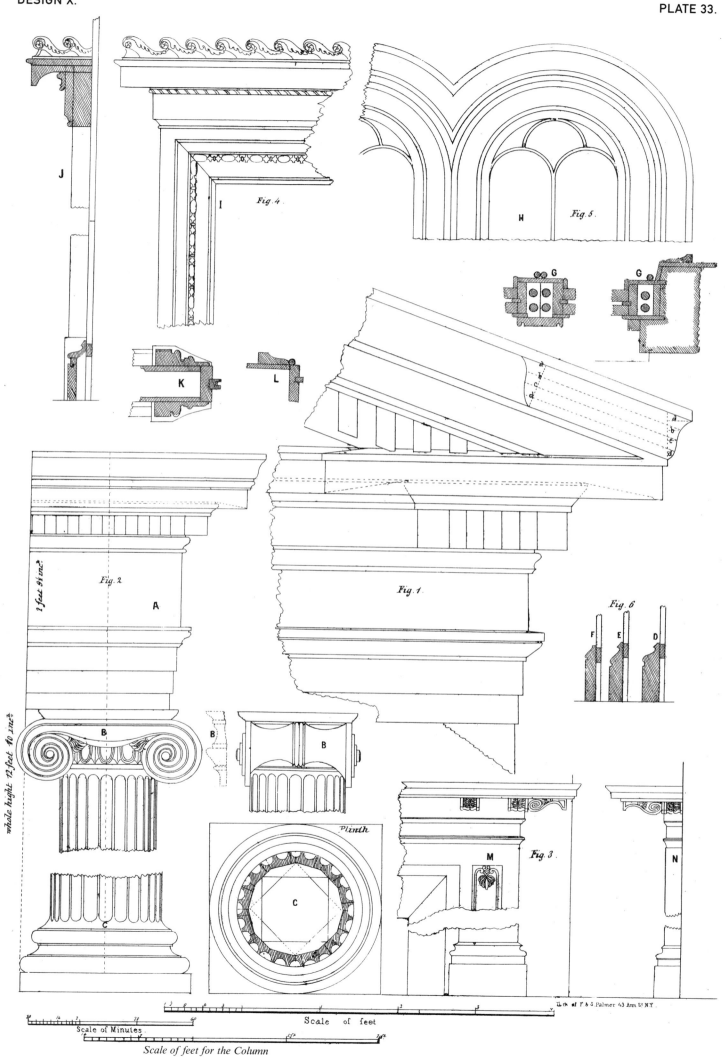

J

Fig. 4

I

Fig. 5

H

G

G

K

L

Fig. 2

A

2 feet 9½ inch.

whole hight 12 feet 40 inch.

B

B

B

B

Fig. 1

Fig. 6

F   E   D

Plinth

C

M   Fig. 3

N

Scale of Minutes.

Scale of feet

Scale of feet for the Column

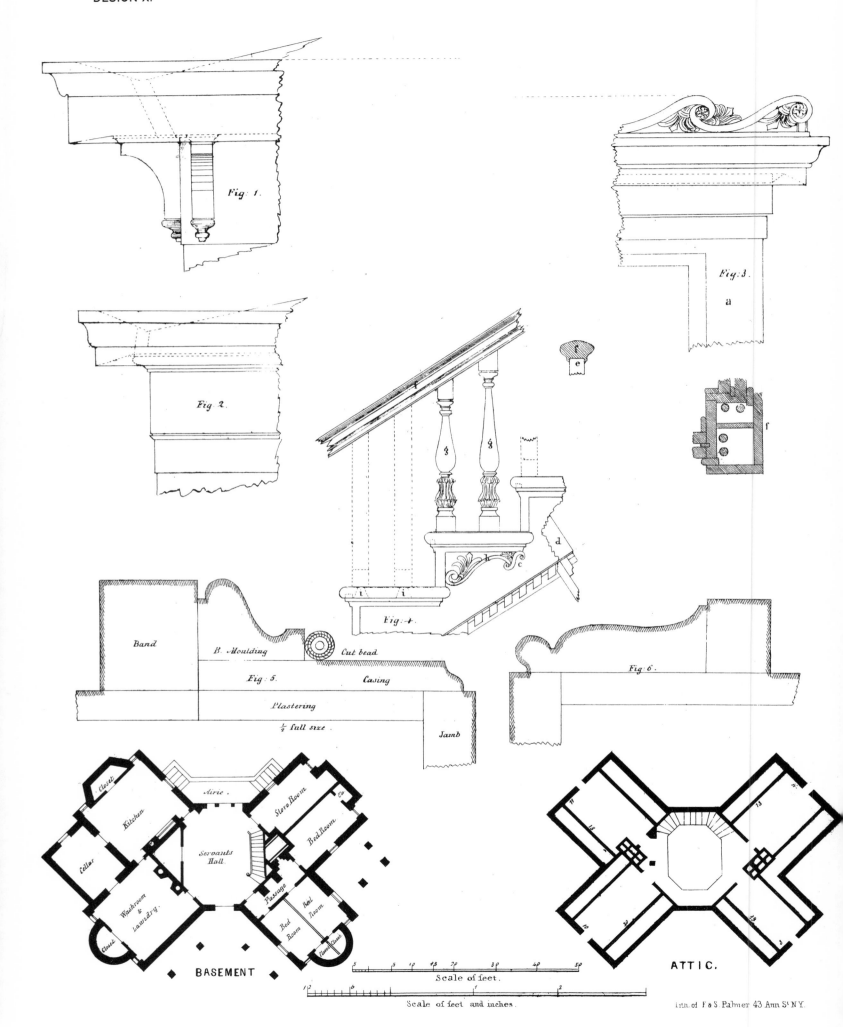

Fig: 1.

Fig: 2.

Fig: 3.

Fig: 4.

a

e

f

d

c

Band

B. Moulding

Cut bead

Fig: 5.

Casing

Plastering

¼ full size.

Jamb

Fig: 6.

Closet

Airie.

Store Room

Kitchen

Bed Room

Cellar

Servants Hall.

Washroom & Laundry

Passage

Bed Room

Bed Room

Closet

Closet

BASEMENT

ATTIC.

Scale of feet.

Scale of feet and inches.

Lith. of F & S. Palmer 43 Ann St N.Y.

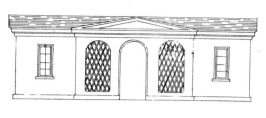

FRONT ELEVATION.

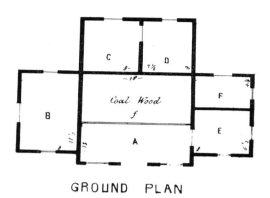

GROUND PLAN

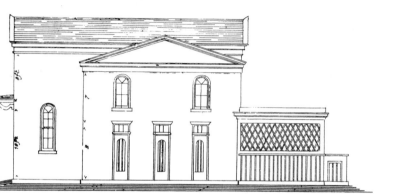

SIDE ELEVATION.

FRONT ELEVATION.

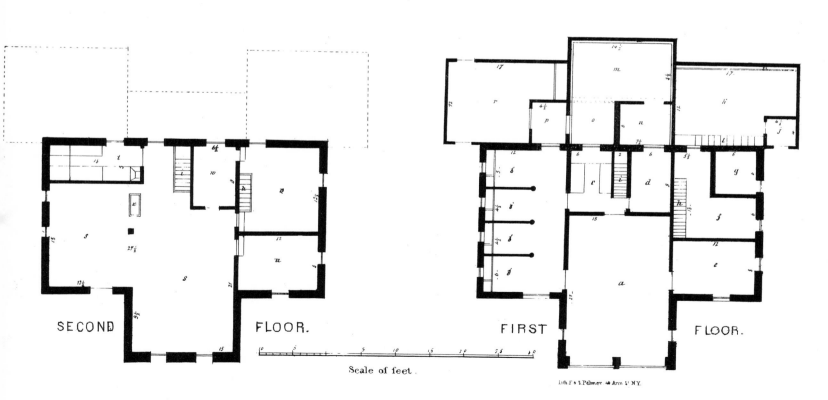

SECOND   FLOOR.   FIRST   FLOOR.

Scale of feet.

Coach house and outbuildings.

PLATE 36.

DESIGN XI.

Drawn by Wm H. Ranlett.

Lith. of F & S. Palmer 43 Ann S N.Y.

SCENIC VIEW.

THE SWISS STYLE.

ARCHITECTURE, having arisen by the necessities of man, is naturally modified and varied by the causes that produced it, as they constantly exist, and are always operating to produce a more perfect adaptation of edifices to the purposes for which they were designed. These necessities are based chiefly on the climate and temperature of the country, and the employments of the inhabitants, and they are greatly varied by manners and customs.

The demands which arise from these facts, have produced the different styles of Architecture, always modified, however, by the facilities at hand for meeting them. Thus, in Egypt, the people were destitute of building timber, and the country furnished an abundance of stone of excellent quality; therefore they were naturally—nay, forcibly, confined to the use of stone and bricks in building. They used much of both, but in the construction of their temples, chiefly stone in large masses, which, with the absence of windows and the closeness of the columns, gave them a cavern-like appearance.

In Greece, where the climate is mild, the air serene, the sky generally clear, and the material, timber, in the origin of their architecture, the style was characterized by a regular outline in the form of a parallelogram, with flat roofs, and pediments; and in more northern climates, where much rain and snow usually fall, the roofs were made high that they might the better throw off the snow and water, and sustain, with greater security, that which should lie upon them.

Switzerland is a cold rugged country, lying between 46 and 48 degrees of North latitude, and traversed by the Alps. The southern part of the country lies among the Alps, and much of it perfectly sterile with cold. The northern part lies on the Swiss Bavarian table land, and has a rugged, hilly surface. A country thus situated, not producing sufficient for its inhabitants, and having limited manufactures and commerce, might be expected to produce a style of architecture peculiarly its own. Their châteaux are considerably larger than their cottages, and they have round towers with conical roofs, and they generally occupy very romantic situations; commanding the most enchanting views of smiling fertile valleys, rushing streams, frightful precipices and towering Alpine peaks crowned with eternal snow.

It would be inconvenient to occupy the basement of a dwelling where the snow often falls to the depth of five or six feet, as it does in Switzerland. This produced the first characteristic of the Swiss style —a basement 6 or 7 feet high, and unoccupied except as a cellar or store room.

The châlets or small huts in the Alpine glens, and often on the hills of Switzerland, are designed for peasants. They are generally built by erecting rough stone walls about four feet high; and the upper part of fir poles and feather-edged boards. Some are, however, of poles, similar to American log cabins. The

51

interior of these huts, they divide into two apartments—one for the family and the other for the cattle. The partition is usually a manger about 18 inches high, to which the cattle are fastened, securing to them the society of the family and comfort of the fire. Thus in a pastoral country, do "men mix with beasts, joint tenants of the shade." The foregoing, are the extremes of Swiss architecture between which we are to look for the body of their style. The same causes operate, to a great extent, on all classes of the citizens, hence high basements are to be met with as a common feature of the dwellings of the middle classes, but the cause that suggested them, forbade the use of them, as apartments for the family. In such mountainous districts, fierce gusts of wind are frequent, especially in winter, and the cold severe, which render it both necessary and difficult to shelter cattle. All this indicated the economical plan of appropriating their basements to their live stock, which is accordingly their mode of life. Such an appropriation of the basements, render it necessary to enter the living apartment outside by steps or step-ladders, and this in its turn indicated, as a useful feature, terraces and galleries, which extended around the house and gave rise to the most marked characteristic of the Swiss style—wide roofs, projecting from six to ten feet beyond the face of the walls, which were supported by large brackets, often carved in ornamental forms. To secure these large roofs against the violent gusts of wind, they placed heavy fragments of rocks upon them. This odd peculiarity of style, is justified in the eye of reason, by its object ; and taste allows it on account of the beauty which it produces after a time, by forming a thin soil on the roof by the accumulation of a species of mould which is common in that country ; in which soil wild flowers spring and flourish, forming with the stones on the roof, a beautiful feature of the edifice. Another characteristic of the Swiss style, is the gallery around the house at the second floor or bed-room story, which is canopied by the projecting roof, and approached by a step-ladder from the terrace.

The Swiss build with wood—usually larch—by squaring and fitting the logs in a horizontal position, not unlike the mode of building the best log houses in our western States. Their windows are horizontal, extending nearly the whole length of the end walls, and sometimes similar ones in the sides, which are filled with small square glass. This style combines well with the wild mountain scenery of Switzerland; for it has an air of convenience and comfort within, while its irregular features without, harmonize in great beauty with rocks, cliffs, glens and hills, and snow-capped mountain-peaks in the distance ; and it is well suited to many portions of our country, especially the extensive Apalachian terrace and table lands in the south, and the rough regions of the lakes and rivers at the north. It is also well fitted for building with wood, which is a common material with us, in all parts of the United States.

CONTRACTING.

This subject is intimately connected with estimating, as a department of building in which there are great abuses that loudly call for correction. Many owners are incapable of judging what would be the most appropriate to their situations, and even what would be the most agreeable to their taste when it is completed. Such are often too frugal in their examinations and determinations to employ an architect to inform them and show them what they need; therefore they will use various means to draw out of an architect or some one who assumes to understand the subject, statements of facts that will serve their purposes, without rendering themselves liable to pay for the information which they seek.

It is too common in building, for proprietors to contract with builders, without the aid of an architect. An erroneous opinion prevails that in this way they can save money. When this course is adopted, it usually proceeds on plans that are not matured, partial specifications and general estimates. The consequences are multiform and disastrous. In the progress of the work, it is discovered that the plan does not comprehend so full an accommodation of the family as is desired, hence deviations from it are likely to be required, which occasion " extra charges." The chief control of the construction which the builder has, and the " low price" at which he has taken the job, induce him to use *cheap materials* and employ *cheap labor*, which turn out a house, *dear* to the disappointed and chagrinned proprietor, who finds, at too late a date, that the " extra charges " and the fated discount in the quality of the edifice, greatly exceed the amount which his *prudence* has saved.

Some proprietors impose as palpably upon builders as others do upon architects. After sketching a plan, and getting some builder to give it a finish, he solicits such proposals as may be received without putting the builders to the trouble of estimating minutely. After the proposals are in hand, differing in many instances from 50 to 100 per cent. as before shown, he will stipulate with his previously chosen builder, to erect the edifice for less than the lowest estimate; making a contract with him to pay, in enstallments, at the completion of certain portions of the work, retaining a percentum on the sums of the payments as security for a faithful performance of the contract.

The builder buys the materials on credit, and proceeds in the erection of the building. After getting the house partly constructed and a large portion of the materials laid in it, he fails; and the proprietor then secures the percentum, and perhaps a full payment for some trifling unfinished portion of the contract; and in this way will retain probably 50 per cent. or more of the price of all the materials and labor that have been appropriated to the building, and justify himself by loud protestations of the damage he suffers by the builder, and false professions of deep regret of the misfortune of the contractor, the men in his employment and dealers of whom he bought the materials; and after all this and more, boasts of the cheapness of his house, and to prove it, he coolly informs his friends that the builder " broke " in erecting it, and lost so much by the job, which is really that amount filched from the pockets of the dealers who trusted the builder for materials, and of the mechanics and laborers for services—and *complaisantly pocketed* by the " lucky proprietor."

A second builder is then employed on the same or similar " principles," and probably with the same specific contract, to finish the structure, and he fails with similar results, affording an additional evidence that it is cheap; all which might be confirmed and handed down to posterity—if the house would last beyond one generation—by an inscription on a marble tablet in the front, of the names of the families of merchants and artisans, who have suffered privation, and perhaps want, by the oppressive and over-reaching schemes of the proprietor.

A thorough knowledge of the expenses and labor necessary to the erection of an edifice, is absolutely essential to a builder who would undertake the construction of a house with safety. Without this knowledge, he is liable to imposition by a proprietor, who is even more ignorant of the subject than himself, for he provides himself by schemes and deceptive language, with landmarks, within the range of which he knows he can proceed with safety to his own pocket, to make a *contract* with the pliant builder who " wants a job." In all this, the contest is between the honest necessities of the half-informed builder and the sordid avarice of the cunning speculator, whose " principles" will allow him to " sleep sweetly" in a comfortable mansion erected by the sweat and substance of the robbed and ruined artisan.

ROOFS.

Much of the comfort, safety and durability of a building depends on the roof, which, if good, does much toward strengthening and sustaining the structure in the resistance of storms. Another consideration of moment, is the prominent part which the roof of a house constitutes in the landscape. It is evident therefore that great care is due to this part of an edifice, that it may best answer its important purpose, and be in good taste.

The pitch of roofs is the principal element by which they differ in their general appearance; and in this they vary from 5 to 60 degrees; the different styles of architecture having various ranges of pitch. In the Grecian, and the styles derived from it—also in the Egyptian and castellated Gothic, the roofs are low, ranging from 10 to 22 degrees. Roofs of 45 degrees form a right angle at the peak, and those from this to 70 degrees are common to the Gothic and the allied styles, and are called high roofs. Medium roofs vary from 22 to 45 degrees, and are common to several styles.

A pitch of one inch to a foot, is the lowest that can be made with safety. A roof of 45 degrees will throw off the snow as it falls, but on one of less pitch, it will lie as a dead weight; therefore a low roof requires greater strength of timber, to sustain with safety, a superincumbent body of snow. The distance between the bearing timbers should not be too great, otherwise the strain on the covering will cause the roof to leak. When the pitch is more than 45 degrees, there is greater perpendicular weight on the plates and less of lateral pressure; and less also on the rafters; but in flat roofs there is greater pressure on the rafters and less on the plates.

Roofs are composed of various materials; as, thatch, tiles, wood, slate, stone, iron, copper, tin zinc and lead. Thatch is still used in many parts of the country where it is difficult to procure shingles. It answers the purpose well for barns, sheds, ice-houses, &c. but for a dwelling, it is not safe on account of its liability to take fire, and it is very unpleasant by the accumulation of insects, for which it constitutes a convenient harbor. The use of tiles is superseded by other materials, especially metals. They make a heavy, durable roof. There are roofs in New York, now good, which were covered with tiles more than a hundred years ago.

Shingles are more generally used in this country, than any other article; and they are the most economical material for country and suburban roofs. To make a good shingle roof, the rafters should be covered closely with boards or plank; and for large shingles, the plank should be tongued and grooved. Shingles differ much in kind and quality. In many parts of the country, they are sawed or cut, by a machine, out of oak, chestnut and poplar; and these, perhaps, are the poorest; and accordingly bear the lowest price. Those which are sawed, are objectionable on account of their roughness, which promotes early decay, and those which are cut, have numerous checks that are made in them by the knife of the machine which cuts them from the block in a lateral direction.

Some roofs are covered with shingles made from oak or chestnut boards half an inch thick, and 6 to 7 inches wide, cut into lengths of three feet each, and nailed on strong strips of plank, so that the upper end of the shingle buts against the lower edge of the strip, laying twelve inches to the weather. A roof well constructed in this way is tight and durable. White pine "bunch" shingles make the tightest roof, cedar and cypress the most durable, but if the latter are put on strips the snow will drive through the crevices badly in time of winter storms. All shingles should be put on three thick, and the nails put in the bands so as to be covered by the next course.

Slates are used to some extent in New York, in covering stores. They should not be put on a roof of less than 30 degrees pitch, otherwise they are apt to break by the action of snow and frost. They are also dangerous in time of fire on account of their liability to break by throwing water on them. The North Wales blue slates are the best, and Westmoreland light green are next in quality. Stones are seldom used for roofs except in very large and expensive buildings. Iron is used for fire-proof buildings, on iron beams; it has to be painted on the outside to preserve it from rust. It renders the upper apartment of a house warm in summer and very damp in winter by condensing the vapor that rises. Copper is an expensive material and liable to damage by the expansion and contraction of heat and cold. Tin is more extensively used for roofing, in the city of New York than any other material, but to make a good roof, it must be put on with great care—with grip-joints from the top downwards, and the cross joints soldered, the under side painted with good white lead and oil, and the grip-joints filled with the same—all the resin should be removed. Tin roofing is apt to rust by the accumulation of dampness under it, and seldom lasts more than ten years, and often not more than five. They are easily damaged by walking over them, and sometimes stripped off by high winds. Zinc roofs have been abandoned on account of their great expansion causing them to crack and leak. They seldom last more than three years. Lead is only used to a limited extent. It is very expensive and easily damaged by holes, unless it is very thick, which makes a very heavy roof.

Galvanized tinned iron plates are the best metal for roofs. Their cost is only about half that of copper, and they are quite as strong—perfectly maleable—expand and contract but little—never require paint and are " proof against rust." A superior fire-proof roof is made by laying these plates on a coat of cement mortar an inch thick on the plank covering. The best method of putting on the galvanized tinned plates is laying them on ridges or triangular ledges. See Plate 40, Fig. 1. Flat roofs, are mostly covered with metal, it being less liable to damage by walking on it. The different metals vary in cost from $8 to $55 per square of 100 feet. The comparative cost of the several materials used for roofing, is as follows :

Roofs of thatch on round poles, per square of 100 ft.	$3 00	Roofs of galvanized tinned iron plates, 1st quality, $14 00
" plain tiles on oak ledges,	14 00	" " " " " 2d " 13 00
" slate, on milled plank	7 50	" " " " " fire proof 22 00
" zinc, " "	13 00	" white pine bunch shingles on hemlock boards, 8 00
" copper, 16 oz. "	32 00	" cedar shingles, 30 in. on oak lath, 8 75
" " 18 oz. "	36 00	" " " " " milled oak plank, 11 75
" tin I. X. " and painted,	9 00	" cypress " 24 inch, on oak lath 7 00
" " I. C. " "	8 00	" " " " " milled plank, 10 00
" lead, 3 lb. per ft. " "	25 00	" covering rafters with milled spruce plank, 3 50
" " 4½ lbs. per ft. " "	32 00	" " " " " hemlock boards, 2 00
" iron, on iron struts or braces "	27 00	" oak lath, 70
" " on iron beams "	55 00	

The prices for the shingle roofs include the planks, boards, and lath ; to the slate, zinc, copper, tin, lead, and galvanized tin, the price of the planks are to be added. Dimensions of metal roofs are taken from the outside and the openings deducted. Of shingle roofs the same, adding 8 in. for valleys, hips, and angular lines.

ESTIMATE.

Materials required for Design XII.

MASON'S.

185 yds. excavation, 12 cts. ; 260 lds. building stone, 75 cts. ; 11,000 salmon brick, $3 00 ; 21 ft. kitchen hearth, 13 cts. ; 132 casks of lime, $1 25 ; 273 loads sand, 42 cts. ; 5 setts brown stone hearth, $4 50 ; 3 setts marble hearth,$5 00 ; 68 bush. hair, 20 cts. ; 34,000 plastering lath, $3 00 ; 3 grates, $20 00 each ; 1 range, $68 00 ; 300 lbs. lath nails, $7 25 ; 20 ft. coping, 14 cts. ; Mason's wages, $1 75 ; laborer's wages, $1 00. 9 stone sills, 75 cts. ; 7,000 hard brick, $4 50 ;

CARPENTER'S.

14796 ft. timber $1 60 cts. ; 425 joists, 14 cts. ; 12 doz. sash pullies, 62 cts. ; 20 lbs. sash cord, 31 cts. ; 110 wall strips, 11 cts. ; 225 lineal ft. basement sleepers, 6c. ; 3 doz. sash fastenings, $3 50 ; 120 ft. 4 in. tin leaders, 15 cts. ; 904 milled plank, 27 cts. ; 280 narrow clear planks, 18 cts. ; 38 ft. 2 in. tin leaders, 9 cts.; 13 gr. screws ⅜, 1, 1¼, 1½, 33 cts.; 6650 shingles, $26 : 150 sq. ft. of lead, 18 cts. ; 33 pair butts, 4 by 4, 22 cts. ; 12 pair butts, 3½ by 3½, 15 cts. ; 5900 ft. sheathing beams, 1½ cts. ; 480 siding boards, 18 cts. ; 20 " " 2⅓ in. 5 cts. ; 8 shutter bars, 21 cts. ; 760 ft. 3 in. plank, 3½ cts. ; 3400 ft. 2 in. plank, 3½ cts. ; 1200 lbs. nails, $4 25 ; 100 lbs. finishing nails, $7 50 ; 1870 ft. 1½ in. " 3½ cts. ; 3840 ft. 1¼ in. " 3½ cts. ; 22 iron braces, 75 cts. ; 24 iron straps, 25 cts. ; 4700 ft. 1 in. and ¾ in. 3½ cts. ; 156 lts. glass, 10 by 16, 20 cts.; 12 mortice locks, $5 63 ; 8 mortice locks, $2 56 ; 120 lts. of gls. 10 by 14, 16 cts.; 36 lts. gls. 9 by 14, 15 cts.; 4 " " $2 63 ; 16 rim locks, $1 31 ; 184 " " 8 by 10, 11 cts. ; 24 " " 6 by 6, 9 cts. ; 7 rim locks, $1 50 ; 55 rolls paper, 75 cts. ; border $19 ; 16 ft. stained glass, 95 cts. ; 902 lbs. sash weights 2 cts. ; 42 rolls paper, 35 cts. ; carpenter's wages, $1 50.

PAINTER'S.

1250 lbs. white lead, in oil, $7 50 ; 62 galls. linseed oil, 82c.; 4 lbs. glue, 20 cts. ; 4 lbs. lamp black, 50 cts. 8 galls. spirits turpentine, 48 cts. ; 35 lbs. putty, 4 cts. ; 2 lbs. bt. umber, $1 ; ½ lb. P. blue, $3 ; painter's wages, $1 73.

Design XII. will cost $5.500 ; XIII. will cost $1,300 ; Coach-house will cost $600.

DESCRIPTION OF PLATES.

PLATE 37.—Design XII. contains the ground plans of the first and second stories of a Villa, and a profile section of the basement wall, timbers, gallery, terrace, roof, &c. *a, a, a,* brackets; *b, b, b,* terrace and gallery posts, and roof pendants; *c, c, c,* beams; *d,* rafter; *e,* main post; *f,* sheathing and weather-boarding; *g,* bracket post of gallery; *h,* main sill; *i,* water table; *l,* main gutter; *m, m,* terrace and gallery bearers; *o,* open space in the brackets; *p,* stone wall.

PLATE 38.—Two geometrical elevations—lawn front and entrance front—of a villa in the Swiss style of architecture, Design XII.

PLATE 39.—Plans of the basement and garret, exterior details and a vertical section of the roof. Fig. 1.—Face and profile of terrace rail, post and filling. Fig. 2.—Face and profile of the gallery rail and filling. Fig. 3.—Section of the roof and bracket. Fig. 4.—Roof and brackets of the several window projections. Fig. 5.—Three sections of a pinnacle.

PLATE 40.—Fig. 1.—A, Section of a roof covered with galvanized tinned iron plates. B, Section, half full size showing the method of putting on the plates; *a, a, a,* roof plank; *b, b, b,* ledges; *c, c,* plates; *d, d,* cletes; *e,* first ledge nailed on the plank; *f,* first ledge covered with the plate, and the cletes put on with one part turned over the plate; *g, g,* both ledges on, the plates turned over between them, and the cletes secured, ready for soldering the joint. Each cross joint to be secured by two cletes in the same manner. [*Directions for Soldering.*— No resin to be used. Take zinc—spelter—break it into small pieces, put it into sufficient muriatic acid to dissolve it, take four parts of this solution, and one part of water—keep it in a leaden vessel—and with a small brush wash the place to be soldered. To clean the soldering iron, dip it into a solution of sal amonia in water.]—c, Section of a roof made of shingles cut out of half in. boards, 7 in. wide and 3 ft. long, nailed on strong plank strips. Fig. 2.—D, Elevation of a door and trimmings for the first story; E, profile of the canopy and casing. Fig. 3.—Mantles; F, for the first story and G, for the second. Fig. 4.—Ground section of jambs and casings of first story doors. Fig. 5.—Ground section of jambs and casings for the second story doors. Fig. 6.—Ground section of a window frame for the first story—in the second story the frames the same, and the casing as in Fig. 5. Fig. 7.—geometrical section of the principle stairs. Fig. 8.—Base, H, for the second story and I, for the first. Fig. 9.—Diagram of the several pitches of roofs, pediments and gables, with a correct elevation of roofs, covered with different materials. The degrees in figures.

PLATE 41.—Design XIII.—Two elevations of a cottage in the Swiss style. The stone walls, brick work, plastering, frame, roofs, weather-boarding—sheathing not included—terrace floor, and studding, the same as for Design XII. All the finishing for the interior of first story same as for second story, in Design XII.—doors, windows and base in the attic neatly finished with mouldings. Two elevations of a wood-house and offices connected, corresponding to the style of the cottage.

PLATE 42.—Ground plans Figs. 6 and 7, of the first and second stories of Design XI. (*in No.* 6.) Similar plans of Design XIII., Figs. 1 and 2. Fig. 3.—A ground plan for the coach house, stables, fowl house and piggery attached. Two elevations, Figs. 4 and 5, of the coach house continued in the style of the cottage, and enclosed with planed boards on the sides of the frame, and the roof with cypress shingles, the corners cut as for Design XIII.

SPECIFICATIONS,

Of the Materials and Labor required for the erection of a Villa according to Design XII.

EXCAVATION,—Eighteen inches deep, and the earth thrown in the rear, and graded.

STONE WALLS,—Twenty in. thick. laid in mortar—the outside, quarry face—joints lined and ridge pointed. The foundation 2 1=2 ft. wide and one foot high. Walls of airie, sunk 20 in. below the surface—the top coped with blue stone, and steps of the same, 10 inches wide and 4 ft. long.

BRICK WORK.—Two double chimneys with 10 fire places, 5 of them finished for wood fires, with brown stone hearths and facings, 3 of them with Berlin grates sett on marble hearths and facings, one with a " Pond's thenion Range" sett complete on a blue stone hearth (3 by 7 ft.), and one large fire place for the wash room, Utops ornamented and open for the flues. The spaces between the studding filled with brick, set on the edge in mortar. Two floors deafened.

PLASTERING,—All the rooms, halls and closets to be lathed and plastered with two good heavy coats of brown mortar, floated true and even, and smoothly slipped for papering and painting.

FRAME,—Of merchantable white pine sawed timber, put together in a good ana workmanlike manner. Twelve posts, 22 ft. long, 4 by 12 in.—4 posts, 11 ft. long, 4 by 8—framing beams, sills, plates and trimmers, 4 by 10—girts, 4 by 7—first and second tier of beams 3 by 10, 16 in. between centers—roof tier, 3 by 8, 30 in. between centers—rafters 3 by 5 and 3 by 7, 30 in. between centers, secured to the plates by iron straps. Sleepers in basement, of cedar, 30 inch between centers. All the timbers for the terrace and gallery, 3 by 8, clear, planed and the corners taken off—posts, 5 by 5, with turned tops and pendants. Studding of 3 by 4 joists, set 16 in. between centers in the second story, garret and basement, and 12 in. in the first story. All the stone walls in the basement to be furred with strips 16 in. between centers, and the upper tier of beams tight furred. Two floors to be prepared for deafening.

ROOFS.—The rafters covered with milled plank, face side down, and 30 in. cedar shingles put on the main roof, three thick, with the corners of the butts cut off. Galvanized tinned plates on all other roofs. Main gutters 5 by 10 in. secured to the rafters by iron straps, the front of the gutters moulded. Roof brackets of two thick= nesses of 2 in. plank put together with 20ᵈ. wrought nails, and cornered. The brackets under the terrace and gallery made in the same manner with 1 1=2 in. plank. Small brackets of 2 in. plank—all the filling of the gallery and terrace rails of 1 1=4 in. plank, opened. Posts secured by 1 =2 in. iron braces— rails, 4 1=2 by 3 inches.

SIDING,—The frame to be enclosed with sound feather=edged boards, put on rough. All the corner boards, water tables and window frames, set on the sheathing, and then sided up with good sound Albany boards planed and rebated—a trus bead on the lower edge, and strongly nailed.

FLOORS,—All the interior floors of good milled white pine plank laid in the best manner. The exterior floors of narrow, clear plank, tongued and grooved, planed both sides—under side beaded and blind nailed.

WINDOWS,——With box frames and the sashes double hung by weights and cord—glazed with single French glass. Sashes in the first and second stories 1 1=2 in. thick—all others 1 1=4. For the size and shape of the glass, see the elevations. Inside shutters to all the windows in the basement.

DOORS,——In the first story, made and trimmed as in Plate 40, Fig. 2—in the second story, 1 1=4 thick, with four panels—the corners filled and moulded. The casings, as in Plate 40, Fig. 5—all other doors made plain, hung by best patent butts—secured by mortice locks with porcelain knobs, "blue coral gilt patern," in the first story, and "blue coral" in the second—rim locks and mineral knobs on all others.

BASE,——In first and second stories, as in Plate 40, Fig. 8—in the basement, 7 in. high.

MANTLES,——Three in the first story as in Plate 40, Fig. 3, F. Four in the second story and one in dining room, Fig. 3, G. Plain plank shelves with brackets in the basement.

STAIRS,——From basement to first story enclosed—a door at the bottom. Principal stair rail made according to Plate 40, Fig. 7, 4 1=2 by 3 in. and continue to the garret; open balusters 1 by 4 in.—steps moulded —terrace steps of 1 1=2 in. plank, moulded—newel, rail and balusters as for terrace.

CLOSETS,——Pantries and wardrobes fitted up with shelves hooks and pins as may be required—dressers with drawers and glass doors in kitchen, and plain dresser in basement.

BELLS,——Five in the first story, and four in the second—the levers corresponding with the lock furniture.

PAPERING,——All the rooms and halls in the first and second stories, to be papered with good American paper—three rooms and a hall in the first story with satin paper costing not less than 75 cents per roll— all other rooms with plain and satin paper averaging in cost not less than 35 cents per roll—the border in each room corresponding with the paper.

PAINTING,——All the wood work outside, except the shingle roofs—and all the trimmings inside, to have two good coats of American pure linseed oil, and Saugerties pure white lead, put on at proper times—the outside to have a third coat of the same body, colored a light French gray—all the ceilings of first and second stories to have three coats of oil paint in such shades of color as may be required—an imitation cornice painted in shades in each of the rooms and halls.

MATERIALS,——All of the best quality and well seasoned—clear for the inside work, and exterior trimmings.

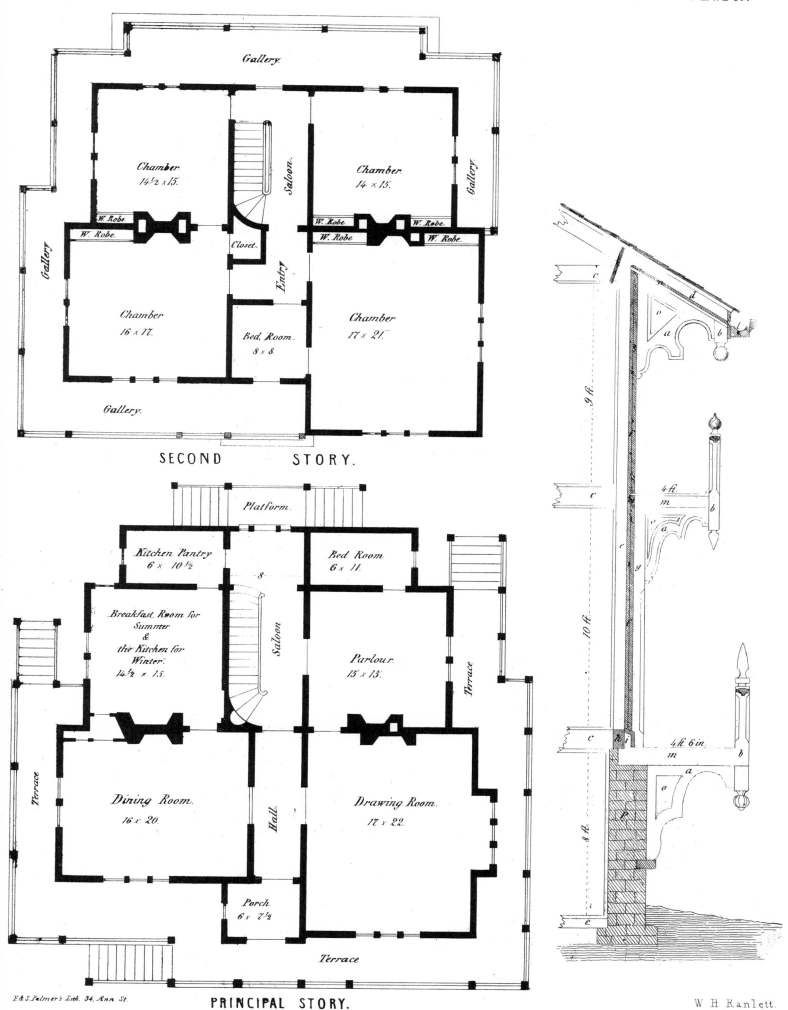

Gallery.

Chamber
14½ × 15.

Saloon.

Chamber
14 × 15.

Gallery.

Gallery.

W. Robe

W. Robe

W. Robe

W. Robe

W. Robe

W. Robe

Closet.

Entry

Chamber
16 × 17.

Bed. Room
8 × 8.

Chamber
17 × 21.

Gallery.

SECOND   STORY.

Platform.

Kitchen Pantry
6 × 10½.

Bed Room
6 × 11.

8

Breakfast Room for
Summer
&
the Kitchen for
Winter.
14½ × 15.

Saloon.

Parlour.
15 × 15.

Terrace

Terrace

Dining Room.
16 × 20.

Hall.

Drawing Room.
17 × 22.

Porch
6 × 7½.

Terrace

9 ft.

4 ft.
m

10 ft.

4 ft. 6 in.
m

8 ft.

F.& S. Palmer's Lith. 34, Ann St.

PRINCIPAL STORY.

W. H. Ranlett.

Scale ⊢───────────────┤ of Feet.

A VILLA IN THE SWISS STYLE.

LAWN FRONT.

Del. & des.ⁿᵈ by Wᵐ H. Ranlett.   Lith F. & S. Palmer 34 Ann St N.Y.

ENTRANCE FRONT.

Exterior Details.

PLATE 39.

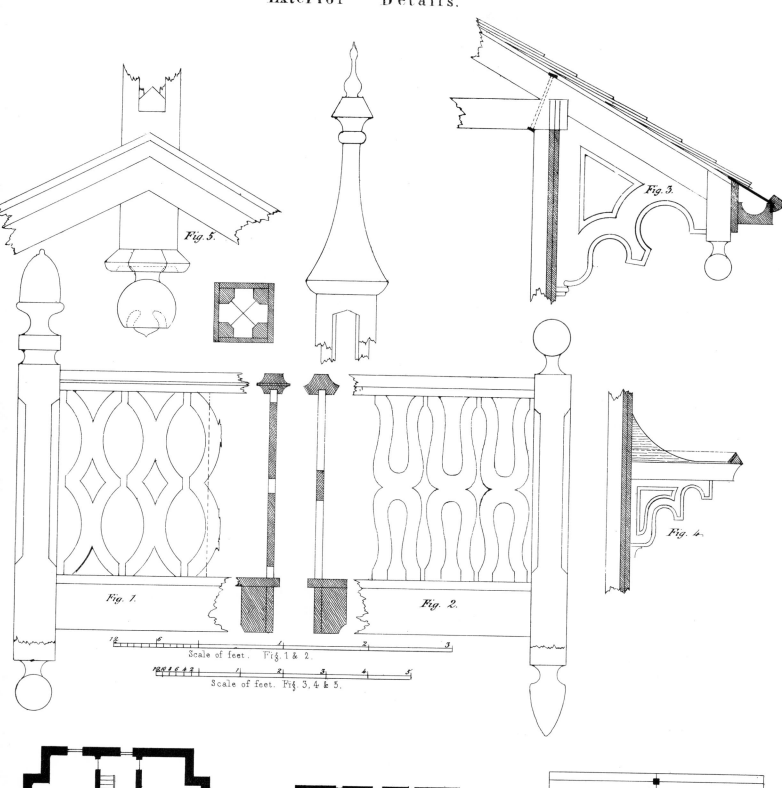

Fig. 5.

Fig. 3.

Fig. 4.

Fig. 1.

Fig. 2.

Scale of feet. Fig. 1 & 2.

Scale of feet. Fig. 3, 4 & 5.

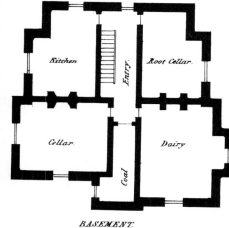

BASEMENT.

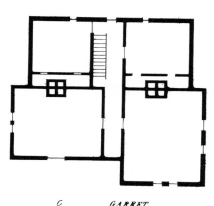

GARRET.

Scale of feet

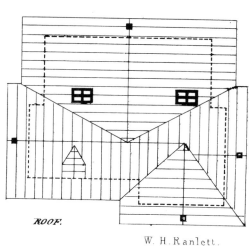

ROOF.

W. H. Ranlett.

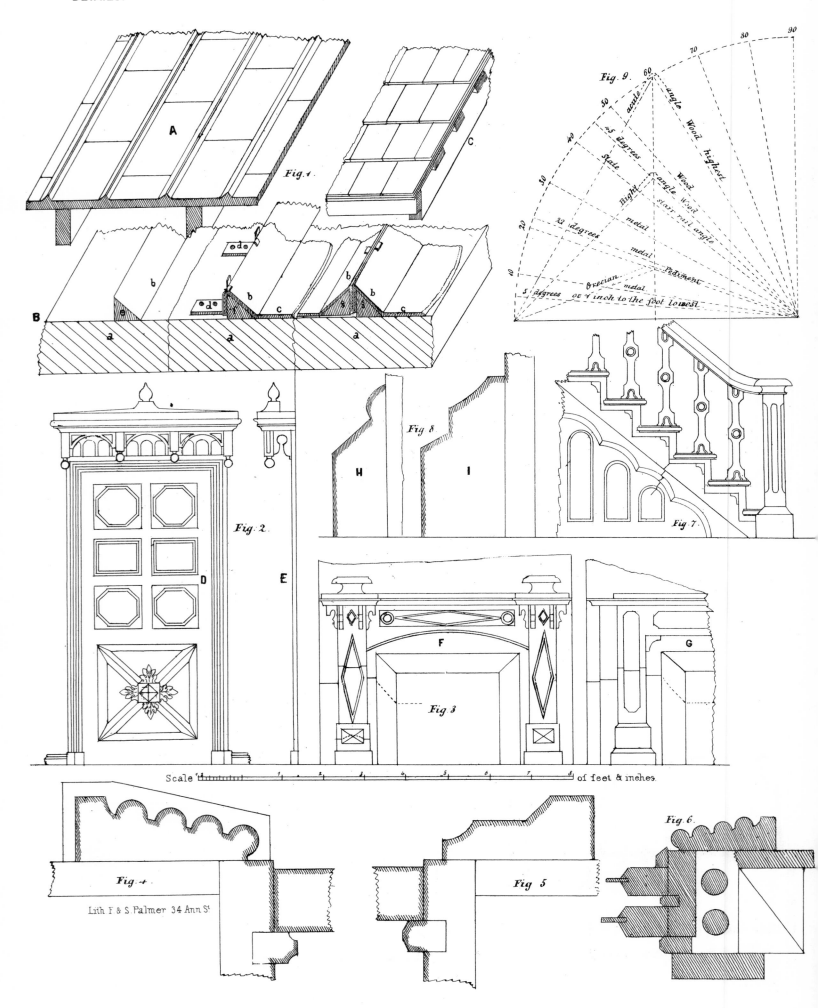

Fig. 1.

Fig. 2.

Fig. 3.

Fig. 4.

Fig. 5.

Fig. 6.

Fig. 7.

Fig. 8.

Fig. 9.

Scale of feet & inches.

Lith F. & S. Palmer 34 Ann St.

A COTTAGE IN THE SWISS STYLE.

ENTRANCE FRONT.

Del & des.ᵈ by Wᵐ H Ranlett

t & S Palmer 34 Ann Sᵗ NY

GARDEN ELEVATION.

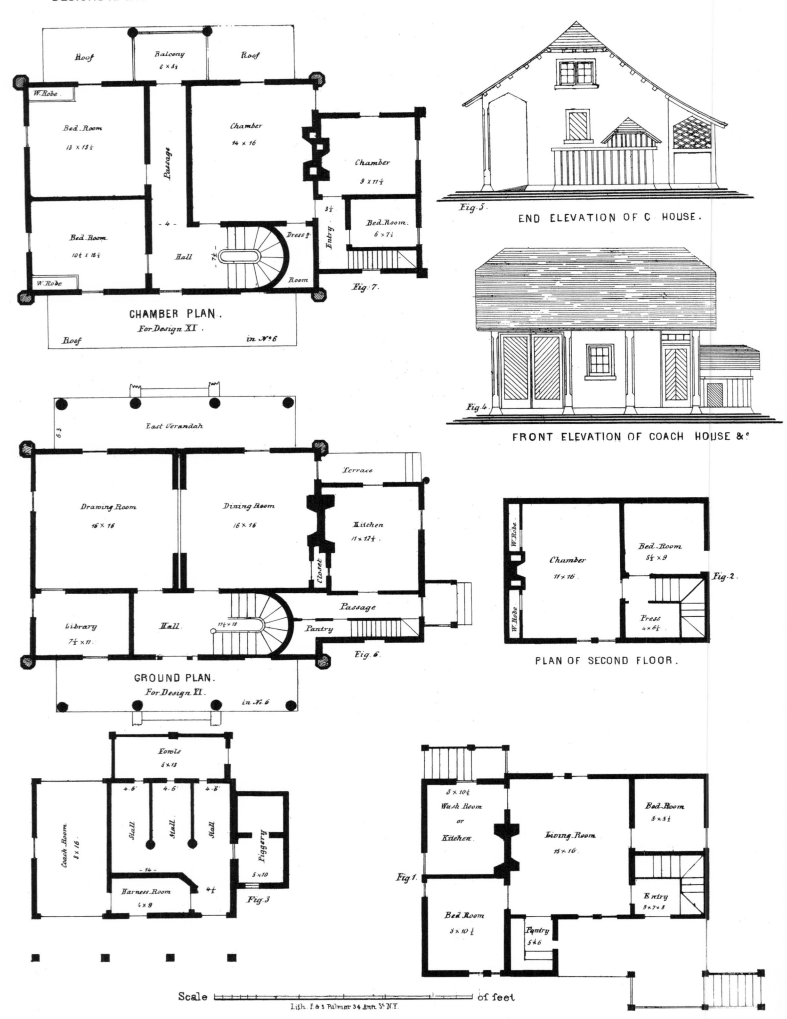

Roof

Balcony
6 × 6¾

Roof

W.Robe

Bed.Room
13 × 13½

Passage

Chamber
14 × 16

Chamber
9 × 11½

Bed.Room
10½ × 13½

— 4 —

Hall

Dress⁹

Entry

3½

Bed.Room
6 × 7½

Room

W.Robe

CHAMBER PLAN.
For Design XI.   in N.º 6

Roof

Fig. 7.

Fig. 5.

END ELEVATION OF C. HOUSE.

6.3

East Verandah

Drawing Room
16 × 16

Dining Room
16 × 16

Terrace

Kitchen
11 × 12½

Library
7½ × 11

Hall

17½ × 18

Closet

Passage

Pantry

Fig. 6.

GROUND PLAN.
For Design XI.   in N.º 6

Fig. 4.

FRONT ELEVATION OF COACH HOUSE &.

W.Robe

Chamber
11 × 16

Bed.Room
5¼ × 9

Fig. 2.

W.Robe

Press
4 × 6½

PLAN OF SECOND FLOOR.

Fowls
5 × 13

4.6   4.6   4.6

Coach Room
8 × 16

Stall   Stall   Stall

Piggery
5 × 10

— 14 —

4½

Harness Room
4 × 9

Fig. 3.

8 × 10¼

Wash Room
or
Kitchen

Living Room
15 × 16

Bed.Room
8 × 8½

Fig. 1.

Bed Room
8 × 10½

Pantry
5 × 6

Entry
8 × 7 × 8

Scale ┠┯┯┯┯┯┯┯┯┯┯┯┯┯┯┯┯┯┯┯┯┯┯┯┯┯┯┈┈┈┈┈┈┤ of feet
Lith. E & S Palmer 34 Ann St. N.Y.

GROUND PLAN OF A COACH HOUSE.   **GROUND PLAN OF A COTTAGE.**

THE INDIAN STYLE.

INDIAN Architecture is said to have arisen from the Mohammedan religion, and it prevails generally in Mohammedan countries, including as its prominent examples, the Oriental edifices of Arabia, Hindoostan, Burmah, Morocco, and other eastern countries, some splendid temples cut into solid rock in the mountains of Ellora, Elephanti, Karli and Salsette. India reached the climax of its glory in the fourteenth century, in which time Architecture received great attention, and a vast number of superb buildings were erected. These improvements were so great in India, that they characterized to some extent, the architecture of Mohammedan countries; hence, the architecture connected with that religion, is generally called Indian. This style is believed to be derived from the Egyptian, to which it bears so striking a resemblance that it is evident they are from one original. The Indian is a pleasing and tasty style, combining much of the details of the Egyptian, Grecian and Roman styles, with the fancy lattice work of the Persian, skilfully blended with general grace and elegance. Great stress was laid on general proportions and symmetry, by Mohammedan architects—so much so, that in some countries, woes were denounced on those who lived in houses that were not well proportioned.

Many ornaments and great splendor characterized this style, especially in public buildings; all, however, appropriated and combined with great skill and exquisite taste, not allowing one ornament to interfere with another. In the public buildings and palaces, the walls were covered with rich Mosaic, and the columns were very light and much varied in forms, and usually of great beauty. Three kinds of arches were used—the circular, that in the form of a horse-shoe and the pointed. The Indian pointed arch was invented by the Arabians at a very early period, but it differs from the Gothic arch in retaining the prevalence of horizontal lines, while the chief characteristic of the Gothic arch is the prevalence of vertical lines. The arches of the Indian, were greatly enriched by foliations around them, similar to Gothic work, but of a much earlier date.

The Indian style is very appropriate for a plain edifice, admitting either regular or irregular outlines, and thereby allowing almost every variety of appropriation for the convenience of the occupants. It also admits of much ornament at moderate expense, and in this particular it has an advantange over most other leading styles. These traits give this style a peculiar adaptation to the taste and economy of our citizens, while its general forms fit it well to our country, being equally appropriate for small cottages, villas and public buildings. The accompanying Design XV. is of a small villa in this style. Its chief peculiarities are a high pointed embattled parapet on a flat roof, and imitation latticed windows, which are in reality, windows with small glass in lead sashes.

VILLAGE SITES.

MANY residences in villages and the suburbs of cities are characterized by a very serious evil which should be corrected as far as possible—the small confined ground plots which are so common. The disadvantages and even damages that often arise out of this improvident feature, are so multiform and great, that special attention should be directed to it, and the people informed and aroused to proper views and efforts on the subject.

The inconveniences of such situations are severely felt by persons of cultivated taste when they are subjected to them. The want of suitable room for stables, cow-houses, poultry-houses, &c. is borne as a great privation; and in very many such sites, yards for domestic animals and poultry, are entirely out of the question. It is not unfrequently the case that lots are so limited as not to allow room for the passage of a wagon or cart for the deposit of fuel at the proper place, or for manuring the garden, if there should be such a department of the premises. To the garden there is entirely too little attention paid in this country generally. It is surprising to observe how many people, who live in villages and the suburbs of cities, have more or less ground that might be cultivated as a kitchen garden, yet it is allowed to lie waste or half cultivated while they buy their vegetables. In farming regions, the garden is the most profitable portion of ground that is cultivated, and it is still more profitable to the villager, for besides having the produce of this portion of soil, above that of his regular business, he has the pleasure of using fresh vegetables instead of the stale ones from the market; and a mechanic of really industrious habits, will cultivate his garden in the " odd spells" that others would waste; all of which is a decided gain in several respects.

The want of a convenient front yard is a great detriment to a residence for which there is no compensation. Such a yard places a house back from the street, and by that means relieves the family of much of the dust and noise by which they would otherwise be annoyed. It adds greatly to the taste and beauty of a dwelling, and thus it renders it decidedly more valuable. It is likewise beneficial to the family by its tendency to foster good taste, especially if it is cultivated with flowers and ornamental shrubs, as a front yard should be. This affords also innocent and useful amusement and pastime and the effects of such employments are always of a genial character, as they cultivate habits of industry and attention, and improve the taste and other fine feelings of our nature.

Another annoying inconvenience of very small lots, is the exposure of many of the domestic operations to the gaze of others. In cities these are secluded by walls and high board fences, but seldom so in villages, hence the importance of having them arranged with sufficient room and buildings for appropriate concealment.

60

Several causes have operated to situate people on small and inconvenient lots. The most common plea is inability to purchase larger ones. A little calculation will, however, show in many cases, that the money which is necessary to purchase a small lot in the populous part of the village, would pay for a much larger one a little out of it. This shows that the *inability* is only the ostensible reason, at least in many instances, and allows the inference that the real one is a want of refined taste and chastened relish for the retired quiet which is so congenial to the cultivation of the domestic virtues and general intelligence. There can be no doubt, however, that limited means have often confined families to small lots.

The most obstinate cause that has served to produce this state of things, is the sordid views and penurious grasping of speculating proprietors of village and suburban property. They proceed with the belief that the greater the number of lots into which they divide an acre of ground, the more money they can realize on it *at the present time ;* and in these matters they allow the future to provide for things of itself. This unworthy disposition has laid the foundation of an immense amount of puerility and deformity in such property, which it is very difficult to remedy in after periods, without the monstrous absurdity of a large house on a small village lot.

It is important in laying out a village, that the plot by which it is first done, should be properly constructed. The smallest lots should be at least 100 feet in front and 150 feet deep. By giving the lots this size, and having an alley in the rear for the introduction of fuel, &c. and at which the stables, coach-houses and other such buildings may be placed, they may be rendered very convenient and pleasant. Then the dwelling should be so placed on the lot, that if the ground should become very valuable, another house may be conveniently built on it, dividing the lot into two equal parts ; and trees should be planted in such positions that they need not be removed nor destroyed.

Another prevailing error is the laying out of village plots in a *regular* form for an uneven surface. Considerable expense is often incurred in grading streets through villages, by which the value of property is really decreased rather than increased, for a village lot that needs much grading, is generally a worthless affair ; and moreover, many persons prefer an elevated site if it has a gradual slope, and others prefer vales on account of their retired, sequestered character.

Designs XIV. XV. XVI. and XVII. are for four cottages to be placed on a plot of village property belonging to Col. N. Barrett of Staten Island ; which plot is so laid out that it illustrates the above views. The plot consists of eight lots with a street in front, and a lane in the rear of each. They are 244 by 151 feet, and the cottages so placed on them that each may be divided into two lots, if such an arrangement should become desirable. See Plate 48.

APPRENTICESHIP.

SKILFUL artisans can be secured to any country only by thorough apprenticeship; and this is, in many cases, prevented by the interest or caprice of individuals, if it is not regulated and protected by legislative acts. In England, men are prevented by law, from practicing any mechanic art, as master-workmen or journeymen, unless they have served an apprenticeship of seven years. In this country any person may practice any trade, whether he has served any time at it or not, and even whether he knows anything of it or not.

Palpable abuses of apprenticeship, are common in our country, and greatly need correction. A fundamental item of these, is the taking of boys to learn trades, without any indentures. This affords the apprentice an opportunity, on a slight pretext or dissatisfaction, to leave his master without the master's having a sufficient basis to correct this ruinous course. It also gives the master the power to make changes if his interest can be subserved or his caprice gratified by such a course, leaving no recourse for the apprentice, for protection or damages. Advantage is often taken of this lax relation between masters and apprentices. A master mechanic who wishes to get along at as cheap a rate as possible, will advertise for a " hand" or " several hands" who have " some knowledge of the use of tools." This presents an opportunity to an apprentice who has obtained some knowledge of the trade he is learning, to procure more wages than he is realizing where he is, and, as he is not indented, he leaves his master and hires himself as a " turnover" which is a rank between an apprentice and a journeyman.

The unavoidable result of this course is the filling of the mechanical trades with pretenders who know very little of the arts which they profess to practice, and the country with bad workmanship. Out of this state of things has grown, the reproachful proverb, that " a mechanic who does not know how to slight his work, has only half learned his trade." It is likewise the reason why foreign mechanics so often have the preference over our native ones ; they having served a regular time at the art, while so many of those of our own country have merely " picked up their trade."

The remedy for this is difficult to prescribe. The statutes of the States should be invoked as one corrective, but how far this can be extended perhaps experience alone would show. Legislation is so very changeable in the United States, that an apprentice could scarcely be expected to commence and end a reasonable apprenticeship under the same statutory regulations. Reliance is probably chiefly to be placed on that great and common corrector of evils in this country—general intelligence.

An apprentice should serve at least five or six years, under competent instructions, before he professes to be a master in his art. The general diffusion of knowledge among our people and the great enterprize that characterizes them, qualify boys to obtain a knowledge of a trade in less time than is required in England. Great pains should be taken by the master to instruct his apprentice in the minutia and science of his art or trade. This is too often neglected to the manifest detriment of both master and apprentice. How often is it the case that young men who have served regular times at their trades, are totally incapable of making estimates in their business.

Every apprentice should be taught at an early period of his apprenticeship, how to estimate the material with which he is employed, and to keep accounts and memoranda ; and then furnished with a book for this purpose and required to note the quantities, qualities and prices of all the materials used in the job at which he is engaged. He should be required to note the chief incidents of the day, and the time that it requires to perform certain portions of work—the difference of the time required by different persons to do the same or similar pieces of work—the amount of work that can be done in a week by one person—by any given number of persons—the difference between the quantities of work that can be done by different persons in a given time, &c. In this way an apprentice will become qualified, in twelve months or two years, to estimate the materials and labor necessary to the performance of any job in his trade.

62

SPECIFICATIONS,

Of the Materials and Labor required for the erection of Designs XIV. XV. XVI. and XVII.

STONE.—Walls of the cellar 7 1=2 ft. high, 18 in. thick, laid in mortar of the best quality, piers of stone to each column, sunk 30 in. in the ground—blue stone steps and coping, 10 in. wide to the airies—blue stone hearth to the cellar kitchen, 2 by 6 ft., same to the kitchens in first story, 1 ft. 6 in. by 5—brown stone hearths 16 in. by 3 ft. 6. to all other fire places; with facings in the parlor. Chimney tops capped with brown stone.

BRICK.—A chimney in each house with 5 fire=places—the flues of each pargetted and topped out with ornamental shafts—the side wall of the stairway to the cellar laid up with brick 8 in. thick.

PLASTERING.—All the walls and ceilings in the first and second stories will be lathed, and plastered with two good coats of the best brown mortar, and hard finished—6 in. plaster cornices in the parlors—the ceilings and partitions of the cellar will have one heavy coat of brown mortar, slipped, and whitewashed two coats. One of "Walker's Cottage Furnaces" placed in the cellar, with three registers in first story, and two in the second.

FRAME.—Of the best sound mill cut white pine timber—substantially framed and braced in every part. Sills and posts 4 by 9—framing beams and plates 4 by 8—girts 4 by 7—first tier of beams 3 by 9, 16 in. between centers—second tier 3 by 8, 16 in. between centers. Roof tier for Design 15, 3 by 8, 20 in. between centers—collar beams, 3 by 6—rafters, 3 by 6, 30 in. between centers—all trimmers 4 in. thick—red cedar sleepers, 2 ft. between centers, in cellar kitchen. Studding, with 3 by 4 joist, 16 in. between centers.

SIDING.—The sides to be sheathed over with sound seasoned pine boards, feather=edged, and then covered with clear 3=4 in. boards, rebated on 1 1=2 in. and to 1=2 an inch thick, and laid 7 in. to the weather—all the door and window frames and corner boards will be set on the sheathing, water tables to project 4 inches.

ROOFS.—The rafters covered with hemlock boards, laid close, the projecting portion with tongued and grooved plank, planed and beaded, and laid face side down, on planed rafters and projecting purlins—best split white pine shingles laid three thick—the valleys open 3 in. and lined with sheet lead 16 in. wide, 4 lb. to the square foot—nails must not be driven through the lead, except within 1=2 an inch of the edge. Roof of Design 15 will be covered with galvanized tinned plates in the usual manner—sufficient 3 in. tin leader to convey the water from the gutters. All the drapery to be made of 2 in. plank cut and opened as represented in the Plates—cornice and mouldings the same—all of best clear seasoned lumber, and put up strong—the gutters put together with white lead in all the joints.

VERANDA.—Roofs of narrow clear planks, edges grooved 1=2 in. deep, and tongues put in with white lead—the joints on the under side beaded—rafters, 3 by 7—purlins, 2 by 6—clear, planed and chamfered gutters of plank, with white lead in the joints—columns of 2 in plank, or of solid seasoned clear timber—parapets and mouldings same as represented and described on the several plates.

FLOORS——*For the interior, of milled pine plank, clear of loose knots, shakes and sap——veranda floors of narrow clear plank, tongued and grooved, joints laid in white lead, and blind nailed.*

STAIRS——*To the cellar will be enclosed with narrow boards, tongued and grooved, a door at the foot——to the second story, moulded steps and string——newell, octagon, paneled——moulded cap and base——rail, 4 1=2 by 2 1=2, moulded——balusters, 1 3=4, center turned——step ladders to attics.*

WINDOW FRAMES——*Of plank, to be made as in Plate 47——sashes 1 1=2 inches thick, filled with best American cylinder glass, set in diamond shape, for Designs 15 and 17, and in squares diagonally for Designs 14 and 16——the sashes in three windows in Design 14, and all the windows in Design 16 to be hung by butts, and secured by locks and bolts——cellar sashes to hang by butts, and all other sashes by weights and cord, and secured by " Jones patent sash locks."*

DOORS——*In first stories of Designs 14, 16 and 17 will be 1 1=2 inches thick, double faced, moulded both sides and the top panels foliated——first story doors in Design 15, as in Plate 46, Fig. 9——front doors 2 in. thick, made and ornamented as in the several perspective views——the doors in second story 1 1=4 in. thick, double faced, moulded one side, and the panel raised on the other——all other doors plain paneled.*

HARDWARE.——*First story doors to be hung by 4 by 4 broad butts, the second story doors by 3 1=2 by 3 1=2 broad butts, all other doors by 3 in. plain butts——the casements by 2 1=2 by 6 in. butts——cellar sashes by 2 1=2 in. plain butts——all patent manufacture. Four in. mortice locks with white porcelain knobs and drops to all the doors in first stories——5 in. rim locks with mineral knobs and bronze drops to all other doors. Mortice sash locks with bolts to the casements——3 in. bolts to the cellar sashes——the blinds hung and secured by "patent lock hinges."*

BASE——*In the first and second stories of Designs 14, 16 and 17, 1 1=4 thick moulded and put down strongly——in first and second stories of Design 15, as in Plate 46, Figs. 11 and 12——all other base 3=4 thick and 5 in. wide, beaded.*

MANTLES——*To four rooms in each house——a neat marble pattern in first story and plain, in the second story. Design 15, as in Plate 46, Figs. 7 and 8——hearth borders to all the fire=places.*

PRESSES, CLOSETS, &c.——*Will be fitted with all the required shelving, hooks, and pins.*

MOVING BLINDS——*Made strong and hung to all the windows above the cellar.*

BELLS.——*Two in first story, with porcelain knob levers, and one in second story with mineral knob pull.*

MATERIALS——*For the doors and interior finish, of the best seasoned clear lumber——all other materials to be of the best quality named.*

PAINTING.——*All the wood=work outside and inside, except shingle roofs and interior floors, to have two good coats of pure white lead and linseed oil, shaded a light brown, different shades for Designs 14, 16 and 17, and a pale straw color for Design 15. The first story of Designs 16 and 17 to be painted in imitation of oak in shades, with oil colors for Designs 14, 16 and 17——the blinds painted the same color as the house, several shades darker——on 15, a Paris green——three coats.*

DESCRIPTION OF PLATES.

PLATE 43.—PERSPECTIVE views of Design XIV. An ornamented cottage in the Elizabethan style; and Design XV. a small Villa in the Indian style. A wash-room and wood-house in corresponding style, attached to each.

PLATE 44.—Ground plans of first and second floors of Designs XIV. XV. XVI. and XVII.—each to have a basement kitchen, store-room and cellar.

PLATE 45.—Perspectives of Designs XVI. in the early English style; and XVII. in the Tudor, appropriate for a parsonage, with the necessary out-buildings and offices near the rear door.

PLATE 46.—Details of the Indian. Fig. 1.—Face section of the main cornice and parapets. Fig. 2.—Profile section of the same. Fig. 3.—A column, cornice, and parapet of the veranda. Fig. 4.—Profile section of the same. Fig. 5.—Ground section of the chimney flues. Fig. 6.—Sections of the shaft and cap of the chimneys. Fig. 7.—Face section of the mantle in the first story. Fig. 8.—Ground section of the same. Fig. 9.—Elevation of a door and trimmings for the principal story. Fig. 10.—Ground section of the same—one half full size. Figs. 11 and 12.—Sections of base for first and second stories.

PLATE 47.—Details for Design XVI. Fig. 1.—Column, cornice and parapet for veranda. Fig. 2.—Main gable drapery and mouldings. Fig. 3.—Profile section of gutter. Fig. 4.—Cornice and parapet of bay-window. Fig. 5.—Ground section of door-frame and trimmings; and Fig. 6, of window-frame and trimmings—the sashes to hang by weights. Fig. 7.—Section of the head and sill of a window frame—the sashes to hang by butts in casements. Fig. 8.—Side section of the same.

Figs. 9 and 10 illustrate a plan for building the sides and divisions of cottages, solid, by cutting inch boards into strips four inches wide, and laying them horizontally on each other, alternately projecting on each side half an inch, each board being nailed down by 10d. nails. The boards must cross at the angles. The roof to project at least 16 inches. The outside to be plastered with one coat of best brown mortar of lime and sand, and one coat cement mortar of clear coarse sand and hydraulic cement, and the inside with one good coat of lime mortar, and slipped. Another plan of finishing is by laying the boards even and planing all the sides smooth, and painting them with two coats of paint, which will fill the crevices and make the walls perfectly tight. The last method is probably the best. Fig. 9.—Framing plan of roof and beams. Fig. 10.—Face and profile of the sides. (The cost of this plan will be given in a future No.)

PLATE 48.—A plot of village property 724 feet by 488. It is divided into 16 lots, with the cottages placed 30 ft. from the street, and a carriage way through from the front to the rear. A wood-house, wash-room, and two water closets under one roof directly in the rear of each house; and stable and coach-house on the rear of the lot at the lane; and near it the poultry-house and yard. The lots are suitably intersected with walks and alleys, and shaded and ornamented by fruit and forest trees and shrubs; with the vegetable gardens near the stables.

65

ESTIMATE.

Of the Materials and Labor required for Design XV.

MASON'S.

170 yds. excavation, - - - 11	$18 70	1 brown stone hearth and facings, -	4 50
112 lds. building stone, - - 70	78 40	2 " " hearths, - - 2 50	5 00
3000 hard brick, 4 00; 2600 salmon brick, 3 00,	19 80	1 " " chimney top - -	18 00
14000 plastering lath, - - - 2 75	38 50	5 blue stone window and door sills, 50	2 50
120 lbs. lath nails, - - - 7 00	8 40	43 ft. " steps and coping, - 14	6 02
124 loads sand, - - - 40	49 60	20 ft. " hearths - - 16	3 20
12 bush. white sand, - - - 12	1 44	Furnace, 130 00; 38 loads carting, 40 cts.	145 20
28 bush. hair, - - - 20	5 60	58 day's mason's wages, - - 1 75	101 50
61 casks Thomaston lime, - - 1 00	61 00	50 " laborer's " - - 1 00	50 00
3 " lump lime, - - 1 75	5 25		
3 " Lubec plaster, - - 1 87	5 61		$628 22

CARPENTER'S.

4632 ft. timber, - - $1 60 per h.	$74 11	460 lbs. sash weights, - - 2	9 20
222 joists, - - - 14	31 08	32 sash locks, 9 cts.; 4 3 in. sash bolts, 10 cts.	3 28
160 ft. cedar sleepers, - 6	9 60	3 bells, 4 00; 100 ft. blinds, 75 cts.	87 00
2800 ft. sheathing boards, - 1½	42 00	2 gross screws ¾, No. 7, - 21	42
305 milled floor planks, - 27	82 35	1 " " 1, " 9, -	27
155 narrow clear milled planks, 18	27 90	3 " " 1¼, " 11 - 36	1 08
3890 ft. 3 in. clear plank and boards, 3½	136 15	10 pair butts, 4 by 4, - 19	1 90
175 best piece plank, - 28	49 00	5 " " 3½ by 3½, - 15	75
345 " " boards, - 19	65 55	9 " " 3 in. - 7	63
500 lbs. nails, 4 37; 20 lbs. finishing nails, 10 cts.	23 85	8 " " 2 in. - 4	32
846 ft. tin roof, - - 13	109 98	9 4 in. mortice locks, - 2 31	20 79
60 ft. 3 in. 12 cts., 24 ft. 2 in. tin leaders, 9 cts.	9 36	9 5 in. rim locks, - - 1 25	11 25
230 super. ft. glazed sashes, - 27	62 10	60 loads carting, - - 40	24 00
36 lights, 10 by 12, - 15	5 40	221 days' carpenter's labor, - 1 50	331 50
5½ doz. pullies, - - 63	3 47		
9 lbs. sash cord, - - 31	2 79		$1227 08

PAINTER'S.

375 lbs. white lead, - - 7 50	28 13	1 lb. chrome yellow; 2 lb. litharge, 18 cts.	54
18 galls. oil, 78 cts.; 2 galls. spirits, 44 cts.	14 92	Carting; 20 days' painter's labor, 1 75,	37 50
2 lbs. glue, 20 cts.; 18 lbs. putty, 3 cts.	94		
			$82 03

ESTIMATE for laying out lots Nos. 1 and 3, as in Plate 48, embracing the cottages, out-buildings, fence, well, cistern, walks, roads, trees, shrubbery, &c.

LOT No. 1.

Design XIV.	$1400 50
273 ft. of front fence with 2 gates, 35 cts. per ft.	95 50
76 ft. of open division fence, 17 cts. per ft.	12 92
122 ft. of tight rear fence, one gate, 25 cts. per ft.	30 50
30 ft. of tight yard fence, one gate, 7 ft. high, 28 cts.	8 40
Wood house, &c. under one roof,	125 00
Coach house, with three stalls, harness room, &c.	450 00
Fowl house, with laying and feeding rooms,	55 00
Well 30 ft. deep, with platform and pump complete,	135 00
Two cisterns with pumps, each $40 and $50,	90 00
250 yards of walks and roads, 8 cts.	20 00
Gravel, spading, seeding, &c.	50 00
100 ornamental and fruit trees, 50 varieties,	42 50

50 ornamental trees and shrubs, 20 varieties,	18 00
Choice raspberries, strawberries, currants, &c.	25 00
Preparing the ground and setting,	25 00
	$2782 97

LOT No. 2.

Design XVII.	1750 00
122 ft. open front fence, with two gates, 35 cts.	42 70
151 ft. " division 17 cts.	25 67
152 ft. of rear and yard fence, one gate,	38 00
Wood-house, coach-house, shrubs and trees, cistern, walks, road, &c. as on lot No. 1,	1035 50
	$2892 77

Design XIV. will cost $1450; XV., $1938; XVI., $1800; XVII., $1750.

. Hight of first and second stories, of each design 9 feet, and of basement, 7 feet—all in the clear when complete.

66

Des. & del. by Wm H. Ranlett

ORNAMENTAL COTTAGE

in the Elizabethan Style.

Des. & del. by Wm H. Ranlett

E. & S. Palmer's lith. 34 Ann St.

A SMALL VILLA

in the Indian Style.

PLATE 44.

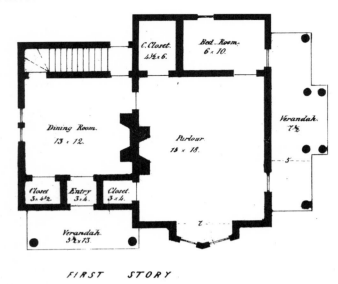

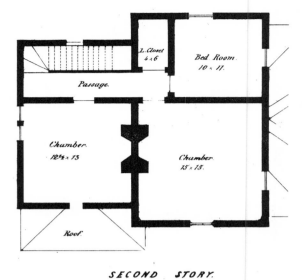

FIRST STORY

SECOND STORY.

DESIGN XIV.

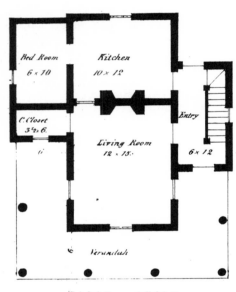

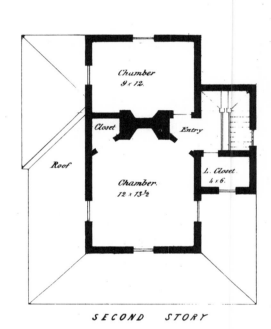

FIRST STORY.

SECOND STORY

DESIGN XV & XVII.

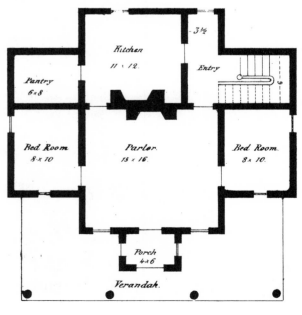

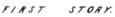

FIRST STORY.

SECOND STORY.

W.H.Ranlett.

Ground Plans.

Des & del. by Wm H. Ranlett.

ORNAMENTAL COTTAGE,

in the early English Style.

DESIGN XVII.

Des & del. by Wm H. Ranlett.

E & S. Palmer's lith. 34. Ann St.

PARSONAGE,

in the Tudor Style.

Fig. 1.

Fig. 2.

Fig. 6.

Fig. 3.

Fig. 4.

Fig. 5.

12 9 6 3 1   1   2   3   4   5   6   7   8   9
Scale of feet and inches.

Fig. 7.

Fig. 8.

Fig. 9.

Fig. 10.

½ full size.

Fig. 11.

Fig. 12.

8 inches.

8 inches.

½ full size.

Wm H. Ranlett.

F & S. Palmer's Lith. 34. Ann St.

INDIAN DETAILS.

DETAILS.

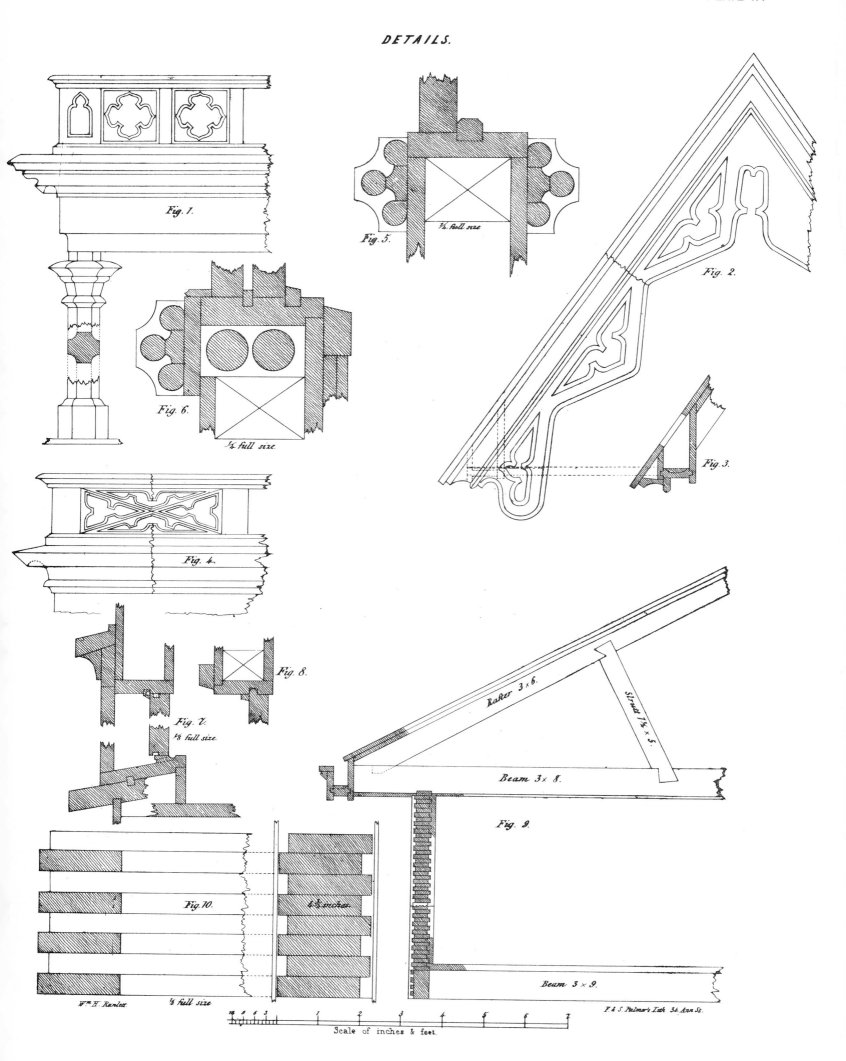

Fig. 1.

Fig. 5.
¼ full size.

Fig. 2.

Fig. 3.

Fig. 6.
¼ full size.

Fig. 4.

Fig. 8.

Fig. 7.
⅛ full size.

Rafter 3 × 6.

Strut 7½ × 5.

Beam 3 × 8.

Fig. 9.

Fig. 10.

4½ inches.

Beam 3 × 9.

Wm. H. Ranlett.

⅛ full size

F. & S. Palmer's Lith. 36 Ann St.

10 9 8 6 3   1   2   3   4   5   6   7
Scale of inches & feet.

PLATE 48.

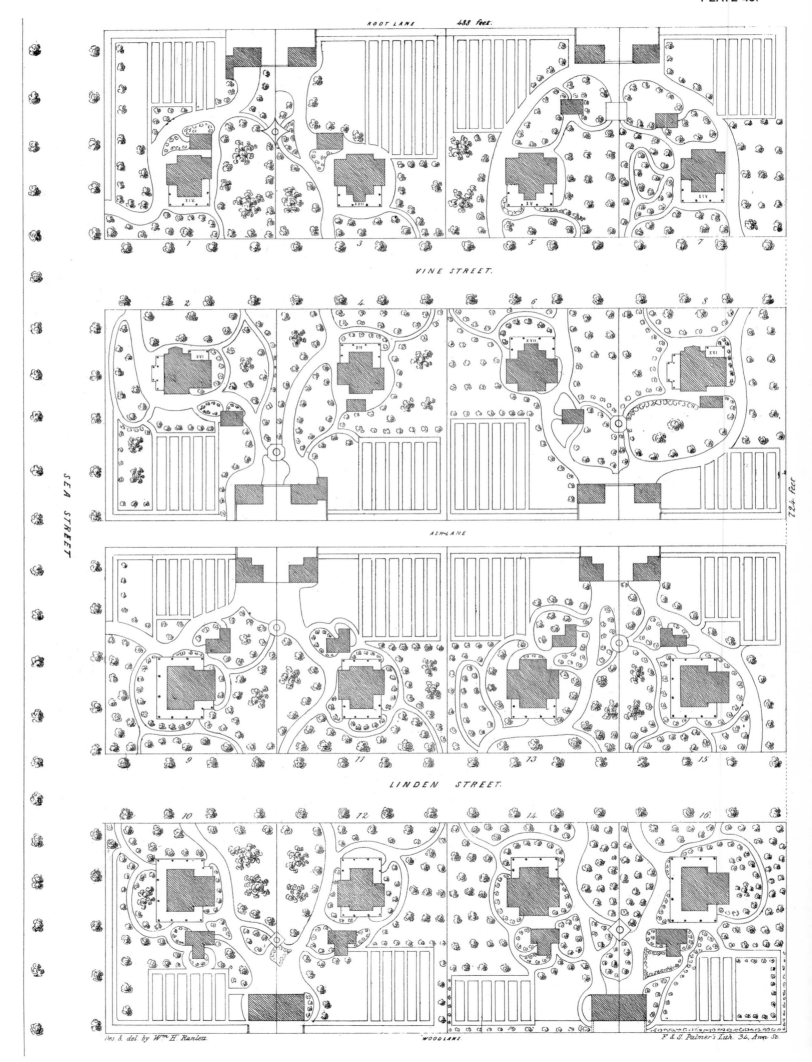

ROOT LANE   438 feet.

VINE STREET.

ASH LANE

LINDEN STREET.

SEA STREET

724 feet

Des & del. by Wm H. Ranlett.

WOODLANE.

F. & S. Palmer's Lith. 34, Ann St.

THE ROMANESQUE STYLE.

THE Romanesque or Byzantine style was introduced in Britain in rebuilding the towns and edifices after the Saxon invasion which occurred about the middle of the fifth century. The country was held by the Roman government, and extensively occupied by their colonies for 500 years. During this period they built many towns. and erected many palaces, public baths, churches, and other public buildings, of stone, in the Roman style; and many of them would have remained to this day, had they not been wilfully destroyed by the Saxons. These towns and edifices continued long in ruins.

This style is—as the title imports—a refined modification of Roman architecture. It arose in Byzantium, in the erection of the splendid church, St. Sophia, in the city of Constantinople, by Constantine. This Emperor, having embraced Christianity, made an attempt to refine the classic architecture of heathen Rome, in the construction of this Christian temple in the early part of the fourth century. It was rebuilt by the Emperor Justinian about the middle of the sixth century, and it is now a Turkish mosque, capable of containing conveniently, one hundred thousand persons. While Justinian was finishing this church, he ordered that of St. Vitale to be erected in the same style at Ravenna in Italy, and contributed towards its erection. The St. Vitale so impressed Charlemagne with its beauty that he had it copied in the erection of a new church in France.

Every system of religion which has become extensively adopted, has produced some specific style of architecture. The Christian religion has produced different styles, particularly the Byzantine and Gothic. The style here noticed is called Romanesque, as above, and Byzantine from the name of the country in which it rose. It has also been called, in the course of its history, the Saxon, Norman and Lombard.

It was introduced in Britain in the after part of the seventh century, by two clergymen, Wilfrid and Benedict. The stone churches with glass windows, erected by these ecclesiastics, were much admired, but did not find many imitators till the after part of the ninth century when Alfred resolved to rebuild the ruined churches and monasteries; and for a long time after Alfred's day, stone was little used, and glass windows seen only in churches—the nobles living in low wooden houses admitting light through holes in the walls, covered with lattice-work. After this, however, the Romanesque was received with great favor and spread all over Europe, and prevailed until the introduction of Gothic Architecture, which began to supersede it in the eleventh century. The Byzantine style was revived under the Stuarts, who recovered the throne of England, in the person of James I., hence it is sometimes called the Stuarts' style.

The characteristics of this style, are circular arches whose archivaults spring directly from the capitals of columns and pilasters, which capitals are little more than square blocks tapering downwards, sometimes ornamented with small foliations. Columns are by no means a common feature, and when introduced, but few are used, which are small, low and plain. The window heads are circular, and the openings small and few, well proportioned and distributed. The members of the edifice are usually massive and heavy. Domestic Romanesque admits verandas, but they are not essential to the style.

WATER.

THE great importance of a plentiful supply of wholesome water, is universally known; but the methods and means of procuring it are less understood, as are also the various qualities and effects of water procured from different sources. The question of water should always be settled in the selection of a site, for if left to be decided at an after period, it may occasion some perplexity. The reader is referred to a paragraph on this subject on page 20.

The common sources of water for domestic purposes, are springs, wells and cisterns. Rain water is the purest natural water. It is produced by condensation of vapor that rises from the surface of the earth by the action of heat and the influence of the atmosphere; hence it is free from the earthy substances which are usually contained in water that is in or on the earth. The facilities now possessed for constructing cisterns, render that mode of procuring water quite convenient, and moderate in expense, while the great superiority of rain water over that generally procured from springs and wells, makes it desirable and economical to provide a supply of this water in addition to that of a well or spring.

Roofs should be constructed with a view to the preservation of the purity of cistern water; for metal roofs will impregnate the water more or less with their qualities, and some of them are very deleterious, especially copper, lead and zinc. Slate is the best material to afford pure water from the roof, as it is the least soluble in water of all articles of roofing; and the purity of rain water renders it the most powerful solvent of all water except distilled. Shingles are the most common article of roofing, especially in the country. They do not materially affect the water in a chemical sense, but particles of the wood are always becoming disengaged in showers, and conveyed to the cistern. Great pains should be taken to keep the roof clean, particularly if the water is to be used for drinking and culinary purposes, and it is decidedly better than hard water for boiling any article of which it is desired to reduce the texture, while hard water is better for boiling articles that should preserve much of their solidity or firmness.

Spring water is apt to contain an admixture of mineral substances, often in solution and sometimes in chemical combination. Sulphate of lime is by far the most common ingredient by which it is impregnated and rendered "hard." It often contains carbonate of lime, and very frequently salts of iron; and occasionally various others. All these are detrimental in some branches of domestic-operations, and some of them in all branches; and others are indifferent in some uses of water, and some of them advantageous in a few. This general view applying to most water from springs and wells, a dwelling should be provided with a cistern unless it has the rare fortune of "soft water," from some other source; and the facilities for constructing good and durable cisterns are so great that few householders have a good reason for being without them.

Wells should be under cover in connection with the house, which is easily arranged by digging the well before building the house; and this should be so done when a well is to be the dependance for water, for it is sometimes found difficult to get good water in this way. It is now common to bore into the earth for the purpose of finding water before digging. This is done at trifling expense and often saves much, for if it is found that water cannot be obtained at a certain locality without digging deeper than it is desired, or if the water should be bad, the spot may be abandoned without much loss; for on these considerations it is sometimes advisable to abandon even a desirable building site.

Artesian wells may be sunk in many places without very heavy expense. A geological view of the region where such a well is desired, will generally afford an idea approximating the truth as to the depth, character of the earth, and consequently the expense of such a well in a given location. They are sometimes sunk even in the beds of rivers, and the facilities that modern improvements have afforded for boring, are so great, that wells of this kind are sunk with convenience to the depth of several hundred feet. If the boring should be through much hard rock, the operation will thereby be rendered proportionably slow and more expensive. The water in Artesian wells is generally very pure. It accumulates in a basin of primitive or other hard rock which is not easily decomposed by water ; and it usually comes from a distance, where the rock forming the basin lies at or near the surface. If a portion of the basin lies higher than the surface where the well is formed, the water will flow out of the top of the well and make a perpetual fountain of pure water.

Another method of procuring water, is by elevating it by means of the " Hydraulic ram," which is an invention by Montgolfier of France, and improved by Benson of Maryland, and further improved by Gatchel of the same State. This machine with a small stream of water having a fall of ten feet, will elevate one eighth of the amount of water to the hight of 60 or 80 feet. The original machine elevated a part of the water used for the power ; and Benson's improvement consists in a provision for elevating water other than that used for the power ; and Gatchel's, for elevating the water from a well or fountain below the ram, and then elevating it as the others ; all by one action of the power. The water is forced up by the action of compressed air; and the whole machinery will not cost more than a well of 25 feet deep. See page 74.

Brooks, creeks and rivers afford water which comes in part from springs and in part from rain, and it usually contains more or less of the dissolved material which is incident to water passing through the upper strata of the earth, and the impurity which is apt to accumulate in flowing on the surface.

Filtering will clear water of sediment and some other impurities to which it is subject. Course filtering is performed by straining liquids through a sieve, cloth or spunge, and a delicate or fine filtering, for chemical purposes, is performed by means of spungy paper. The ordinary processes of filtration for domestic purposes, are between these modes. It is accomplished by passing the water through sand or other material of which the pores are too minute to allow the particles suspended in the water, to pass through. Various plans have been invented for this process. Spunge makes a good filter by compressing it into the orifice through which the water is to percolate, and it is convenient, for it can easily be taken out, cleaned and replaced. Porous stone is often used ; but charcoal produces the most thorough defecation, for besides extracting the extraneous particles, it absorbs the carbonic acid gas and coloring matter, which are often contained in water, and decidedly deleterious in their effects. Water cannot be defecated of salts by filtration. This can be done only by chemical re-agents, which merely substitute one impurity for another.

DRAINS.—The plan of a house should include a plan of drains sufficient to keep it dry to the bottom of the cellar, which state is very important for the preservation of the house, and still more so for the health of the occupants. They should not only conduct the water from the basement or cellar, but they should extend through the whole area of the house under the ground, pavement or floor in the lowest apartment. They should conduct the water to considerable distance from the house and discharge it into a branch or brook, if possible ; but if this cannot be done, it should be into a sesspool which should be placed at a distance from the house, properly walled, covered and marked, and the foul air kept out of the drain by a " stench trap " in a stone basin, and a plan of the drains should be kept in the house, that it may be known where to open them, in case of necessity.

WATER CLOSETS.—This is an important appendage to a dwelling, touching which there is a most egregious lack of good taste in our country. It is very frequently a " privy " or small box-like affair, placed in the yard or garden, separate from all other buildings, and often in a conspicuous part of the grounds, with a straight walk from the door, or a *continuation of the main hall*, even by an ornamental grape arbor ; and it is sometimes ornamented with a screen, or consecrated by a miniature steeple, as if it were feared that the public eye might not recognize its use !

A water-closet should be a room in the main edifice or in an out building, so that its use may not be displayed to the public eye. It is better not to be constructed over a sink, but with a basin in the seat, from which a soil-pipe extends to the drain, that conveys the sediment to a sesspool at a distance from the house. The drain should be so constructed as to receive the waste water from the house, which will be sufficient to keep it clear. But it is better to have running water conveyed by a pipe to the basin and soil pipe, if convenient. The drain should be sufficiently deep to prevent its freezing ; and the whole so arranged as to prevent the stench from escaping into the closet or from the drain at any other point ; which is easily done by a stench-trap in a properly constructed basin, and a small copper gate in the lateral drain.

JOURNEYMEN.

THE transition from apprenticeship to the rank of what is technically called a " turnover," has been shown in a former article. The aspiring candidate for a trade, can graduate as easily from the grade of a turnover to that of a journeyman, as through the former " transition state." This slack polity in the mechanic arts, produces many incompetent journeymen, and the evils resulting are many, multiform, and often disastrous, affecting interests both private and public. The incompetency of many journeymen makes it necessary for the foreman to give particular jobs to select workmen, which prevents that equality of rank and distribution of work that is so desirable, and the want of which produces so much dissatisfaction.

A journeyman should have a thorough knowledge of his trade, which means more than mere ability to fit a piece of lumber or make a good joint, or even to commence and finish, in an approved manner, a specific job. It implies ability to comprehend the whole plan and scheme of the construction in which he is employed, so as to see the end from the beginning; including a critical perception to discover defects, and a master's skill to remedy them. E. g. a journeyman is employed to put on the casings of a door, make the door, and hang it; and he finds that it does not fit; on examination, it is ascertained that the door-frame was allowed, by carelessness or incompetency, to be out of plumb half an inch: a half an inch is not much, to be sure, but the consequences are very considerable; and if the proprietor has to bear them, he should, rather than allow so heavy a damage, pay off the journeyman, throw away the work he has done and the material he has wasted, and employ a competent workman, who will see that his *basis is right*, and then proceed secundum artem.

The above illustration is only one of many that might be given, which often occur, and produce more or less damage. Suppose, for instance, that the foundation walls of a large house be laid in an improper manner—" not sufficiently bound " —it is liable to give way, by which the whole building would be damaged or destroyed. It is thus manifest that the results of the bad workmanship of a job, involves consequences vastly beyond the value of the job itself. *Expedition* is another important point in journey-work. It depends much on the mode of operation, and is more manifest in the contrast between foreign and native mechanics, than in any other general feature of mechanical labor.*

Thus it is manifest that the qualifications of journeymen have an important bearing on the interests of employers, in the character and despatch of their workmanship; on the proprietor, in the style and durability of his property; and on the country, in the value and influence of its improvements; and the style of improvements generally, is of such a character at the present day, that artisans have the strongest inducements to use their best efforts to attain excellence in their respective trades. Public taste also is rapidly improving; and its demand of satisfactory qualities in artistical productions, must be met; hence our artisans must be qualified to produce such workmanship, or others will be called in to occupy the ground which the incompetent might have secured by proper diligence.

---

* Take, for example, their different modes of dressing lumber. A foreigner will first go through the lot, facing each piece, deciding whether the face is in a plane, by placing a couple of planes on it and looking across them—then through squaring one edge—then through gaging it—then through dressing the other side and edge; while the native workman would take a piece upon his bench and face it, judging its parallelism by the eye, then square one edge, then run his gage twice along it, and then dress off the other side and edge—all before laying it away: thus he would do the work on a lot of trimmings in handling it once over, that a foreigner would do in handling it over from four to six times; and the work in the two cases would be done with equal exactness, but one would require considerable more time than the other.

SPECIFICATIONS,

Of the Materials and Labor required for the erection of Design XVIII.

EXCAVATIONS——*Properly made, and the earth graded around the building, cistern, and sink.*

STONE WORK.——*Cellar walls 18 in. thick and 7 ft. high, on a broad foundation, 10 inches deep. Walls of the airie 18 in. thick, and founded 18 in. below the pavement at the bottom. The steps and coping of blue stone, 10 inch. wide. Stone footings to all the piers. Kitchen hearth of blue stone, 2 by 6 ft.——blue stone neck to cistern, a stone sesspool 5 ft. diameter by 9 ft. deep, for the water closet——a sink 10 ft. deep, 5 by 6 ft. in clear.*

BRICK WORK.——*In the cellar, 6 piers, 8 by 12 in. 7 ft high, and 17 piers, 8 by 12 in. under the columns. A chimney with five fire-places——each flue well plastered and topped with proper elevation above the roof——the fire-place in the cellar 5 ft. wide and 2 ft. deep, with eyes for a crane. All the exterior walls filled between the studs with brick set on the edge and bracketed on every fifth course. A cistern 10 ft. deep, 8 ft. diameter, arched top, properly cemented inside.*

PLASTERING.——*Lathed and three coats, scratch, brown, and hard finish, on all the walls and ceilings in the first and second stories. The ceiling of the cellar lathed and plastered with one coat of brown mortar, and whitewashed. A ten-inch moulded cornice of plaster in two rooms and the hall in the first story.*

MANTLES.——*Two veined marble mantles in the second story, to cost not less than $20 each, and one in the dining-room, of white or Egyptian marble, to cost not less than $40. One grate in the dining-room, and one in a chamber, to cost $9 and $12——all to be set complete. "Walker's furnace" set in the cellar with pipes and registers to five rooms.*

MATERIALS——*All of the best quality for their specific uses. All the mortar for the stone and brick walls, and plastering, of proper proportions and well mixed.*

FRAME——*Of best seasoned white pine milled timber, properly framed and well braced in all its parts. The sills, posts and plates, 4 by 10——framing beams, 4 by 9——girts, 4 by 7——first tier of beams, 3 by 10, 16 in. between centers——second tier, 3 by 9, 16 in. between centers——roof tier, 3 by 8, 3 ft. between centers all trimmers 4 in. thick. Two girders in the cellar, 5 by 9. Studding in the exterior walls, 3 by 4, 12 in. between centers——in partition 16 in. between centers. Veranda timber: floor beams, 3 by 8——sills, 4 by 8——rafters, 3 by 9——purlins, 3 by 7. Second floor beams prepared for deafening, and both floors cross bridged.*

SIDING.——*With clear tongued and grooved plank, 1 1-4 thick, rabbeted 1-4 inch deep and one in. wide, put up with white lead in the joints, and nailed with 12d nails, the corners overlapped by boards 7-8 thick, mitered and bevelled, same as drawn on the elevations.*

ROOFS——*Of hemlock boards laid close, and covered with best split, clear white pine shingles, laid 3 thick—— the valleys open 2 in. and lined with sheet lead, 16 in. wide, weighing 3 1-2 pounds to the square foot. The* projections from the main house to be covered with galvanized tin, the edges secured to the plank by close nailing —4 in. tin leaders to convey the water to the cistern and waste.

CORNICE.—Main cornice as in Plate 53, Figs. 1 and 3. All the exposed joints to be put together with white lead. Water table 8 in. high, and project 7 inches from the sills.

VERANDA ROOF—Of narrow, clear white pine plank, 1 1=4 thick, planed on both sides, tongued and grooved, and beaded on one side, laid in white lead and blind nailed—the rafters and purlins planed, and the corners run with a 3=4 bead—the columns solid, of seasoned clear white pine—the caps and bases as in Fig. 5, Plate 53.

FLOORS—Of veranda, of narrow clear white pine, 1 1=4 in. thick, with the joints laid in white lead and blind nailed. All the interior floors of sound white pine milled plank, laid in courses, and the joints made smooth on the completion of the house—the ceiling in the second story to be tight furred with 3 in. strips 1 1=4 thick.

BASE—As in Plate 53, first story, Fig. 9, and second story, Fig. 8.

STAIRS.—From the first story to the second, with moulded string and steps, and risers not over 7 1=2 in. with brackets—a moulded rail 4 1=2 by 2 1=2 in., to terminate with a scroll, and rest on 2 in. turned balusters and a 4 in. newel of best St. Domingo wood. Cellar stairs with strings 2 in.—steps 1 1=4 in. and risers 7=8 in. thick, put up in the strongest manner and enclosed at the head by a door and panel=work under the main stairs. Suitable steps well made to the several outside doors.

WINDOWS.—In the cellar, 6 windows, each 8 lights, 10 by 12—the sashes 1 1=4 thick, hung by butts, and secured by 4 in. flat bolts. Six double and 3 single windows in the first story, and six double and four single windows in the second story—the sashes 1 1=2 in. thick, and double hung, with circular heads—the glass in the first story, 10 by 15 ; and in the second story, 10 by 14 ; and that in the heads as in the elevation. A circular, ornamented window, with a sash 1 1=2 thick, in each pediment.

DOORS.—In the first story, 1 3=4, thick 8 ft. high, 8 panels, and moulded on each side, with circular heads —front door in two parts, top panels of stained glass, the side door with a stained glass head. In the second story, 1 1=2 in. thick, 7 ft. high, 4 panels and moulded on both sides. Jambs, 1 1=4 thick, 5 3=4 wide, set before plastering. The stops glued in grooves. Saddles, 1=2 in. thick and 6 in. wide. Butts, 4 by 4, in first story, and 3 1=2 by 3 1=2 in second. Mortice locks, 4 1=2 in. with porcelain furniture, of "Victoria gold sprig" pattern, in the first story, and in the second, 4 in. mortice locks, porcelain furniture, "Victoria white."

ARCHITRAVES—In first story, of 2 in. plank, moulded as in Plate 53, Fig. 7—in second story, of 1 1=2 in. plank, 4 in. wide, put on after the plastering is done.

CLOSETS AND PRESSES.—All to be fitted with shelves, drawers, and brass hooks and pins for the required uses. A water=closet fitted up in the best manner with a basin, soil=pipe, a pipe from the cistern, and a force pump to convey the water to a lead lined reservoir, to contain 30 gallons.

BELLS.—To each of front and side doors ; the drawing=room, dining=room and three chambers each to have one— the lever knobs corresponding with the lock furniture respectively. A speaking tube in the hall, to the kitchen.

MANTLES.——*A neat wooden mantle, marble pattern, in the kitchen. Hearth borders to all the hearths.*

BLINDS——*To all the windows in the first and second stories, made in the stongest manner and hung by welded hinges, and secured by best patent fastenings.*

PAINTING.——*All the wood work, except the shingle roof, interior floors and mahogany; to have three good coats of pure white lead and linseed oil, put on at proper times; and, if required, the two last coats may be colored a French gray, or light granite on the outside, and a light straw color inside. The blinds to have three coats of best Paris green. The stair rails and balusters to have four coats of varnish, rubbed each time, and finished with the fifth, or flowing coat.*

MATERIALS——*All of the best quality. The lumber for the veranda, cornices, and all other trimmings, outside and inside, to be clear and well seasoned.*

DESCRIPTION OF PLATES.

PLATE 49.—Design XVIII.—Two—front and side—entrance elevations of an ornamented Villa, in the Romanesque style.

PLATE 50.—Design XVIII.—Plans of the first and second stories, and a section of the hights of ceilings.

PLATE 51.—Design XIX. Two elevations and two ground plans of a cottage with solid walls and partitions, and a frame section of the hights of the ceilings, and elevations of the rafters. For the walls, see Figs. 9 and 10 in Plate 47, and for roof, C, Fig. 1, Plate 40.

PLATE 52.—Details of Design XVIII. Fig. 1.—Elevation of a window. Fig. 2.—Mantle for the first story. A, a section of the front elevation ; B, a section of the ground plan ; C, a profile section. Fig. 3.—A section of siding with the corner boards. A, the face ; B, profile ; C, ground sections. Fig. 4.—A profile section of siding, cut by a patented machine, one half full size. Fig. 5.—A circular window for the pediments.

PLATE 53.—Details for Design XVIII. Fig. 1.—Profile of main cornice, one fourth full size. Fig. 2.—Face of the crown block. Fig. 3.—Face section of the main cornice. Fig. 4.—Profile section of the main cornice, rafters, shingles, &c. Fig. 5.—Face section of veranda cornice, column, cap and base. Fig. 6.—Elevation of a door for the first story. Fig. 7.—Architrave for the first story, one half full size. Fig. 8.—Base for the second story. Fig. 9.—Base for the first story.

PLATE 54.—Fig. 1.—A brick cistern, 10 feet deep and 10 feet diameter ; capacity 4800 gallons : *a*, main section ; *b*, ground plan ; *c*, outlet ; *d*, sesspool ; *e*, stone neck ; *f*, rack ; *g*, wooden neck. Fig. 2.—A filtering cistern, 8 feet in diameter and 10 feet deep ; capacity 3080 gallons : *a*, main section ; *b*, ground plan of receiver ; *c*, section of filter ; *d*, the filtering material, which is of round or irregular stones, 3 in. diameter, covering the bottom and overlaid with coarse gravel, 4 in. deep, and then with alternate layers of charcoal and coarse gravel, 4 or 5 in., each course to the depth of 2 ft. 8 in., the top layer being of gravel. The charcoal should be clear of all dust and made very compact. *e*, is the draw-pipe, 1 in. diameter, with the end inserted in the material, and a strainer of lead or copper to prevent the particles of coal or gravel, from passing into the pipe ; *f*, the receiving pipe of lead, 5 in. diameter ; *g*, the stone neck ; *h*, the stone cover ; scale, ⅛ of an in. Fig. 3.—A round sewer of brick, 12 inch. diameter in the clear. Fig. 4.—An oval sewer, 12 by 18 in. in the clear. Fig. 5.—A square sewer, 12 by 12 in., top and bottom of blue flagging. Fig. 6.—A square sewer 8 by 8 in., top and bottom of flag. Fig. 7.—A right angled drain, 4 by 8, top and bottom of flagging. Fig. 8.—A square drain, 4 by 4 in., of brick. Fig. 10.—A triangular drain of brick, each side of 5 in. Fig. 11.—A common drain of field stone, 6 by 12 in. in the clear. All the above drains and sewers to be laid in mortar. Scale, 1 inch to the foot, for the drains and sewers, and ⅛ in. to the foot for the cisterns.

ESTIMATE.

Of the Materials and Labor required for Design XVIII.*

MASON'S.

160 yds. excavation,	- - -	11	$17 60	
170 lds. building stone,	- -	70	119 00	
10900 hard brick, 4 00; 17500 salmon brick, 3 00,			96 10	
24000 plastering lath,	- - - 2 00		48 00	
216 lbs. lath nails,	- - - 7 00		15 12	
222 loads sand,	- - -	40	88 80	
30 bush. white sand,	- - -	12	3 60	
48 bush. hair,	- - -	20	9 60	
97 casks Thomaston lime,	- - 1 00		97 00	
9 " lump lime,	- - 1 75		15 75	
8 " Lubec plaster,	- - 1 87		14 96	

2 marble mantles, $20; 1 marble mantle, $70,			110 00
12 ft. kitchen hearth,	- -	16	1 92
44 ft. steps and coping,	-	14	6 16
7 blue stone window and door sills,		50	3 50
2 grates, $9 and $12,	- -		21 00
Cistern neck, $3 50; crane eyes,		50	4 00
Furnace, 180 00; 122 loads carting, 40 cts.			228 80
113 days' mason's wages,	- - 1 75		197 75
82 " laborer's "	- - 1 00		82 00
			$1180 66

CARPENTER'S.

13500 ft. timber,	- - $2 00 per h.		$270 00	
430 joists,	- - -	14	60 20	
410 milled floor planks,	-	27	110 70	
726 narrow clear milled planks,		18	120 68	
372 siding planks,	- -	33	122 76	
10230 ft. clear planks, 3, 2, 1½, 1¼, 1, ¼ in.		3½	358 05	
150 best piece plank,	-	28	42 00	
150 " " boards,	-	19	28 50	
320 hemlock boards,	-	13	41 60	
28 bunches shingles, $2 50; 52 ft. mahogany, 10 cts.			75 20	
46 balusters, 12 cts; newel, $2 25,	-		7 77	
80 ft. blinds, $1 25; 46 ft. blinds, $1 00,	-		146 00	
1000 lbs. nails, 4 37; 50 lbs. finishing nails, 10 cts.			48 70	
317 ft. galvanized tin roof,	-	14	44 38	
92 ft. 4 in. 12 cts., 51 ft. 3 in. tin leaders, 10 cts.			16 04	
165 lights, 10x15, 170 lts. 10x14, 48 lts. 10x12,			130 00	
4 pediment sashes,	-	7 00	28 00	
21 ft. stained glass,	- -	75	15 75	

10½ doz. pullies,	- -	63	6 62
12 lbs. sash cord,	- -	31	3 72
626 lbs. sash weights,	- -	2	12 52
Speaking tube, $3 50; 7 bells, $4 50			35 00
6 flat bolts, 10 cts.; 3 10 in. bolts, 25 cts.			1 35
2 gross screws ¾, No. 7,	-	21	42
1 " " 1, " 9,	-		27
3 " " 1¼, " 11,	-	36	1 08
20 pair butts, 4 by 4,	-	19	3 80
8 " " 3½ by 3½,	-	15	1 20
10 " " 3 in.	-	7	70
1 doz. brass hooks, $3 00; 2 doz. iron hooks, 42 cts.			3 84
93 ft. sheet lead,		25	23 25
Water closet and fixtures,	- -		90 00
55 loads carting,	- -	40	22 00
365 days' carpenter's labor,	-	1 50	547 50
			$2429 60

PAINTER'S.

800 lbs. white lead,	- -	7 50	60 00
40 galls. oil, 65 cts.; 4 galls. spirits, 44 cts.			27 76
4 lbs. glue, 20 cts.; 25 lbs. putty, 3 cts.			1 55

1 lb. chrome yellow, 35 cts.; 3 lbs. litharge, 6 cts.		53
Carting, $3 00; 47 days' painter's labor, 1 75,		85 25
		$175 09

ESTIMATE for Design XIX.

100 yards excavation, $10 00; 54 loads stone, $37 80; 2000 hard brick, $8 00; 3500 salmon brick, $10 50; 30 casks lime, $30 00; 4 casks cement, $6 00; 60 loads sand, $21 00; 20 bushels hair, $4 00; 2 hearths, $3 00; carting, $10 50.

3100 ft. timber, $53 75; 193 milled plank, $50 18; 795 roof boards, $111 30; 1331 wall boards, $159 72; 1100 ft. clear lumber, $38 50; 90 plank, $27 00; 76 boards, $15 29; 174 lights glass, $24 36; 500 lbs. nails, $22 00; 27 ft. tin roof, $3 50; sash weights, cords, and pullies, $12 00; 11 locks, $9 68; 11 pair butts and screws, $14 00.

Lead and oil, $27 00; painter's labor, $16 00; carpenter's labor, $129 00; mason's labor, $42 00; laborer's, $18 00.

Design XVIII. will cost $3785 35; XIX., $903 39.

* An attic may be made in Design XVIII. with three rooms, each about 12 by 14 feet, without raising the posts or any other alteration of the general plan. The cost would be $185 00. The right hand chimney may be based on a large flag on the main partition. If the kitchen be placed on the first floor, in should be in the room marked dining-room.

SIDE ENTRANCE ELEVATION

Romanesque Style.

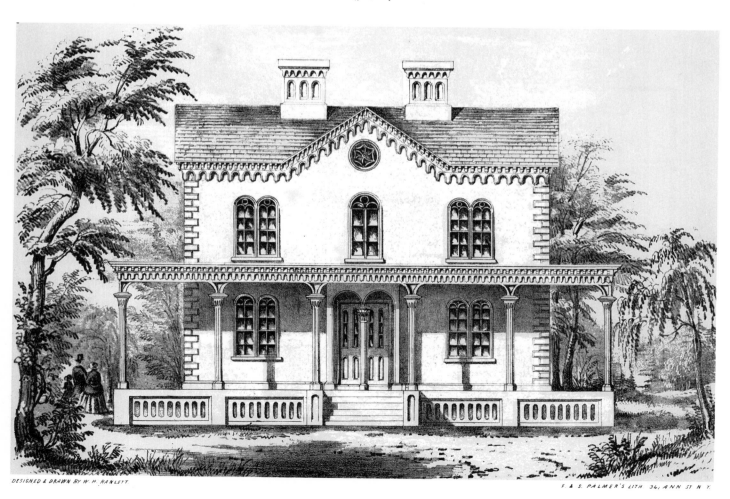

DESIGNED & DRAWN BY W. H. RANLETT.

F. & S. PALMER'S LITH. 34, ANN ST N.Y.

FRONT ENTRANCE ELEVATION

PLATE 50.

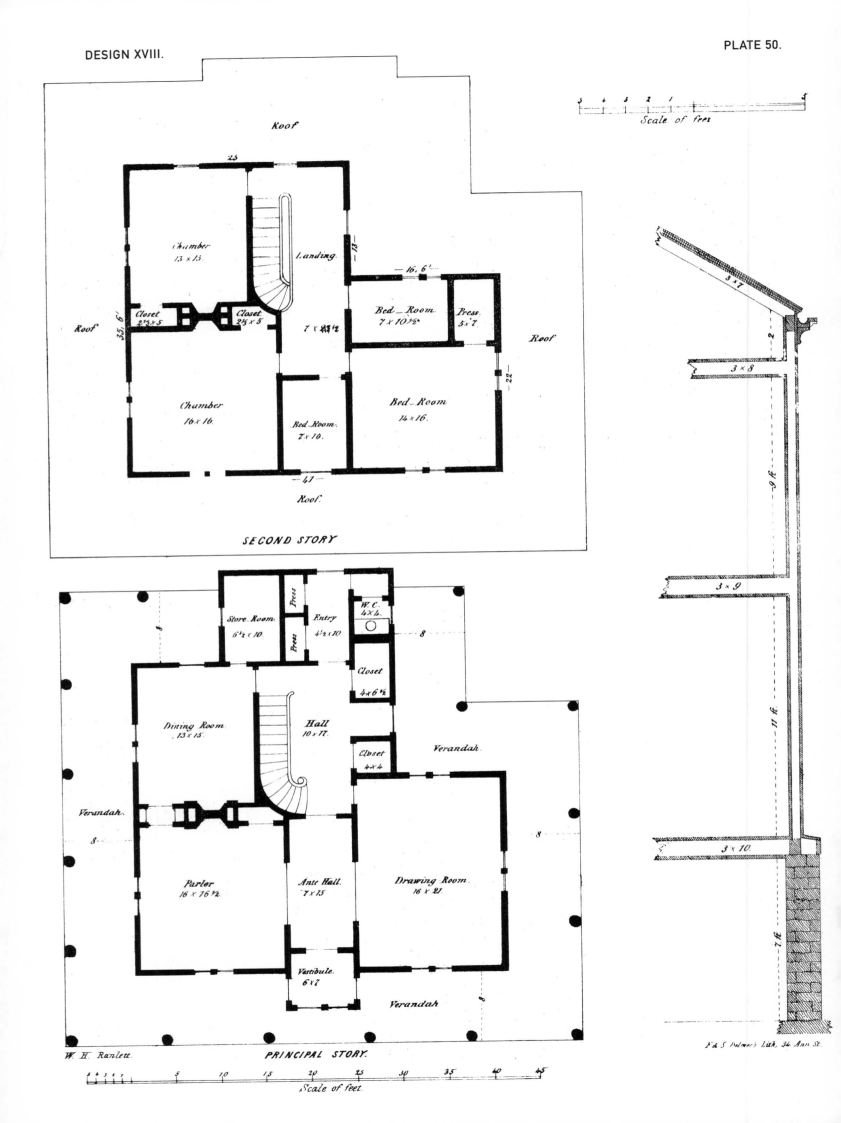

Scale of feet

Roof

23

Chamber
13 x 13

Landing

— 16. 6'

Roof

35, 6'

Closet
2'3 x 5

Closet
2'5 x 5

7 x 23'2

Bed — Room.
7 x 10½"

Press
5 x 7

Roof

Roof

Chamber
16 x 16

Bed — Room.
7 x 10.

Bed — Room.
14 x 16

— 22 —

— 47 —

Roof.

SECOND STORY

3 x 7

2

3 x 8

— 9 ft. —

Store Room.
6½ x 10.

Press

Press

Entry
4½ x 10.

W. C.
4 x 4.

8

Closet
4 x 6½.

3 x 9

8

Dining Room.
13 x 15.

Hall
10 x 17.

Verandah.

— 11 ft. —

Closet
4 x 4

Verandah.

8

8

Parlor
16 x 16½.

Ante Hall.
7 x 15.

Drawing Room.
16 x 21.

3 x 10.

Vestibule.
6 x 7

8

— 7 ft. —

Verandah.

W. H. Ranlett.

PRINCIPAL STORY.

F. & S. Palmer's Lith, 34 Ann St.

5   10   15   20   25   30   35   40   45

Scale of feet.

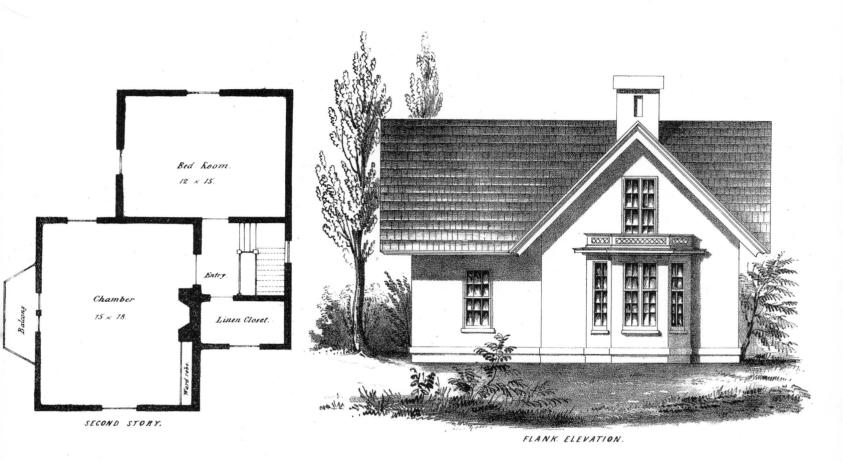

Bed Room.
12 × 15.

Chamber
15 × 18.

Entry.

Linen Closet.

Balcony

Ward robe

SECOND STORY.

FLANK ELEVATION.

SECTION.

Kitchen.
12 × 12.

Kitchen Pantry
7½ × 3.

Closet
3½

Dining Room.
15 × 18.

Hall
8 × 12.

FIRST STORY.

ENTRANCE ELEVATION.

Designed & drawn by W. H. Ranlett

Lith of E & S Palmer, 34 Ann St. N.Y.

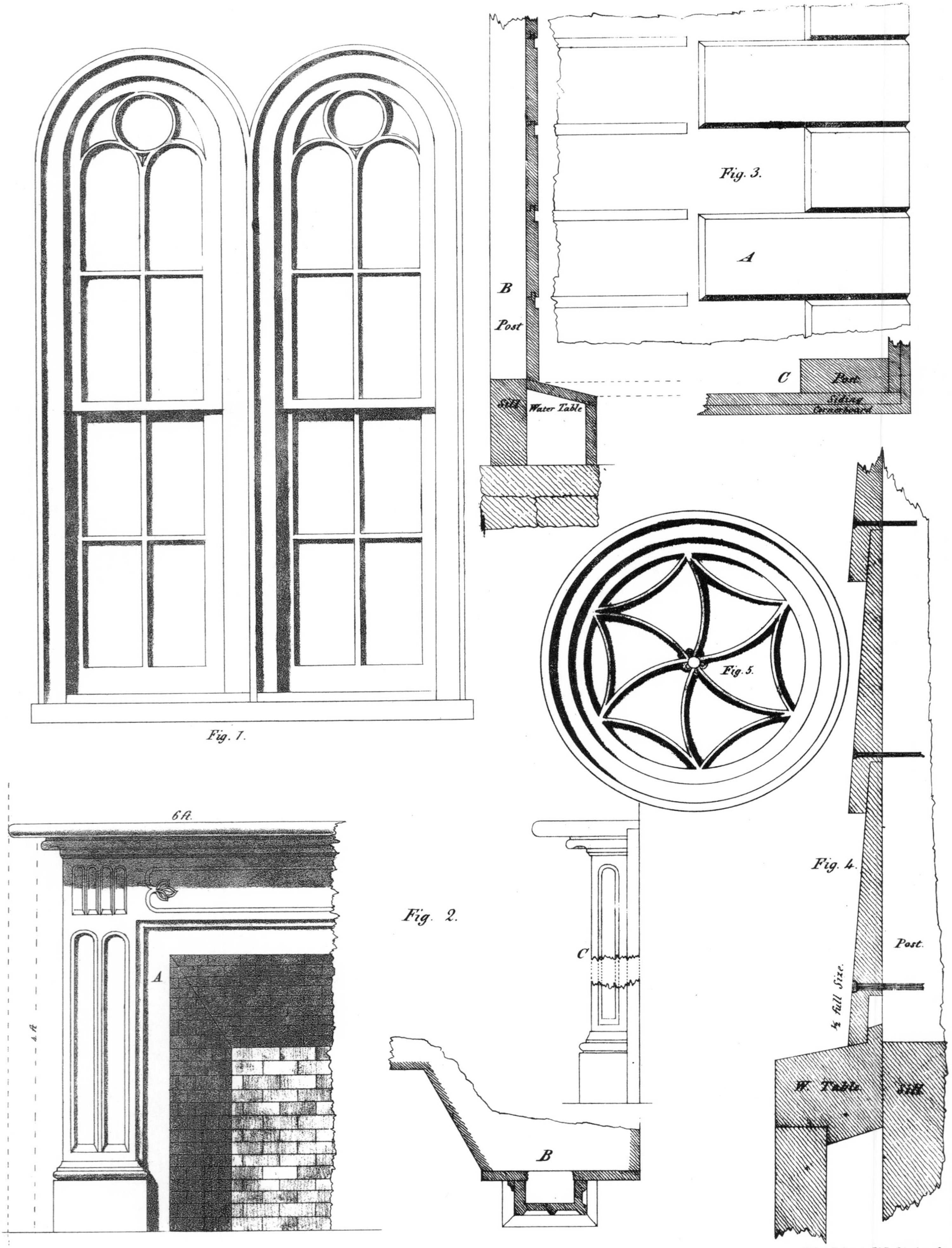

Fig. 3.

A

B
Post

C   Part
Siding
Groundwork

Sill   Water Table

Fig. 7.

Fig. 5.

Fig. 4.

½ full Size.

Post.

W. Table   Sill.

6 ft.

A

4 ft.

Fig. 2.

C

B

Scale 1 Inch

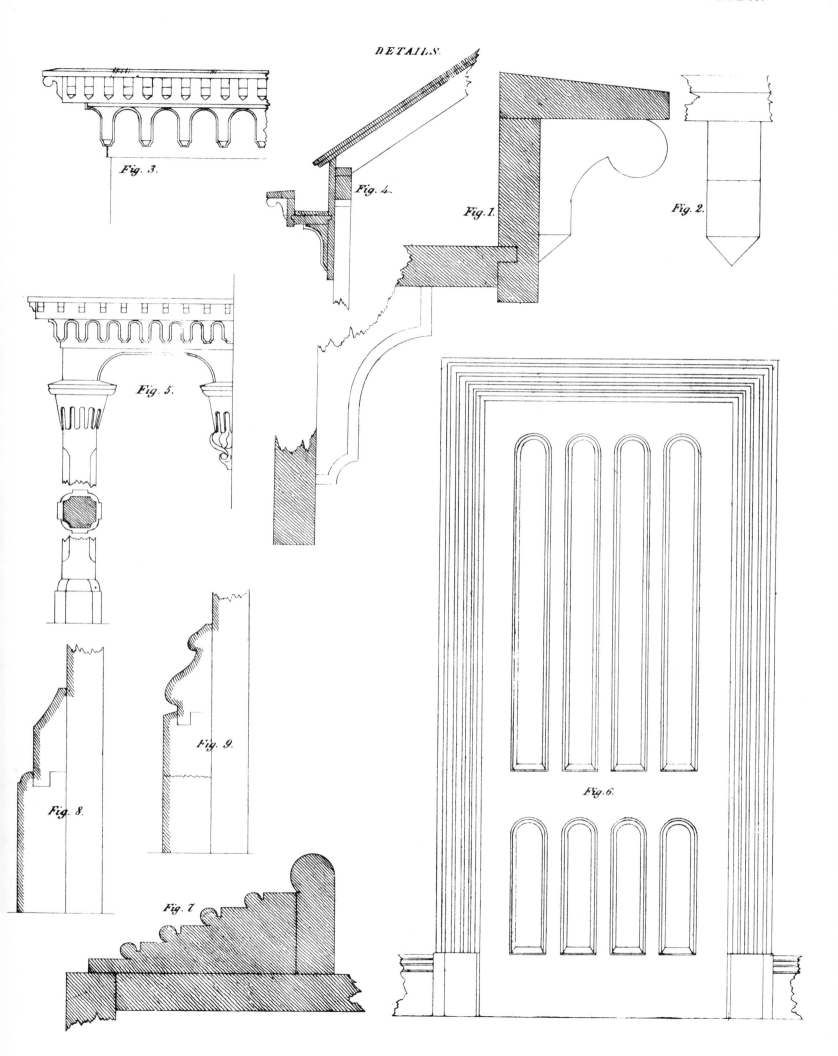

DETAILS.

Fig. 3.

Fig. 4.

Fig. 1.

Fig. 2.

Fig. 5.

Fig. 6.

Fig. 8.

Fig. 9.

Fig. 7.

PLATE 54.

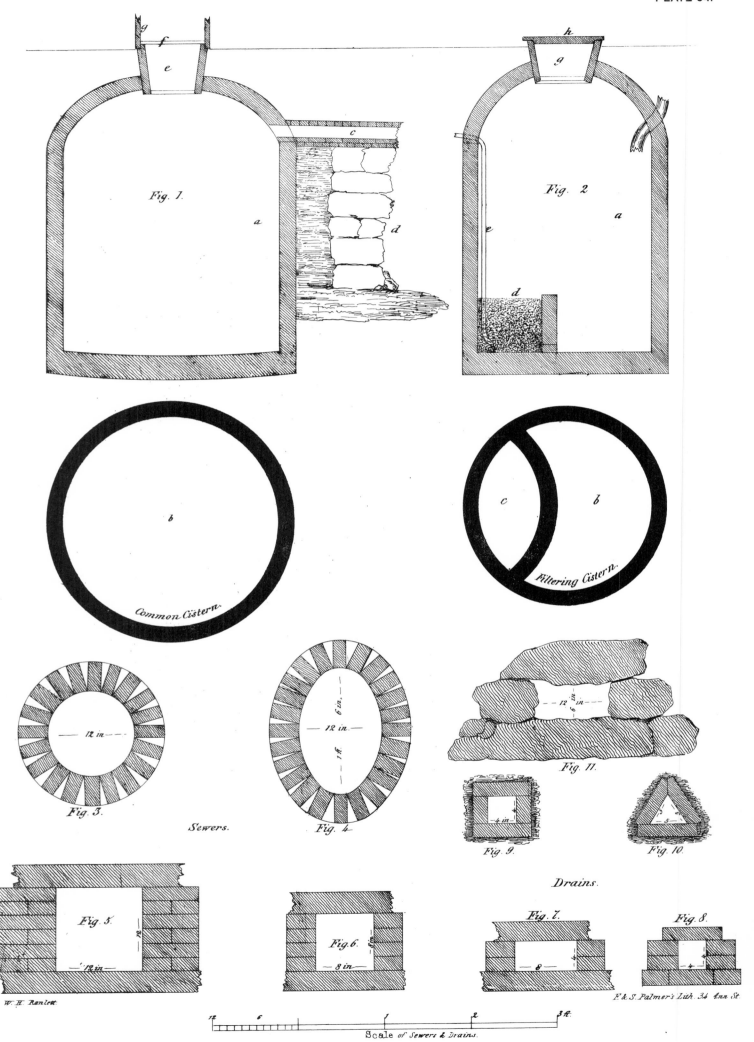

Fig. 1.

Fig. 2.

Common Cistern.

Filtering Cistern.

Fig. 3.

Sewers.

Fig. 4

Fig. 11.

Fig. 9.

Fig. 10.

Drains.

Fig. 5.

Fig. 6.

Fig. 7.

Fig. 8.

W. H. Ranlett.

F. & S. Palmer's Lith. 34 Ann St.

Scale of Sewers & Drains.

FRENCH ARCHITECTURE.

THE French have, in the course of their history, imitated different styles of architecture, particularly the Italian, Byzantine and Gothic; but possessing a native genius that enables them to excel in everything they undertake, they have produced a style which may, with the greatest propriety, be called their national architecture. It partakes of the different styles which they had imitated.

It embraces regular, irregular, and even curved outlines, in general plans. It admits columns sparingly, of the Grecian and Roman orders. The palace of Versailles has Ionic columns in the second story, but none in the first. The style admits numerous windows of medium size—some with angular heads, others with circular, and many with heads slightly curved, somewhat in imitation of the low pointed arch. These give the windows a pleasant variety in their appearance.

The roofs are very irregular, and partake more of the Gothic than any other style, being quite high. They are usually hipped, and terminate with attic bands and railings. Light is admitted through the principal planes of the roofs by dormer windows of various shapes. The cornices are heavy, and supported by ornamented brackets, trusses and cantalivers, and the whole surmounted by high open balustrades. The details are often embellished by figures and flowers, and the outlines much broken. They have but few regular gables, and seldom any pediments.

The general configuration of French edifices is in the best taste, comprising pleasing proportions, and thoroughly relieved by well-chosen irregularities of outline. This style, being the product of French taste and skill, admits, of course, of much ornament—of which the French are very fond; for they often ornament even the roofs of their buildings. The style allows a convenient and agreeable distribution and finish to the interior, comprising much of the details of the Gothic and Byzantine, but latterly with the rich and gorgeous style of Louis XIV. which originated in the reign of that monarch. Peasants cottages or huts are built of stone, without taste or ornament—destitute of gardens and other kindred conveniences, and the occupants live in them on floors of earth, and almost without furniture. Cottages and small villas are coming into fashion in France. They are constructed in imitation of English cottages, in their general appearance, also in the finish and decorations. Chateaux are generally well arranged and elegantly constructed; usually without enclosures, but accompanied by gardens laid out in good style, and well set with vines and shrubbery.

The French have attained great perfection in the construction of bridges and public edifices. Paris, being situated on both sides of the Seine, has afforded great opportunities, and offered strong inducements

75

for the construction of the best bridges.   Add to this the sentiment, that the building of bridges was an act of charity to the people, and piety to God, which formerly prevailed in that country ; and we behold the French nation possessed of the strongest impulses to excellence in architecture.   One of the most curious and most admired relics of ancient art, is the bridge across the Rhone, near Avignon, which was built in the 13th century.   It appeared so wonderful to the inhabitants of that age, that they supposed Benedict, the Architect, to have been inspired in producing it ; and therefore had him canonized by the title of St. Benedict or Benezet.   So high was their estimate of the pious work of building bridges, that a company was formed under the title of *La Fraternité des Ponts*—The Brotherhood of Bridges—who employed themselves in building bridges from motives of piety.

Design XX. is for a villa in a style peculiar to the French in the construction of their suburban chateaux.   It partakes of the details of some of their chief features, and it is believed that this style will suit the taste of some gentlemen who object to the high points and ornamented gables of the Gothic, the low regular roofs of the Grecian, and the diminutive details of the Italian.

The French style is well adapted to the vicinities of cities and large commercial towns.   It is desirable that the views should comprise considerable water, hence it is well adapted to the shores of bays and rivers.   This design properly carried out on a suitable site will combine elegance of appearance, with comfort, convenience and economy.   The rooms are large and lofty, well lighted and thoroughly ventilated ; and the whole finished in a becoming and graceful manner, while the materials and mode of construction will render it a durable edifice.

This style is so well adapted to many portions of our country, and to the taste and habits of our citizens, that it will not be a matter of surprise, if it should become a favorite style with us in the course of a few years.   Our utilitarian and tasteful eclecticism might, certainly with great propriety, include it in our selection of Gallican excellencies and elegancies.

The French style will harmonize well with portions of our country, and our citizens will find it to accord well with their taste and convenience.

DUTIES OF ARCHITECTS.

The Architect is the *responsible* man in the construction of an edifice. If the builder should proceed improperly—put in poor material, employ incompetent workmen, or adopt any other measure that would be likely to produce damage to the proprietor; the Architect has the authority to arrest his course, and he should do it promptly. It is his duty to keep himself well informed of the material, workmanship, and indeed of all the facts and circumstances in the progress of the erection; for the proprietor entrusts to him an important power touching his estate, and the exercise of this power is destined to have an important bearing on him in profit or damage; therefore it cannot be said that any man sustains that trustworthily, who has not kept himself thus acquainted with the subject of his charge.

The integrity of the Architect is a matter of great moment to the proprietor, for he has to rely very much on his decisions; all which heightens the importance of his reputation to himself, hence it is of the first moment to him that he be prepared to carry out the trusts committed to him in a manner which is proper in itself, and satisfactory to the parties, which he cannot do unless he keeps himself informed of the work as above, for he is to pass upon the materials and work, by giving a certificate of approval before the builder can draw his pay. All these considerations go to show the importance of the Architect's relation to the edifice, in view of the interest of all concerned in it, and hence the necessity of prompt action on his part to arrest any improper measure or means in the course of the erection.

Another point that Architects should keep in view, is to avoid as, far as possible, alterations in the original design; for out of this great dissatisfaction often arises. This should be done by having the plan made in a proper manner; and this point can be reached, in many instances, only by his showing the proprietor what he needs and what will suit his taste, and be adapted to his situation, that all these may be provided for in the plan. This will avoid the demand for alterations, and preserve the symmetry of the edifice. These considerations show it to be wholly within the province of the Architect to procure a faithful fulfilment of the contract and execution of the plan: hence it follows, that if there is a deficiency in the structure, the blame is to be attached to the Architect, unless he has been prevented from doing his duty by the proprietor, which, unfortunately, is too often the case. This is the basis of another duty of the Architect, which is to resist such interference with his prerogatives, on the part of those who employ him. He may not, indeed, dictate in an absolute manner, to those who employ him: but he should remonstrate against their changing the plan or interfering in any way with the progress of the work.

One of the prominent features of quackery in architecture, is the practice of many who have thrust themselves into this profession, to connive at defective materials, or improper workmanship in buildings, and approve them in contravention of every principle of honor and justice; and in some instances receive of the contractor a bonus, in view of his generosity in passing his performance, notwithstanding its defectiveness. This is outright perfidy, to which no man of intelligence and integrity could submit; for it renders a man unworthy of confidence. Indeed the money thus procured from a proprietor, is worse than filched from his pocket, for besides procuring that for which no equivalent has been rendered, the property has been damaged to a considerable extent.

This is, indeed, a high charge to lay against "professional men" to whose hands important trusts are often committed, but the instances are at command by which it may be verified. From all this it is perfectly obvious that it is a matter of the first importance to a proprietor to employ an Architect who is both *competent* and *honest*.

It often happens also, that the frugality or parsimony of proprietors, so circumscribes the prerogatives of the Architect, that he cannot produce the result that he desires; and for which he is well qualified. Against such restrictions, he should always protest, for it is a great waste of money and effort to construct an edifice under such

77

limitations as prevent the effects that might be secured by a little additional means; and the want of which produces such lasting defects in the beauty, convenience and durability of the structure; and always injures deeply the reputation of the Architect.

These considerations go far to show the necessity of cultivating architectural science among our citizens, that they may be prepared to appreciate the traits and qualities of improvements, and avoid impositions. They also indicate the necessity of scientific intelligence, chastened taste, firm integrity, and practical skill in the Architect.

ARCHITECTURAL SCIENCE.

The general intelligence of the citizens of this country prepares them for extensive enterprise in the various pursuits and improvements of the age. One of the benefits of this intelligence is a knowledge and appreciation of the necessity of skilful and scientific professional talent in the production of artistical improvements, that they may possess becoming beauty and profitable durability. The advance of architectural science has been greater in this country than it ever was in any other, in the same period of their history; so that our country compares advantageously with older ones in its architecture, considering its comparative age.

Notwithstanding all this there is a vast amount of quackery on this subject. And if this wasteful policy were confined to pseudo-economists, who, to save a little in the erection of an edifice, will sacrifice five times the amount in the permanent value of their property, it would be far less mischievous to the country than it is under existing circumstances. Many who become candidates for public favor, as architects and builders, are deplorably ignorant of the subject; and, worst of all, some who set themselves up as teachers of the public mind, and guides and patterns of the public taste and architectural refinement, are so destitute of everything like the science of architecture, and so saturated with the vulgarisms of the shop, the kitchen and the street, that it would be the grossest misnomer to call the productions of their pens, *literary;* though they be embellished by two-penny imitative drawings.

What can be expected in the science and literature of the most difficult of the fine arts, from one who cannot write a page of plain English without marring it, not only by solecisms, but also by gross barbarisms?

The disposition of so large a portion of our community, to rely upon cheap publications, gives a great advantage to incompetent adventurers on this, as on other subjects, and the demand produces the supply; for men who have spent little time and less money to procure an education adequate to the business, can manage "to get up" some imitations accompanied by the parlance of apprentice boys, executed with little expense and less taste, which can be sold cheap because they cost little. If such persons ever had any just appreciation of the importance of their calling, they must suppose that the mass of the people have not, and that they are therefore lawful game.

Our utilitarian character ought to lead the community to take a comprehensive view of this subject, and to adopt such aids and guides as will give the best results, not merely in the present expense, but in the beauty, fitness, and permanent future value of our improvements. Unscientific guides in Architecture, like cheap and common school teachers, leave their products characterized by their own vulgarities, and marred by deformities which they were incapable of preventing, and which can be remedied only by the dissolution of the subject.

It would be an easy matter to give numerous examples and proofs of the above positions, were it necessary. The remedy for the people in such cases, is the common corrective for similar evils—the intelligence of our citizens; where this fails, they must learn by experience, if they will not by precept and observation.

Much is now doing for the information of the people, through the various publications of the day; and if they will take a little pains to avoid impositions, and provide themselves with the scientific productions of genuine skill and enlightened literature on the subject, they will find themselves provided with safe guides to the most desirable results in their domestic improvements—the durability, tasteful beauty, comfort and convenience of their "Home—sweet Home."

SPECIFICATIONS,

Of the Labor and Materials required for the erection of Design XX.

EXCAVATION.—Four ft. deep, and the earth graded to a terrace 12 ft. wide, from the veranda.

STONE WORK.—The foundation for the main walls, 2 ft. 6 in. wide, and 1 ft. deep, of large flat stones. Foundations for partitions and chimneys, and piers 18 in. square and project 6 in. from the uprights. Main walls 20 in. thick and 8 1=2 ft. high. Airie walls 18 in. thick, and founded 18 in. below the pavement. Sink and sess=pool, each 10 ft. deep and 6 ft. in diameter, covered with blue flag stones. Hearths in the kitchens of blue stone 3 by 8 ft. Blue stone flagging, coping and steps 10 in. wide, to the airie. Lintels over the kitchen fire=places, 5 in. thick and 16 in. high. Sills and lintels to the doors and windows in the basement, of blue stone. Water table and the sills and lintels above the water table, all of sound brown stone, polished. The hearths and facings of two fire=places, of brown stone.

BRICK WORK.—The main walls 12 in. thick, wing walls 8 in. thick, the corners and facias to project 4 inches from the walls. Four chimneys with 11 fire=places, two for kitchens, 3 for wood fires and 6 for grates. Brick piers 12 by 12 in. under the columns.

PLASTERING.—The first and second stories to be lathed, and plastered with two coats of brown mortar and hard finished. The basement lathed and plastered, with two coats of brown mortar, slipped and white=washed. All the interior above the second story, to be lathed and plastered, with one heavy coat of brown, and hard finished. The outside of the brick walls to be covered in the very best manner, with mastic cement, and laid out in blocks to imitate brown stone. The floors deafened in the first and second stories. Neat moulded 12 in. cornices in the parlor and dining room. A 9 in. ornamental cornice in the main hall—a 16 in. full enriched cornice in each drawing room—and 5 plain 9 in. cornices in the second story.

MATERIALS.—The foundations and basement walls to be of quarry stone. The brick to be good hard pavers except three fire=places—that in the kitchen, and the two for wood, which are to be laid with face brick in white mortar. All the mortar to be made with proper proportions. The lath 1 1=4 in. for the ceiling, and 1 1=2 in. for the walls.

MARBLE MANTLES.—Two of statuary marble, and two of black and gold, in the first story; and four of veined marble in the second story. All set complete; and to cost not less than $ 45 each for parlors and dining room, and $ 100 each for drawing rooms; the veined $ 20 each.

GRATES.—Two ornamental and two plain, in the first story, to cost $ 32 and $ 18 each; and two plain, in the second story, to cost each $ 13 when set. Pond's third sized range set in one kitchen, and a copper boiler of the capacity of 40 gallons, and a three feet iron grate in the other fire=place.

TIMBER.—*All of the best quality of milled white pine.   First tier of beams 3 by 12—second tier, 3 by 11—third tier, 3 by 10—all 16 in. between centers—trimmers, 4 in. thick—main plates 5 by 10—top do. 4 by 8—rafters, 3 by 8, 2 ft. between centers—veranda-sills of chestnut, 4 by 6, beams, 3 by 8 ; rafters of pine, 4 by 9, purlins and plates, 3 by 8—basement sleepers of chestnut, 6 by 6, 2 ft. between centers.   Locust sleepers on the sink and sess-pool.   Partition studs, 3 by 4—door studs, 4 by 6.*

FLOORS.—*In the first story and verandas, of narrow, clear yellow pine, 1 1-4 thick, tongued and grooved and blind nailed.   All other floors of best quality white pine milled plank.*

ROOFS.—*The principal roof to be covered with best Welsh slate, on milled pine plank.   All other roofs to be covered with first quality Naylor's patent galvanized tinned plates, laid on milled plank—all the gutters to be lined with the same—4 in. leaders to the main house and wing, and 2 1-2 in. to the verandas.   The plank on the veranda roof to be clear of loose or hard knots and shakes—laid face side down on rafters, and purlins planed and moulded.*

CORNICES, &c.—*All the cornices, columns, brackets, cantalivers, railings and balusters to be made of perfectly clear lumber.   See details in Plate 57.*

WINDOWS.—*All the frames made of 2 in. plank, and the sashes to hang by patent butts, and be secured by grip turn bolts.   All the sashes in the first and second stories 1 3-4, and all others 1 1-2 in. thick.   Four windows of 20 lights, 14 by 22—5, of 16 lights, 14 by 20—6, of 20 lights, 12 by 22—6, of 16 lights, 12 by 20—11, of 12 lights, 10 by 16—4, of 4 lights, 10 by 16—8, of 6 lights, 12 by 18—10, of 8 lights, 10 by 12.   French plate glass in all the sashes—double thickness in first and second stories, and single in basement and two dormer stories.*

DOORS.—*In the first story, three pairs of sliding doors, with cast ways, 6 in. brass sheaves and flush bolts—front door in two parts, to fold on a mullion—back door with side and head lights, and 6 passage doors, all to be 2 inches thick, and each to have 8 panels moulded on both sides.   Six sash doors, each having 4 panels, 1 5-8 thick—the glass in these and the side and head lights to be enameled, with stained borders.   The passage doors to be hung by butts 5 by 5 in. and have 5 in. mortice locks—sash doors, by 4 by 4 butts, and to have 4 in. mortice locks.   All the lock furniture in the first story to be porcelain, "blue coral gilt" pattern.   In the second story, the doors 1 3-4 thick, 8 panels, moulded on both sides, hung by butts 4 by 4, and secured by 4 1-2 in. mortice locks—lock furniture, porcelain, "blue coral" pattern.   All other doors 1 1-4 thick, 6 panels, moulded on one side, hung by 3 by 3 butts, and secured by 3 1-2 in. mortice locks with mineral knobs.*

STAIRS.—*From basement, with steps one and a quarter in. thick, enclosed with narrow plank, tongued, grooved, and moulded.   The stairs from the first floor, to the attic or dormer story, with a double landing on the second and attic floors—open and blocked strings—steps one and a half in. thick—moulded risers with brackets to continue on the galleries—the rails to be of black walnut, six in. wide and three thick, moulded, with scrolls on five in. carved newels—two and three quarter in. balusters turned—an enclosed step ladder to the garret and roof.*

BASE.—*In the first and second stories as in Plate 58, Figs. 6 and 7—in basement and dormer story one and a quarter thick, eight in. high, moulded.*

CLOSETS & PRESSES——*All to be fitted up in the best manner with drawers, doors, shelves, strips, hooks, pins, &c., each for such purpose as may be required.*

ARCHITRAVES——*In the first and second stories, as in Plate 58, Figs. 4 and 5——in the basement and dormer stories, 3 1=2 in. wide and 1 1=4 in. thick, moulded.*

SHUTTERS & BLINDS.——*Shutters four fold inside to all the windows in first and second stories——Soffit's back linings, elbows and backs——all to have moulded panels corresponding with the door panels——strong moving blinds made and hung to the windows in the second and dormer stories. the hinges to be welded and best patent fastenings.*

FURRING.——*All the stone and brick walls with 2 by 4 in. strips, 12 in. between centers in first, and 16 in. in basement and second stories——the ceilings in dormer stories tight furred, 16 in. between centers.*

BELLS.——*Five in first. and six in second stories, with pulls and levers corresponding with the lock furniture.*

PAINTING.——*All the wood=work outside and inside, except interior floors and black walnut, to have 3 coats of pure lead and American linseed oil, put on in dry weather——thirty days intervening between putting on the first and second, and the second and third coats——the last coat on the exterior trimmings and veranda floor to be colored——the doors in first story to have two extra coats and polished——the stair rails and balusters to have seven coats of varnish, rubbed each time and polished——the blinds to have three coats of paint, a dark brown, and varnished two coats.*

DESCRIPTION OF PLATES.

PLATE 55.—Two geometrical elevations of a Villa in the French Style.   Design XX.

PLATE 56.—Ground plans of the first, second and dormer stories, and a section of the hight of stories.   Design XX.

PLATE 57.—Exterior details for Design XX.   Fig. 1.—Main cornice and balustrade.   Fig. 2.—Attic cornice and railing.   Fig. 3.—Wing cornice and roof.   Fig. 4.—Veranda cornice ; blocking course and column.   Fig. 5.—Dormer window head.

PLATE 58.—Interior details.   Design XX.   Fig. 1.—Elevation of a door for the first story.   Fig. 2, for the second story.   Fig. 3.—Elevation of a window for the first story.   Fig. 4.—Plan of door architrave for the first story.   Fig. 5, for the second story.   Fig. 6.—Section of base for the first story.   Fig. 7, for the second story.   Fig. 8.—Face section and plan of the mantle-piece for the drawing-rooms.   Fig. 9.—Plan for the sliding-doors.   Fig. 10.—Ground plan of basement.

PLATE 59.—Two geometrical elevations of a cottage in the French Style.   Design XXI.

PLATE 60.—Ground plans of the principal and dormer stories, section for framing the roof—hights of stories, and a section of the gallery rails, post and filling.

Design XXI. is intended for a gardener's lodge for Design XX., to be built of wood—the frame of sound pine timber—sills, posts, plates, framing-beams and trimmers, 4 by 8 ; beams, 3 by 8 ; rafters, 3 by 6 ; and studding, 3 by 4—the sides sheathed with feather-edged boards and covered with Wykoff's patent siding.   See Plate 52, Fig. 4—roof, of best split pine shingles, laid on hemlock boards, and milled plank—the dormers with galvanized tin—floors, of milled pine plank inside, and narrow clear milled, outside—windows with good glass, sashes hung by butts, and secured by bolts—doors, six panels, 1¼ in. thick, moulded on one side, secured by mortice locks and mineral knobs—moulded casings—moulded base—closets shelved—stairs, with mahogany rail and balusters—neat mantles.   Painted two coats of best lead and oil, colored outside, and completed in every part neat and substantial.

ESTIMATE
Of the Materials and Labor required for Design XX.

MASON'S.

Item	Rate	Amount
560 yds. excavation, - - -	18	$100 80
370 lds. building stone, - -	75	277 50
140200 hard brick, - - -	4 00	560 80
290 casks Thomaston lime, - -	1 00	290 00
40 " finishing do. - -	1 50	60 00
45 " Lubec plaster, - -	1 75	78 75
20 " marble dust, - -	1 75	35 00
640 loads sand, - - -	35	224 00
60000 plastering lath, - -	1 88	112 80
550 lbs. fine lath nails, - -	7	38 50
120 bush. hair, - - -	20	24 00
238 feet brown stone, w. table, -	50	119 00
20 brown stone window sills, 108 ft.	45	48 60
2 " hearths and jams, - 5 00		10 00
4 " chimney tops, - 10 00		40 00
82 ft. blue stone steps and coping, -	16	13 12
2 kitchen hearths, 48 feet, - -	18	8 64
2 " lintels, 12 ft. - -	40	4 80
24 sills and lintels, 88 ft. - -	20	17 60
120 ft. flagging, - - -	10	12 00
2 marble mantles, - - -	$100 00	200 00
2 " " - - -	45 00	90 00
4 " " - - -	20 00	80 00
2 ornamental grates, - - -	32 00	64 00
2 plain " - - -	18 00	36 00
2 " " - - -	13 00	26 00
"Pond's" range, - - - - - -		52 00
Copper boiler, - - - - - -		45 00
Iron grate, - - - - - -		12 00
530 yards mastic cement, - -	1 00	530 00
553 loads carting, - - -	30	165 90
370 days' mason's wages, - -	1 75	647 50
359 " laborer's " - -	1 00	359 00
		$4383 31

CARPENTER'S.

Item	Rate	Amount
25150 ft. timber, - -	$1 75 per h.	$440 12
660 joists, - - -	13	85 80
950 wall strips, - - -	11	104 50
1250 lineal ft. chestnut sleepers, -	5	62 50
40 " locust "	10	4 00
3200 ft. hemlock boards, -	1¼	40 00
21950 ft. clear plank, ¾, 1, 1¼, 1½ and 2 in.	3½	768 25
940 yellow pine narrow planks,	24	225 60
975 white " milled " -	27	263 25
770 spruce " " " -	20	154 00
225 ft. black walnut, - -	8	18 00
2 carved newels, - -	5 00	10 00
210 balusters, - - -	25	52 50
65 roof " - -	30	19 50
144 cornice brackets, - -	65	93 60
33 " " - -	50	17 50
44 " " - -	45	19 80
16 rosettes, - - -	50	8 00
4 attic posts, - - -	1 50	6 00
80 lights glass, 14x22, - -	75	60 00
96 " " 14x20, - -	66	63 36
120 " " 12x22, - -	70	84 00
96 " " 12x20, - -	55	52 80
48 " " 12x18, - -	44	21 12
148 " " 10x16, - -	24	35 52
80 " " 10x12, - -	20	16 00
24 " " 9x12, - -	14	3 36
6 sash doors, - - -	12 00	72 00
1 sett of side and head lights, -		15 00
178 ft. blinds, - - -	1 00	178 00
4210 ft. galvanized tin roof, -	13 00	547 30
4096 ft. slate roof, - -	7 50	307 20
11 pairs 5x5 broad butts, - -	30	3 30
16 " 4x4 " " -	19	3 04
22 " 3x3 " " -	11	2 42
44 " 4½ nar. " -	16	7 04
16 " 3 " " -	7	1 12
100 " 2½ " " -	5	5 00
4 gross screws, 1½ in. -	36	1 44
8 " " 1¼ in. -	32	2 56
9 " " 1 in. -	27	2 43
10 " " ¾ in. -	22	2 20
3 setts sliding door trimmings, -	23 00	69 00
9 5 in. mortice locks, -	5 00	45 00
10 4½" " " -	2 63	26 30
6 4 " " " -	2 56	15 36
22 3½" " " -	1 44	31 68
24 rail screws, - -	8	1 92
1 pair welded hinges and chain, - -		1 60
44 iron grip bolts, - -	3 50	154 00
44 shutter bars, 7 in. - -	21	9 24
150 ft. 4 in. leader, - -	15	22 50
120 " 2½" " - -	12	14 40
900 lbs. nails, - -	4 50	40 50
2 water closet fixtures, -	30 00	60 00
40 ft. soil pipe, - -	50	20 00
20 " waste pipe, - -	25	5 00
60 " supply pipe, - -	20	12 00
196 loads carting, - -	40	78 40
845 days carpenter's labor, -	1 50	1267 50
		$5753 53

PAINTER'S.

Item	Rate	Amount
1150 lbs. white lead, - -	7 50	86 25
45 galls. raw oil, - -	80	36 00
5 " boiled oil, - -	95	4 75
1½ " varnish, - -	4 00	6 00
3 " spirits turpentine, -	45	1 35
15 lbs. putty, - - -	4	60
4 " glue, - - -	20	80
6 " litharge, - - -	6	36
2 lbs. burnt umber, - -	30	60
2 " raw " - -	20	40
4 " Venetian red, - -	6	24
½ " Prussian blue, - -	1 50	75
1 " lamp black, - - -		50
Carting, $5 00; 92 days' painter's labor, 1 75,		166 00
		$304 60

Design XX. will cost $10,441 44. Design XXI. $1,450.

A VILLA IN THE FRENCH STYLE.

Side Elevation.

DES & DRAWN BY H. H. RANLETT   LITH OF F. & S. PALMER 34 ANN ST N.Y.

FRONT ELEVATION.

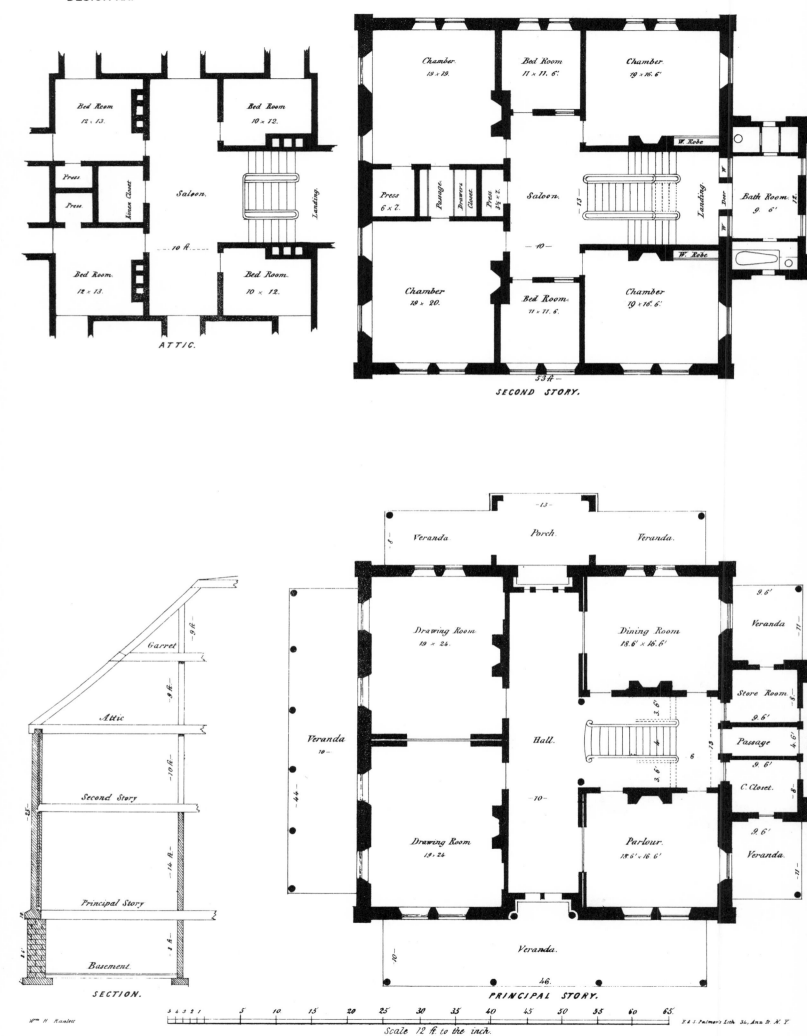

ATTIC.

SECOND STORY.

SECTION.

PRINCIPAL STORY.

Scale 12 ft. to the inch.

Fig. 1.

Main cornice.

Fig. 2.

Attic cornice.

Fig. 3.

Wing cornice.

Verandah cornice.   Fig. 4.

Cap.

Column.

Shaft.

Base.

Fig. 5.

INTERIOR DETAILS.

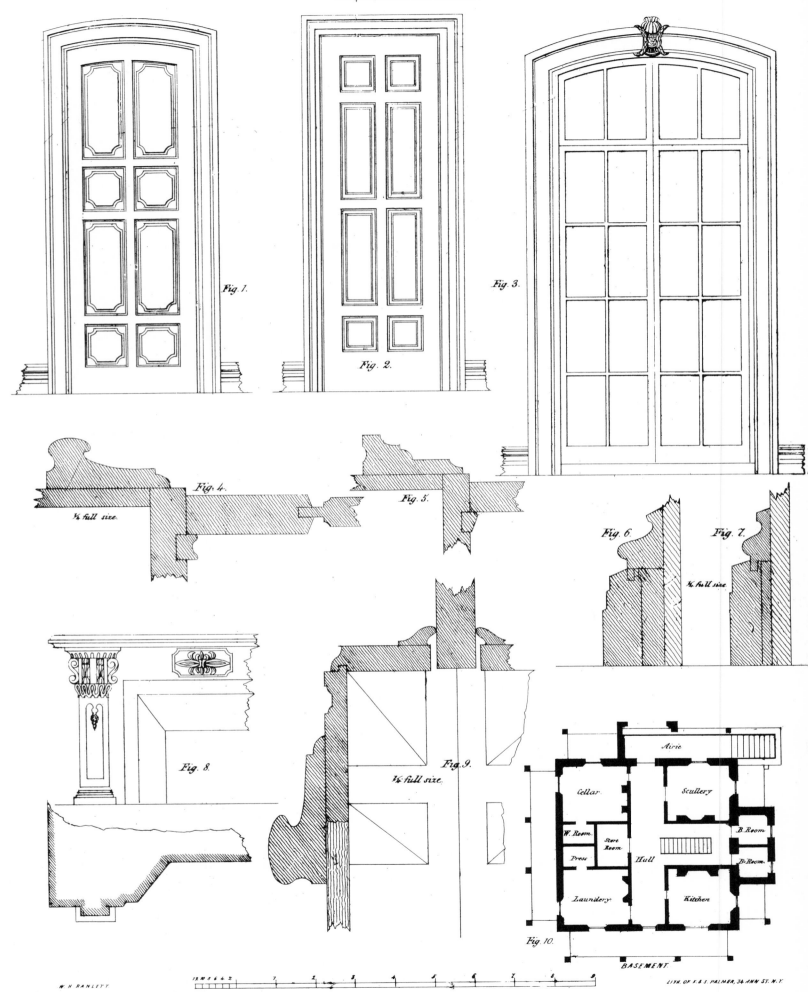

Fig. 1.

Fig. 2.

Fig. 3.

Fig. 4.

¼ full size.

Fig. 5.

Fig. 6.

Fig. 7.

¼ full size.

Fig. 8.

Fig. 9.

¼ full size.

Fig. 10.

Airie.

Cellar.

Scullery.

W. Room.

Store
Room.

B. Room.

Press.

Hall.

B. Room.

Laundery.

Kitchen.

BASEMENT.

W. H. RANLETT.

LITH. OF F. & S. PALMER, 34 ANN ST. N.Y.

COTTAGE IN THE FRENCH STYLE,
Side Elevation.

ENTRANCE ELEVATION.

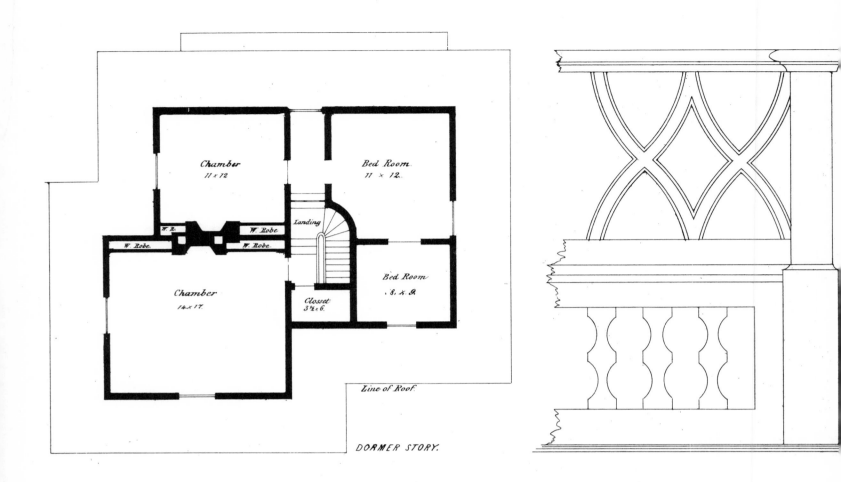

Chamber
11 × 12.

Bed Room.
11 × 12.

W. R. W. Robe. Landing

W. Robe. W. Robe.

Chamber
14 × 17.

Bed Room
8 × 9.

Closet
3½ × 6.

Line of Roof.

DORMER STORY.

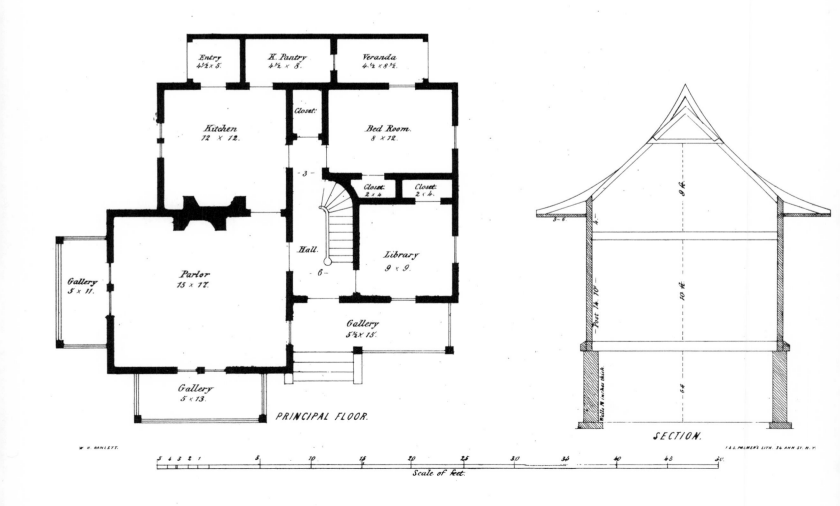

Entry
4½ × 5.

K. Pantry
4½ × 8.

Veranda
4½ × 8½.

Closet.

Kitchen
12 × 12.

Bed Room.
8 × 12.

- 3 -

Closet
2 × 4

Closet
2 × 4

Gallery
5 × 11.

Parlor
15 × 17.

Hall.

- 6 -

Library
9 × 9.

Gallery
5½ × 15.

Gallery
5 × 13.

PRINCIPAL FLOOR.

SECTION.

W. H. RANLETT.

5 4 3 2 1   5   10   15   20   25   30   35   40   45   50.

Scale of Feet.

ADVERTISEMENT.

THIS work has been projected to supply a systematic treatise on Rural Architecture, with scientific and practical developements of various styles adapted to the United States. The want of such a work has long been felt, and it will be alike useful to the professional architect, operative artisan and private citizen.

The first volume is now completed, which consists of ten numbers, and contains twenty-one original designs of rural residences—cottages and villas—exemplifying twelve different styles of architecture. These residences will vary in the cost of erection, from nine hundred to twelve thousand dollars. Each design comprises full ground plans and elevations, and many of them perspective views, projected ground plots—exterior and interior details, accompanied by specifications and estimates;—it contains also divers historical sketches of differen styles, and essays on ventilation, the appropriation of light, heat, water, &c. also on contracting, workmanship, and various other topics connected with building.

The volume contains 60 plates—19 of them tinted in a style of lithography which will commend itself to every judge of the art. The most difficult of them being executed on the stones by Mrs. F. PALMER, who stands at the head of the art; and the ground plans and details by F. MEYER, whose superiority in this department of lithography is generally admitted. The plates are from the well-known lithographic press-room of Messrs PALMER. The stereotype plates and printing, by the enterprising firm of SNOWDEN & PRALL. The paper is manufactured expressly for this work by Messrs. BURNAP & BABCOCK.

The work will consist of two volumes—the second to contain a series of numbers similar to that of the first, the issue of which will commence immediately. The whole will constitute a scientific and practical guide for the erection of country and suburban dwellings of all grades, from plain cottages to elaborate and ornamental villas in the most approved styles of rural achitecture, also for laying out and improving the grounds connected with them.

W. H. RANLETT, ARCHITECT,

170 *Broadway.*

NEW-YORK, JULY, 1847

INDEX.